SEVENTH EDITION

LOCATING AND CORRECTING READING DIFFICULTIES

James L. Shanker
California State University, Hayward

Eldon E. Ekwall
late of University of Texas at El Paso

Merrill,
an imprint of Prentice Hall

Upper Saddle River, New Jersey   Columbus, Ohio

Library of Congress Cataloging-in-Publication Data

Shanker, James L.
  Locating and correcting reading difficulties / James L. Shanker,
Eldon E. Ekwall. — 7th ed.
    p.   cm.
  Ekwall's name appears first on the 6th edition.
  Includes bibliographical references and index.
  ISBN 0-13-862962-5
  1. Reading—Remedial teaching. I. Ekwall, Eldon E. II. Title.
LB1050.5.E38 1998
372.43—dc21   97-33467
                                                         CIP

Editor: Bradley J. Potthoff
Production Editor: Julie Peters
Production Manager: Pamela D. Bennett
Production Coordination: WordCrafters Editorial Services, Inc.
Cover Design Coordinator: Karrie M. Converse
Cover Designer: Proof Positive/Farrowlyne Assoc., Inc.
Illustrations: Steve Botts and Carlisle Communications, Ltd.
Director of Marketing: Kevin Flanagan
Marketing Manager: Suzanne Stanton
Advertising/Marketing Coordinator: Julie Shough

This book was set in Century Schoolbook by Carlisle Communications, Ltd., and was
printed and bound by R. R. Donnelley & Sons Company. The cover was printed by
Phoenix Color Corp.

 © 1998 by Prentice-Hall, Inc.
Simon & Schuster/A Viacom Company
Upper Saddle River, New Jersey 07458

Printed in the United States of America

10 9 8 7 6 5

ISBN 0-13-862962-5

Prentice-Hall International (UK) Limited, *London*
Prentice-Hall of Australia Pty. Limited, *Sydney*
Prentice-Hall Canada Inc., *Toronto*
Prentice-Hall Hispanoamericana, S. A., *Mexico*
Prentice-Hall of India Private Limited, *New Delhi*
Prentice-Hall of Japan, Inc., *Tokyo*
Simon & Schuster Asia Pte. Ltd., *Singapore*
Editora Prentice-Hall do Brasil, Ltda., *Rio de Janeiro*

To my wonderful mother-in-law
Blanche Edelman
and to the memory of
my father-in-law Arthur Edelman
and my dear Aunt Mollie.

Preface

The seventh edition of this book, like the previous editions, is designed to give busy reading specialists, teachers, and students in reading education specific, concrete methods for locating and correcting reading difficulties. It can be used in developmental, corrective, and remedial situations. The major features of previous editions have been retained, with new, up-to-date information added to most chapters. The importance of direct instruction, motivational learning activities, and abundant practice in the act of reading is stressed. As in the previous editions, instruction in individual reading skills is recommended where appropriate; however, emphasis is also placed on the use of strategic approaches to the teaching of reading.

NEW TO THIS EDITION

This new edition contains additional concrete methods for teaching students how to read. In response to comments from reviewers and readers of the book, the chapter entitled "Useful Methods for Teaching Students with Reading Difficulties" has been expanded and moved to the beginning of the book. This chapter provides information on important principles of effective instruction for students who have reading difficulties. It is hoped that these principles will guide your reading through the remainder of the book. The introductory chapter also includes a description of a number of especially useful techniques or approaches for students with reading difficulties. The section on the language-experience approach has been expanded to include many practical applications for the use of this method in the classroom. Also, the section on effective oral reading activities now includes descriptions of dyad reading, group-assisted reading, paired repeated reading, Reader's Theater, and the shared book experience. These and other oral reading approaches have been shown to be unusually effective not only in helping students with the initial task of decoding, but also in developing students' reading efficiency or fluency.

The basic format of each chapter remains the same. As with previous editions, the Reading Diagnosis Chart matches the logical development of various reading abilities and corresponds to the order of the chapters.

New material is also included throughout the book on a host of topics, such as procedures for assessing and teaching phonemic awareness, helpful charts for understanding how phonics and structural analysis aid students in decoding, and new techniques for teaching the various decoding and comprehension skills. However, the most significant additions to this edition can be seen in the number of practical new appendices provided and the reorganization of the appendices to make them more easily accessible to the user.

IMPROVED APPENDIX MATERIAL

This edition contains three informational appendices (A-1 through A-3). The first presents comprehensive charts listing the scope and sequence of reading skills as presented in typical basal readers. A redesigned phonics primer is also provided, along with suggestions for interviewing parents of disabled readers.

This book has been created so that reading specialists, teachers, and students in reading education courses can use the materials in the appendices for locating reading difficulties (B-1 through B-11) to construct their own diagnostic kits. These appendices include information on a code for marking in oral diagnosis and materials for assessing students' knowledge of the alphabet, basic sight words and phrases, phonics, structural analysis, the use of context clues, and reading interests. These appendices clearly describe how to prepare diagnostic materials for classroom or clinical use. Specific directions and important points to remember are included for administering each test or survey instrument.

Other materials included in the appendices for locating reading difficulties are the Quick Check for Basic Sight Words, which quickly tells you whether a student should be given an entire basic sight word test; the Quick Survey Word List, which provides a rapid assessment of a student's ability to use phonics and syllabication skills to decode multisyllable words; materials for testing knowledge of contractions; and information on the use of the cloze procedure.

To further aid the teacher in locating reading difficulties, two new batteries of prescriptive, easy-to-administer tests have been provided: one for phonics and the other for structural analysis. Each of these test batteries includes unique subtests that evaluate a student's ability to apply the specific decoding skills (either phonics or structural analysis) *while reading passages in context.* Another new addition to the appendices for locating reading difficulties is the Reading Interest Survey. This test is designed to assess the student's attitude toward reading and school, areas of reading interest, reading experiences, and conditions affecting reading in the home.

Appendices have also been provided for correcting reading difficulties. The popular phonics instructional program entitled "Phonograms and Words for Use in Teaching Phonics" has been retained. Immediately following this appendix is a new appendix: "Words, Sentences, and Stories for Teaching Structural Analysis." As the title implies, this appendix provides teachers with practical, field-tested, effective materials for teaching students to decode words of more than one syllable. These word lists, sentence lists, and stories are keyed to the new Structural Analysis Assessment, which was mentioned earlier.

The appendices for correcting reading difficulties also include a list of 110 sentences for teaching the basic sight words. These materials are keyed to the

Preface

The seventh edition of this book, like the previous editions, is designed to give busy reading specialists, teachers, and students in reading education specific, concrete methods for locating and correcting reading difficulties. It can be used in developmental, corrective, and remedial situations. The major features of previous editions have been retained, with new, up-to-date information added to most chapters. The importance of direct instruction, motivational learning activities, and abundant practice in the act of reading is stressed. As in the previous editions, instruction in individual reading skills is recommended where appropriate; however, emphasis is also placed on the use of strategic approaches to the teaching of reading.

NEW TO THIS EDITION

This new edition contains additional concrete methods for teaching students how to read. In response to comments from reviewers and readers of the book, the chapter entitled "Useful Methods for Teaching Students with Reading Difficulties" has been expanded and moved to the beginning of the book. This chapter provides information on important principles of effective instruction for students who have reading difficulties. It is hoped that these principles will guide your reading through the remainder of the book. The introductory chapter also includes a description of a number of especially useful techniques or approaches for students with reading difficulties. The section on the language-experience approach has been expanded to include many practical applications for the use of this method in the classroom. Also, the section on effective oral reading activities now includes descriptions of dyad reading, group-assisted reading, paired repeated reading, Reader's Theater, and the shared book experience. These and other oral reading approaches have been shown to be unusually effective not only in helping students with the initial task of decoding, but also in developing students' reading efficiency or fluency.

The basic format of each chapter remains the same. As with previous editions, the Reading Diagnosis Chart matches the logical development of various reading abilities and corresponds to the order of the chapters.

New material is also included throughout the book on a host of topics, such as procedures for assessing and teaching phonemic awareness, helpful charts for understanding how phonics and structural analysis aid students in decoding, and new techniques for teaching the various decoding and comprehension skills. However, the most significant additions to this edition can be seen in the number of practical new appendices provided and the reorganization of the appendices to make them more easily accessible to the user.

IMPROVED APPENDIX MATERIAL

This edition contains three informational appendices (A-1 through A-3). The first presents comprehensive charts listing the scope and sequence of reading skills as presented in typical basal readers. A redesigned phonics primer is also provided, along with suggestions for interviewing parents of disabled readers.

This book has been created so that reading specialists, teachers, and students in reading education courses can use the materials in the appendices for locating reading difficulties (B-1 through B-11) to construct their own diagnostic kits. These appendices include information on a code for marking in oral diagnosis and materials for assessing students' knowledge of the alphabet, basic sight words and phrases, phonics, structural analysis, the use of context clues, and reading interests. These appendices clearly describe how to prepare diagnostic materials for classroom or clinical use. Specific directions and important points to remember are included for administering each test or survey instrument.

Other materials included in the appendices for locating reading difficulties are the Quick Check for Basic Sight Words, which quickly tells you whether a student should be given an entire basic sight word test; the Quick Survey Word List, which provides a rapid assessment of a student's ability to use phonics and syllabication skills to decode multisyllable words; materials for testing knowledge of contractions; and information on the use of the cloze procedure.

To further aid the teacher in locating reading difficulties, two new batteries of prescriptive, easy-to-administer tests have been provided: one for phonics and the other for structural analysis. Each of these test batteries includes unique subtests that evaluate a student's ability to apply the specific decoding skills (either phonics or structural analysis) *while reading passages in context.* Another new addition to the appendices for locating reading difficulties is the Reading Interest Survey. This test is designed to assess the student's attitude toward reading and school, areas of reading interest, reading experiences, and conditions affecting reading in the home.

Appendices have also been provided for correcting reading difficulties. The popular phonics instructional program entitled "Phonograms and Words for Use in Teaching Phonics" has been retained. Immediately following this appendix is a new appendix: "Words, Sentences, and Stories for Teaching Structural Analysis." As the title implies, this appendix provides teachers with practical, field-tested, effective materials for teaching students to decode words of more than one syllable. These word lists, sentence lists, and stories are keyed to the new Structural Analysis Assessment, which was mentioned earlier.

The appendices for correcting reading difficulties also include a list of 110 sentences for teaching the basic sight words. These materials are keyed to the same words and phrases that are tested in the locating reading difficulties section. In addition, you will find the following materials in these appendices: lists of prepositional phrases; lists of meanings, examples, and uses of prefixes and suffixes; charts for graphing students' progress in using the technique of repeated readings; a description of and charts for graphing students' progress in using the precision reading technique; and charts for graphing words per minute and comprehension.

ACKNOWLEDGMENTS

Special thanks are extended to Cheryl Milner, Director of Assessment and Staff Development in the San Mateo/Foster City (California) School District, for her willingness to share the materials she developed and field-tested for the teaching of structural analysis. Part of her instructional program is presented in Appendix C-3.

I greatly appreciate the conscientious work of the following individuals who reviewed this edition of the text: Lois C. Catrambone, Concordia University; Elizabeth Darvas, Nova Southeastern University; David C. Little, Samford University; Donna Ortiz, Fort Hays State University; and Marla Slack, University of Phoenix. They, and reviewers of previous editions, have offered their insights, thoughtful comments, and constructive suggestions to make this a more useful text.

I wish to give special mention to my immediate family: my fantastic wife, Susan, and my two terrific sons, Michael and Kenny. More than anything, their love and support make life worthwhile.

J. L. S.

Contents

How to Use This Book

Begin by skimming the next section, "Definitions of Terms," to be sure you are familiar with these terms before you read the text. Then examine the Reading Diagnosis Chart (p. xix), which lists 28 reading or reading-related abilities. Because these abilities are keyed to the specific chapters in the book, they are numbered from 1 to 28. After looking over the Reading Diagnosis Chart, you may wish to skim the book from beginning to end to ensure familiarity with the contents. Each of the 28 chapters on reading or reading-related abilities has a similar organization. First, an explanation is given on how to recognize the difficulty with the specific ability. Then a brief discussion explains any pertinent problems. Specific recommendations for correcting any weaknesses in each of the abilities follow the discussion. Finally, in some chapters, a list of games and exercises is presented to help correct these reading difficulties. In most cases you will not be able to attempt everything listed as a recommendation; however, you can choose the techniques that seem most appropriate for your situation.

The Reading Diagnosis Chart is constructed to give you an opportunity to check each of the 28 abilities three times during the year. The time period between checks will depend on the intensity of the help or the normal teaching program. It could be as often as once a month or once during each semester of the school year. You should attempt to locate student difficulties as early in the year as possible. The "Recognized By" section in each chapter will be helpful in determining whether certain skills are deficient. After determining which abilities are weak, tally the total number of students who are weak in each area. If possible, group the students who need reading instruction in similar areas. In some cases, you may base your instruction on those areas in which the class as a whole is weakest. Then turn to the "Recommendations" and the "Games and Exercises" sections to use the suggestions given there.

Before initiating actual instruction, read the section entitled "Principles of Effective Instruction" at the beginning of the introductory chapter. The information in this section is based on the authors' reading and research and more than 50 years of combined experience in helping students learn how to read. It is hoped that these suggestions will guide you in selecting the most appropriate recommendations in each chapter for your student or students.

The checklist does not categorize reading difficulties by the severity of the problem. Be aware, however, that some of the items listed are more serious than others. Each discussion section explains how to determine whether the difficulty needs treatment or is only a symptom of a more serious problem. For example, word-by-word reading, improper phrasing, and repetitions usually are symptoms of more serious problems, such as difficulty in one or more of the following areas: decoding, efficiency skills, or comprehension. In this situation, treatment for these larger problems probably would cause the symptoms of word-by-word reading, improper phrasing, and repetitions to disappear automatically. Read each discussion section carefully to ensure adequate diagnosis and to determine the proper techniques for instruction.

After noting on the Reading Diagnosis Chart the skills in which your students are weak, turn to the Contents. This will help you to quickly locate corrective procedures for each of the problems listed. The numbers on the Reading Diagnosis Chart correspond to the chapter numbers for each difficulty noted. For example, students who have difficulty with basic sight words can be helped by using the corrective procedures in Chapter 12, while those who are unable to skim or scan can be helped by using the procedures in Chapter 25, and so on.

Following the Reading Diagnosis Chart is a section entitled "Making Your Own Diagnostic Kit from the Appendices." Become familiar with this section, so you can make your own diagnostic kit as you read the various sections for which testing or assessment materials are included in the appendices. After becoming familiar with the text, you may wish to reproduce copies of the Reading Diagnosis Chart so you will have a record for each member of the class, or for each student with whom you are working. It will be easier to locate certain difficulties if you use the code for marking in oral diagnosis, which is described in Appendix B-1. This code will enable you to find exactly what type of mistakes students make in their reading. With a little practice, you will become adept at transcribing the student's oral reading. You will, of course, need a copy of what the student is reading (preferably double-spaced) to mark as the student reads. You will also find this marked or coded copy useful in rechecking a student's reading to record progress in overcoming earlier difficulties. In selecting material for the student to read, try to find material that will cause the student to make 5 to 10 errors per page. If the material is too easy and the student is able to read it without error, you obviously will be unable to determine the nature of his reading difficulties. On the other hand, if the student makes more than about 10 errors per page, the material may be so difficult and frustrating that he will guess wildly and lose his ability to apply the reading skills he does possess. This guideline applies to the selection of reading material *for testing/diagnosis purposes* only. The difficulty of other reading material will vary according to the purpose for which it is used. The student should be able to decode at least 95% of the words in material you use for instructing the student and at least 98% of the words in material that the student reads independently.

Sometimes a particular suggestion will be appropriate for a younger child but inappropriate for an older student. We have not listed the various suggestions as appropriate for certain grades or age levels. Exercise your own judgment based on the severity of the problem and the age and attitude of the child. We have, however, noted that some problems are beyond the beginning reading stage.

Definitions of Terms

Affixes   The verb *affix* means "to fasten"; the noun form is usually applied to suffixes and prefixes collectively.

Alphabet Knowledge   The ability to discriminate, recognize, and name the letters of the alphabet.

Basal Reader   A reading textbook designed for a specific grade level. These usually contain material designed to enhance specific skills, such as word-attack, vocabulary, and comprehension skills, along with teacher's manuals and a wealth of other teaching/reinforcement materials.

Basic Sight Word Phrases   These are basic sight words that are grouped together in phrase units. When students learn to read these phrases quickly and smoothly, they usually transfer their ability to recognize basic sight words in isolation to reading them in context.

Basic Sight Words or **Basic Sight Vocabulary**   These are words that appear most often in reading material written for children and adults. For a student to master a basic sight word, she must recognize and pronounce the word instantly (in 1 second or less) every time she sees it. One of the most common basic sight word lists is the Dolch Basic Sight Vocabulary, which contains no nouns but is a 220-word list of "service words." In Appendix B-4 you will find a modified version of this list, along with instructions for assessing students' knowledge of these words.

Choral Reading   Reading done orally by two or more students from the same passage at the same time.

Cloze Passage   A reading passage of approximately 250 words in which, beginning after the 25th word, every 5th word is omitted. Students read the original passage, then fill in the exact word, if possible. Independent, instructional, and frustration levels may be calculated based on the percentage of correct words filled in.

Cloze Procedure   A process of matching students to materials at their appropriate grade level. *Cloze passages* may be used to test the students' comprehension of selected passages to determine placement, to teach context clues, or to teach students to better comprehend what they read.

Comprehension   Meaning gained from what is written on a page (when read) or heard (when spoken).

Consonant Blend   Combinations of two or three consonants blended together into sounds while retaining the sounds of the individual letters, for example, *cr* in *crayon* and *pl* in *plate*.

Consonant Cluster A term referring to both *consonant blends* and *consonant digraphs*.

Consonant Digraph See Digraph.

Context Clues Clues to the meaning and/or pronunciation of an unknown word derived from the words preceding or following that word. For example, one can use context clues to determine that the missing word in the following sentence is *dog:* The _____ was barking all night and kept me awake.

Critical Reading Evaluating on the basis of the reader's experience the meaning and implications of what is read.

Decoding The process of taking words in print and changing them to spoken words. This is accomplished when the reader applies one or more of the following: sight word recognition, phonics, structural analysis, and context clues.

Diagnosis A careful investigation carried out to determine the amount and sequence of remediation needed by a student with reading difficulties.

Digraph A combination of two letters recording (representing) a single sound. There are *consonant digraphs* and *vowel digraphs*. An example of a consonant digraph is *ph* in the word *digraph*. In this case, the *ph* stands for the /f/ sound. (When a letter is found between two slash marks, as the *f* above, it means the sound for which the letter stands.) An example of a vowel digraph is the *ea* in the word *each*. In saying the *phoneme* (sound) represented by the letters of a digraph, one does not change the position of the mouth from the beginning to the end of the sound.

Diphthong A combination of two vowel letters that are both heard in making a gliding sound, for example, *ow* in *cow* and *oy* in *boy*. In pronouncing a diphthong sound, the position of the mouth is moved from the beginning to the end of the diphthong. (The word *diphthong* is pronounced: /dif'/ /thong/. The consonant digraph *ph* is pronounced as /f/.)

Direct Instruction A teaching approach that is academically focused, sequential, and structured. The teacher presents information to the students and monitors the pacing and learning of the material.

Dyad Reading An adaptation of the neurological impress method whereby proficient readers are paired with struggling readers to assist them as they read from one shared book.

Echo Reading Also called *imitative reading;* a recommended technique for improving efficiency skills in reading. This technique can work on a one-to-one basis or with a tape recorder. Students may also use this technique when reading in pairs. The teacher reads a passage aloud; then the student attempts to duplicate the passage using the same phrasing and intonation.

Efficiency Skills Beyond the ability to merely decode words, the ability to use punctuation and other cues to read smoothly and easily, with proper speed, accuracy, and phrasing. This term is often used synonymously with *fluency.*

Engaged Time or **On-Task Time**   The amount of time a student is involved or engaged in the learning task.

Flexible Reading   Adjusting reading speed to fit the requirement of understanding the text. The purpose for reading and the type of material to be read dictate appropriate speed.

Fluency   See **Efficiency Skills.**

General Sight Words or **General Sight Vocabulary**   *Any* word that a reader has seen many times in the past and is able to recognize instantly without using word-attack skills. This term should not be confused with the term *basic sight words,* which refers only to words that appear on a list of the most frequently occurring words.

Grapheme   A grapheme is the written representation of a phoneme; for example, the word *dog* has three distinct sounds that are represented by the graphemes *d, o,* and *g.* The word *straight* also has three phonemes that are represented by the graphemes *str, aigh,* and *t.* See **Phoneme.**

Group-Assisted Reading   A modification of the dyad reading method to be used with groups of struggling readers. The reading material is large enough for all to see, and the teacher and students read it out loud together, with the teacher pointing to each word as it is read.

Holistic Approach   A teaching-learning approach that emphasizes wholes of subject matter. A completely holistic approach to teaching reading would include few or no subskills of reading and an emphasis on the teacher as a facilitator of learning rather than one who provides direct instruction. Also called *whole-language approach.*

Interactive Model of Reading   A model that describes reading as being both concept- and text-driven, in which the reader and the text work together to elicit meaning. The reader comprehends through the use of both decoding skills and prior knowledge.

Kinesthetic Method or **Tactile-Kinesthetic Method**   The use of touch, hearing, sight, and muscle movement to teach letters or words. The approach usually involves tracing over words with the index and middle fingers while sounding the part being traced.

K-W-L Technique   For reading in the content areas, a direct-instruction comprehension strategy in which the teacher elicits what the students *know* about the subject to be read (*K*), what they *want* to learn (*W*), and finally what they *learned* from reading the passage (*L*).

Language-Experience Approach (LEA) The student's or group's own words are written down and used as material for instruction in reading, writing, spelling, listening, and speaking. The approach relies on children's oral language background to develop their reading skills and is considered more personalized and motivating, though less systematic or sequential, than other approaches.

Letter Knowledge See **Alphabet Knowledge.**

Letter-Sound Correspondence The relationship between a letter and the sound it stands for.

Levels of Reading

Independent or **Free reading level** The student can function adequately without the teacher's help at this level. Comprehension should average 90% or better, and word recognition should average 99% or better.

Instructional reading level The student can function adequately with teacher guidance and yet be challenged to stimulate his reading growth. Comprehension should average 75% or better, and word recognition should average 90% or better.

Frustration reading level The student cannot function adequately. In reading at this level, the student often shows signs of tension and discomfort. Vocalization is often present. Comprehension averages 50% or less, and word recognition averages 90% or less.

Literature-Based Reading Program Teaching reading using children's stories, nonfiction pieces, and poetry. This may range from an in-depth study of core literary works to extension of core work together with recreational and motivational reading that is based on the student's natural curiosity.

Meaning Vocabulary Sometimes called simply *vocabulary;* refers to the student's knowledge of the *meanings* of words in her listening, speaking, and reading vocabularies. A large and growing meaning vocabulary is critical to reading comprehension as students progress through the grades.

Metacognition Knowledge of one's own thought processes while reading. This implies that the student can select reading strategies that will help her to comprehend the material.

Modeling Strategies for Paragraph Meaning The teacher models, then directs students in the use of, a code for marking reactions to selected paragraphs. This is one of the most effective methods to teach students to improve their comprehension by monitoring their thought processes when reading.

Neurological-Impress Method (NIM) The teacher sits beside the student and points to each word, reading it aloud. The student follows along with her eyes and reads aloud with the teacher.

Paired Repeated Readings Students are paired. They read the selection silently, then each reads it out loud three times while the other listens and provides assistance. The reader evaluates his or her performance and the listener provides a critique.

Phoneme The smallest unit of speech sound in a language; for example, in the word *dog* there are three phonemes: /d/, /o/, and /g/.

Phonemic Awareness Also called *phoneme awareness, phonological awareness,* or *oral phonemic segmentation;* the understanding of and the ability to manipulate phonemes.

Phonic Elements Initial consonants, consonant digraphs, consonant blends, vowels, vowel combinations, or special letter combinations to be learned in the study of phonics.

Phonics The application of *phoneme-grapheme* (sound-symbol) relationships to the teaching of reading; usually used in beginning reading because phonics is a helpful tool for decoding one-syllable words.

Phonogram A series of letters that begin with a vowel and are often found together; for example, *all, ell, old, ime,* and so on. A phonogram is sometimes referred to as a *rime, graphemic base, word element, word family, vowel family,* or *graphoneme.*

Precision Reading A method used to help students overcome difficulties with reading efficiency. A segment of a book is selected and the student is told to practice reading these sentences as accurately as possible. Later, the oral reading of the sentences is scored and the results are graphed.

Reader's Theater After practicing, students read their parts from a script in front of a group. The material read is highly motivating and not too difficult.

Reading Programs

    Developmental The normal classroom instructional program followed by the teacher to meet the needs of students who are progressing at a normal rate in terms of their capacity.

    Corrective A program of instruction usually conducted by a classroom teacher within the class setting to correct mild reading difficulties.

    Remedial A program of instruction which may be carried on either inside or outside the regular classroom to teach specific reading skills to students with severe reading difficulties.

Reading Recovery A program developed by Marie Clay for the early intervention of reading difficulties. This one-to-one instructional program is designed to help 6-year-olds overcome a slow start in reading. It is a registered trademark in the United States. Reading Recovery teachers receive extensive training prior to certification.

Repeated Readings The student is given a selection of 50 to 200 words, practices reading it, and is timed. Reading rate and number of errors are noted. The student then rereads the selection along with a recording and is retested.

Semantic Mapping   Organizing concepts into a cognitive structure or hierarchy for better comprehension.

Shared Book Experience   Also called *shared reading,* this strategy was developed by Don Holdaway to provide young children in the classroom with experiences similar to those they might experience in a warm and literate environment at home. Big books are used by the teacher to help the youngsters learn to read by following along as the teacher reads with enthusiasm and runs his or her hand under the words as they are read. Repetitive, familiar texts are often used. The shared book experience is a step between reading to children and independent decoding by the children.

Story Frame   A device used to build comprehension. It provides structure to a variety of content material. In a story frame, the teacher begins a sentence about the story's content and the student must complete the sentence. Story frames may become more elaborate and deal with character, plot, and setting as students become more skilled in completing them.

Structural Analysis   Often referred to as *morphology;* the study of meaning-bearing units such as root words, prefixes, suffixes, possessives, plurals, accent rules, and syllables. Structural analysis is a critical skill that enables students to decode multisyllable words.

Vocabulary   Most often, and most appropriately, this term is synonymous with *meaning vocabulary.* Sometimes it is used to refer to the number of words a reader recognizes, or the reader's *sight vocabulary.*

Whole-Language Philosophy   Reading and writing instruction that uses complete texts in communicative situations, as contrasted with focused skills practice or the use of phonics or isolated drilling of language. This philosophy or approach to reading/language instruction may also incorporate speaking, listening, and spelling, and may use materials such as newspapers, children's books, notes, and memos. It usually deemphasizes grouping by ability and teacher-directed instruction.

Word-Analysis Skills   Sometimes called *word-attack skills,* these are the skills a reader must use to determine how to pronounce a word when it is not recognized instantly. (The three important word-analysis skills are phonics, structural analysis, and context clues.)

Word-Recognition Skills   The ability of a reader to recognize words; usually refers only to recognition by sight or recognition without the aid of word analysis.

Reading Diagnosis Chart

1	Lacks Phonemic Awareness and/or Alphabet Knowledge	Pre-Reading		
2	Word-by-Word Reading	Oral Reading		D—Difficulty recognized
3	Incorrect Phrasing			P—Pupil progressing
4	Poor Pronunciation			N—No longer has difficulty
5	Omissions			
6	Repetitions			
7	Inversions or Reversals			
8	Insertions			
9	Substitutions			
10	Guesses at Words			
11	Voicing-Lip Movements, Finger-Pointing, and Head Movements			
12	Basic Sight Words Not Known	Decoding		
13	General Sight Vocabulary Not up to Grade Level			
14	Phonics Difficulties: Consonants			
15	Phonics Difficulties: Vowels			
16	Phonics Difficulties: Blends, Digraphs, or Diphthongs			
17	Structural Analysis Difficulties			
18	Contractions Not Known			
19	Inadequate Ability to Use Context Clues			
20	Vocabulary Inadequate	Comprehension		
21	Comprehension Inadequate			
22	Low Rate of Speed	Study Skills		
23	Inability to Adjust Reading Rate			
24	High Rate of Reading at the Expense of Accuracy			
25	Inability to Skim or Scan			
26	Unable to Locate Information			
27	Undeveloped Dictionary Skills	Other		
28	Written Recall Limited by Spelling Ability			

NAME _____ GRADE _____

TEACHER _____ SCHOOL _____

1st Check   2nd Check   3rd Check

The items listed above represent the most common difficulties encountered by pupils in the reading program. Following each numbered item are spaces for notation of that specific difficulty. This may be done at intervals of several months. One might use a check to indicate difficulty recognized or the following letters to represent an even more accurate appraisal:

Making Your Own Diagnostic Kit from the Appendices

Materials are included in Appendices B-1 through B-11 for developing your own diagnostic kit for use in locating students' reading difficulties. Most of these appendices are organized as follows:

Preparing for the test. In this section, you will find instructions for preparing the material in this book for use in testing. In most cases, the directions include removing an answer sheet, which is to be duplicated. Directions are also included for removing and laminating a stimulus sheet. It is suggested that you file the materials from each of these appendices so that you may easily retrieve them. You may wish to file each test or assessment device in a large manila envelope and then label each envelope like a file folder. These may then be kept in a portable file box, and easily transported from place to place as needed in various testing situations.

Specific directions for giving each test or assessment device. In this section, you will find specific directions for administering each test or assessment device.

Important points to remember. In administering any test or assessment device, there are certain techniques that you will find helpful and others that should be avoided. This section, found in each appendix, includes this information.

Following is a list of appendices and testing or assessment devices that you should have in your kit when it is completed.

Appendix B-1: Code for Marking in Oral Diagnosis
Appendix B-2: Testing Letter Knowledge
Appendix B-3: Quick Check for Basic Sight Words
Appendix B-4: Testing Basic Sight Words and Phrases
Appendix B-5: Quick Survey Word List
Appendix B-6: Phonics Assessment
Appendix B-7: Structural Analysis Assessment
Appendix B-8: Testing Knowledge of Contractions
Appendix B-9: Testing Ability to Use Context Clues
Appendix B-10: Reading Interest Survey
Appendix B-11: Using the Cloze Procedure

It will *never* be appropriate to give all of these tests or assessment devices to any one child. Which tests you use with a particular student will depend on the student's current reading level and the amount of information you wish to obtain. With some experience in conducting individual diagnostic testing, most examiners can do a thorough evaluation in 20 to 60 minutes.

PART ONE

INTRODUCTION

Introduction: Useful Methods for Teaching Students with Reading Difficulties

In this chapter you will find information on some important principles of effective instruction for students who have reading difficulties. Consider these principles when you are organizing your instruction and selecting techniques to use from various chapters in this book. Next, you will find information on the use of several techniques or approaches that are especially helpful with students with reading difficulties. The first of these approaches is the language-experience approach. Although this approach is used by most primary-grade teachers in a regular developmental reading classroom, certain procedures emphasized here are particularly appropriate for disabled readers of any age. A number of highly effective oral reading techniques are then described.

PRINCIPLES OF EFFECTIVE INSTRUCTION

Students often fail to learn to read because large class sizes and multiple demands on the time of classroom teachers make it difficult or impossible for teachers to give students the concentrated instruction they need. Our reading of the considerable literature in the field of reading instruction and our experience in the roles of classroom teacher, reading specialist, school administrator, college teacher, and director of university reading clinics have persuaded us that, with reasonable conditions and appropriate instruction over time, nearly every disabled reader can make significant progress.

The teaching of reading is not a mystical process. Although much remains to be learned about how we can best help those who are failing, we do know which practices succeed most often. The recommendations provided in this book will be most effective if you are mindful of the following principles:

1. Most students require a certain amount of systematic, sequential skill instruction to learn how to decode or pronounce unknown words fluently. The amount of this type of instruction required varies considerably from student to student.

2. Most students require *direct instruction,* in which the teacher presents information to the students in small increments of learning, guides the instruction, and monitors the pace of student learning of new material.

3

3. All students should be taught, and should practice, reading at an appropriate level of difficulty so that they can experience frequent success. All too often, disabled readers are expected to read material that is much too difficult for them. From this experience they learn only frustration, instead of how to read successfully.

4. All students need substantial amounts of practice in the act of reading to ensure that important skills are learned and utilized and to promote an appreciation for the value and joy of reading.

You will notice that some of the recommendations in this book require the teacher to interact with the students in order to guide them in developing strategies to improve their reading abilities. These techniques may require the teacher to describe or model a strategy, assist the students in using it, then provide the students with opportunities to use the strategy on their own. These recommendations are usually the most important and most effective. Other recommendations, while valuable, are less critical. For example, in most chapters you will find suggestions for worksheets, games, or other activities that will give students independent practice on certain skills. These activities may be motivating and may give students beneficial practice when they are working alone or in small groups without the teacher present. But they cannot replace the direct instruction provided initially by the teacher.

For students to benefit most from their reading instruction and practice, activities must be presented at the appropriate level of difficulty. When reading independently, students should be able to decode at least 98% of the words on their own. (A procedure for helping students determine whether reading material is too difficult is presented in Chapter 21 under "Procedures for Improving Overall Comprehension," item A. If the level of instruction is too high or the material is too difficult, students will become frustrated. If such frustration occurs frequently, then the "assistance" provided to students may actually do more harm than good. When in doubt, have students read easier material. Even if it is too easy, they will benefit from the practice in reading it.

For new learnings to transfer and become permanent reading abilities, it is essential that students have abundant opportunities for practice in the act of reading. Such practice must consist of the reading of whole, contextual material, not merely flash cards, word lists, or items on a worksheet. This practice should occur both in and out of school and may include both oral and silent reading of magazines, stories, books (both fiction and nonfiction), poems, instructions, recipes, newspapers, child-authored books, manuals, and so forth. As a teacher of reading you should make every effort to motivate students to read for information and pleasure. While engaged in the act of reading, students put the pieces of reading instruction together and gradually develop the fluency that makes reading an automatic process. Such fluency is also required for adequate reading comprehension.

A number of unusually effective techniques or approaches are presented in the following sections of this chapter. Each of these techniques or approaches embodies the principles we have described.

THE LANGUAGE-EXPERIENCE APPROACH

The **language-experience approach (LEA)** combines all of the language arts—listening, speaking, reading, and writing. When using the language-experience approach, one need not be concerned about whether the material being read is in the learner's background and will be too difficult to comprehend or whether the student will be interested in the subject. One also need not be concerned about whether the reading material will appear too "babyish" for the student. This is because in the language-experience approach, the reading material is generated by the student.

The language-experience approach can be used with a single student or with a group of students. Much has been written on the use of the language-experience approach, and varying procedures for its use have been suggested. The material presented here indicates how it might be used with an individual and with a group. Certain procedures are also stressed that may seem unimportant at first. However, certain aspects of the language-experience approach are extremely important for its success, and we recommend little variation from these specific procedures. The material that follows is divided into five sections: (1) the theory behind the success of the language-experience approach; (2) using the language-experience approach with individual students; (3) using the language-experience approach with small groups of students; (4) important procedures and information about the use of the language-experience approach; and (5) a description of a number of highly motivating language-experience activities.

The Theory behind the Success of the Language-Experience Approach

The language-experience approach uses the language of the students as the basis for writing materials that will later be read by those same students. When a student dictates something to the teacher or writes something herself, it will naturally be something in which the student is interested and will also be something that the student will understand with no difficulty. Furthermore, it will be written at a reading level appropriate for the student, and its content will not insult the student regardless of age.

Using the Language-Experience Approach with Individual Students

In using the language-experience approach with individual students, the teacher should follow this general procedure:

1. Tell the student that you would like her to dictate a story to you, so she will have something to read immediately. Spend some time discussing topics that interest her about which she would like to talk or write.

2. When she has chosen a subject, ask the student what she would like to use as a title for the story. You may wish to make suggestions; however, it is much better to get the student to use her own language. The student may wish to write about some experience that she has had lately, or she may wish to write about a favorite pet or a brother or sister. There are often hands-on experiences that have taken place in the classroom setting about which the student may wish to write; for example, a science experiment or something the student is making as an art project or social studies assignment.

3. When the student has decided on an appropriate title, begin to write. Use either manuscript or cursive writing, depending on the age/grade level of the student and what she has previously been taught. If the student has done very little writing of any kind, or if you are in doubt, then you should use manuscript writing. As you write each word, make sure the student is watching. Say each word as you write it. As soon as you have finished writing the title or any sentence, stop and bring your finger down on each word and read it back to the student. It is important to bring your finger down on each word for two reasons. First, it will help the student understand that each set of letters stands for a particular word; second, it will set a pattern for the student to follow when she begins to read. It is also important that you read the material first, so that the words will again be emphasized. This will give the student a second chance to learn each written word.

4. Ask the student to read the title to you. Make sure that the student brings her finger down on each word as she reads it. This will ensure that the student again notes each word carefully and sees each word as a part of the overall title or sentence. In most cases, a student will be able to read the title or a sentence back to you without carefully looking at what has been written. Having the student bring her finger down on each word will also ensure that she is actually looking at the word she is pronouncing and not saying one word while looking at another. If you allow the student to slide her finger under the words as she reads, she may have a tendency to read ahead of or behind where her finger is pointing. Students are hesitant to do this at times; they may have had a teacher who told them not to point to words as they were reading. A student may also resist raising her finger up and bringing it down on each word. Insist that it be done this way and you will, in most cases, find that any initial resistance is quickly overcome.

5. Continue to do the rest of the story as you did the title. Stop after you have written each sentence and point to each word as you reread the sentence. Bring your finger down on the word and say it at exactly the same time your finger comes down on the word. After reading the sentence, have the student do it in the same manner. Then add a sentence at a time until you have finished the story.

6. After finishing the story, point to each word and read the entire story. Then have the student do the same. If she miscalls a word, quickly correct her and continue. Depending on the student and her ability to remember, it may be advisable to read the story several times.

7. The length of each story will depend on the characteristics of the student who is dictating it. However, in the beginning stages, be careful not to make the stories too long. The student will lose accuracy in rereading a particularly lengthy story, thus defeating the purpose of having her create her own material. As students continue to improve their reading, you are likely to find that they begin to dictate longer stories.

8. At this point you may let the student illustrate the story or apply stickers or appropriate pictures from other sources.

9. Next, type or print the story using a word processor. If you use a typewriter, use primary or pica type, whichever is appropriate to the age/grade level of the student. If you use a word processor, you may be able to select from a number of fonts and sizes. The student should have the ability to transfer knowledge of words from manuscript or cursive writing to printed type.

10. After a period of time, such as would elapse after doing another activity, have the student reread the original story and then the typewritten or printed copy. You may wish to have the student take the original illustrated story home and practice reading it to someone in her family. Some students may lose their stories, and having prepared and saved it on a word processor will ensure that all stories remain intact.

11. When next meeting with the student, ask her to again read the story written in the previous session. If she reads it without errors, write another story and use the same procedure. Continue this sequence, that is, rereading all previous stories and writing another one each time you meet.

12. After the student has written a number of stories, you may bind them into a booklet and let the student illustrate the cover.

13. After the student has built up a considerable sight vocabulary and has developed some beginning word-attack skills, you may have her gradually begin to read basal readers or general books.

Using the Language-Experience Approach with Small Groups of Students

In using the language-experience approach with small groups of students, you may wish to follow a sequence such as the following:

1. Find some event or subject of interest to the group, and tell the students that you would like to help them write a story about the event or subject.

2. Ask students to decide on a title for the story. When they have agreed on a title, write it using the exact words given by the students. As you write it, say each word. After finishing the title, instruct the students to watch carefully as you read it. Point to each word as you read it. Be careful to bring your finger down on each word and read it only as your finger touches the word. Then ask the students to read the title as you point to each word. You may have several students read it individually.

3. When writing the story, use these general guidelines:

    A. Use the type of writing to which the students are accustomed, that is, either manuscript or cursive.
    B. Use the language that the students suggest and make very few, if any, changes.
    C. Write on something that can be saved for future use. Use 24″ × 36″ lined chart paper if it is available.
    D. Use a felt-tip pen or marker that will make broad, readable lines.
    E. In the beginning stages, use one-line sentences and gradually increase the length of the line as students' reading improves.
    F. Emphasize a left-to-right movement.
    G. Make sure students see all words as they are written.

4. After the story has been finished, read it to the class, being careful to point to each word as you read it. Be sure to read the story with enthusiasm.

5. Have the students read the story as a choral exercise as you point to each word.

6. Have individual students come to the chart and read the story. The chosen student should point to each word as she reads it, exactly as you have been doing. While this student points and reads, the rest of the students should read the story quietly as a choral exercise. (Although this may seem like a lot of reading of the same story, you will find that it is excellent practice and the students will enjoy participating.)

7. Use a typewriter or word processor to prepare a printed copy of the story after it is finished. Also, have the students copy the chart in its exact form.

8. If possible, duplicate the story and give each student a copy to take home to practice reading to someone in her family.

9. After a period of time, ask students to reread the story. You may have students take turns reading a sentence at a time.

10. After the students have practiced reading the story a number of times, you may also duplicate the story on a large piece of tagboard. The tagboard may then be cut into strips with one sentence on each strip. Either you or the students may then place the strips in a pocket chart to re-create the original story. At this time, make sure each student can read each sentence in isolation. After you have done this, you may cut the strips of sentences into words and re-create the original story by placing each word in the pocket chart.

11. Each time you meet with the group, read the previously written story and then write another one. Continue this process until stories have been read many times and students know all, or nearly all, of the words as sight words.

12. As students grow in their ability to read, let them begin to write and illustrate their own stories. Then bind these into booklets and let the students illustrate the covers. Let students exchange booklets and read each other's stories.

13. Let students begin to read commercially written materials as their sight vocabulary and word-attack skills permit.

Important Procedures and Information about the Use of the Language-Experience Approach

1. Teachers should remember these important procedures about the language-experience approach:

   A. When students dictate stories, attempt to use the exact language of the students. However, if you are concerned about students' incorrect usage or inappropriate language, you may modify the transcription of the dictation slightly and tell the students, "That's a good thought; another way we might say this is . . ." (See item 4.)

   B. Make sure that both you and the students point to each word as it is being read. Doing this in the beginning stages of using the language-experience approach ensures that each word is memorized as a separate entity as well as a part of an entire story.

   C. Keep words clearly spaced, so students will recognize the difference between *words* and *letters*.

   D. In the beginning stages, be sure to use only one-line sentences. Then gradually expand the length of the sentences as the students become more adept at reading.

    E. Emphasize a series of events, if possible, so students will see the development of the story.

    F. If possible, use 24″ × 36″ chart paper, so capital letters are 2″ high and lowercase letters are 1″ high.

    G. Make sure students see the words as they are being written.

    H. Duplicate the chart so students can take the materials home to be practiced with another member of the family.

    I. Emphasize left-to-right direction and the return sweep in writing and reading the stories.

2. Keep in mind that there are certain limitations to the language-experience approach. For example, a teacher using this approach almost exclusively is not likely to follow a sequential program in teaching word-attack skills. Many studies have shown that structured programs tend to produce better overall achievement from students. For this reason, you would probably want to use the language-experience approach in conjunction with a basal reader program or as a supplemental program for students with reading difficulties.

3. Different types of charts may be written in essentially the same manner as has been described in the preceding material. Some types of charts and their uses are the following:

    A. *Summarizing chart.* This chart shows a series of events on a field trip or a step-by-step procedure for doing an experiment in science.

    B. *Story chart.* This chart describes an event in the life of a group or an individual.

    C. *Planning chart.* This chart lists plans for such things as an anticipated trip or some other event in which the entire class will participate.

    D. *Direction chart.* This chart gives specific directions, such as for the assembly of a toy or paper-folding exercises.

    E. *Dictionary chart.* This chart lists new words that students have learned in science, social studies, or other subject areas.

4. There has been considerable controversy over the shaping of the language of students who are using the language-experience approach. For immature speakers and students whose language is somewhat divergent from what might be considered standard English, the question sometimes arises as to whether the teacher should correct certain usage errors made by these students. It is probably true that more fuss is made over this issue than is necessary. If the teacher chooses to modify the students' language slightly, as indicated in the preceding directions, and if this is done gently, then no damage to either the children's self-esteem or their reading progress need occur.

5. It should be remembered that unless students begin to read trade books and other types of materials as they develop their sight vocabu-

laries, their reading vocabularies will, of course, be limited to only those words in their speaking vocabularies. Therefore, students using the language-experience approach should be encouraged to read other materials along with their language-experience charts and books.

Twenty Language-Experience Activities

Listed here are a number of language-experience materials created by children. Most of the items in the list are examples of individual descriptions of illustrations done in a group setting. With this approach, the teacher motivates the students and leads a brief discussion on the topic. The children then draw pictures of the topic. Some sample topics for this type of activity for beginning readers might be:

1. Happiness is . . .
2. Sadness is . . .
3. A friend is . . .
4. I feel afraid when . . .
5. If I were the teacher I would . . .
6. If I had a million dollars I would . . .

The children decide how they will finish the sentence and begin their illustrations. (These are sometimes called *model sentences*.) The teacher (and other adults, if available) circulates quickly about the room and writes down the children's words, such as "A friend is my Daddy," or "A friend is someone who rides bikes with you," or "A friend is a big yellow zebra." The teacher writes down the exact words the student says. With practice, the teacher can catch all the students' responses while they illustrate. Then, the teacher collects the pictures and binds them and the sentences into a book that the children can read later.

A collection of these student books often becomes the single most popular item in the classroom. The students eagerly read them many times and learn to recognize not only their own words but also the words dictated by their peers. Variations on these examples can be created for virtually any grade level.

The student books can be made from simple materials. The most common type uses a fabric cover around construction paper pages. Here are the directions for making this type of book.

Materials: A piece of fabric, approximately 22″ × 16″
Sheets of 12″ × 18″ construction paper (you'll need one sheet for every four pages of the book, plus one sheet to attach to the cover)
One sheet of 12″ × 18″ tagboard for the cover
Needle and thread
Rubber cement or equivalent

Procedure:

For Pages:
Fold construction paper pages in half.
Sew pages in the middle from bottom to top.
Do not sew through the tagboard cover.

For Cover:
Put rubber cement around inside edge of tagboard.
Put fabric around cover; cement overlap on inside edges of cover.
Fold cover in half.

To Attach Pages to Cover:
Put rubber cement on outside of front and back pages.
Cement outside of pages to cover.

Some Ideas for the Beginning of the Year

1. *Our Class:* You will need one page for each student. The student selects a precut circle of the appropriate color for her face, then draws in the face and the body around it. The student dictates a couplet, which the teacher copies along with the student's name. If one is available, the teacher adds the child's actual picture from a class composite. Examples: "My name is Russell and I have a big muscle," "My name is Brenda Lee and I got stung by a bee," "My name is Ted and I fell out of bed."

2. *All about Us:* Originally these were individual projects that were placed on bulletin boards or around the room. Later they were put together in a large class book. Each student creates her face, arms, and legs out of construction paper that is pasted to a large tagboard sheet. Each student also makes hair out of yarn. The body is 9″ × 12″ construction paper with writing paper on the inside. The construction paper is folded to make the body, then unfolded to read the dictated story.

3. *All about Me:* In this case, each student makes her *own* book, consisting of many pages. Pages may be done one per day and then bound into an individual student book when finished. Example pages: Page 1—All about Me. The student colors the page and writes her name. Page 2—My name is _____ . This is me. The student draws a picture of herself, writes her name, and learns to read a few words. Other pages may include: This is my house; This is my family; I like _____ ; I would like to be a _____ ; My best friend is _____ ; I like to eat _____ ; I don't like to eat _____ ; I like to play _____ ; I am afraid of _____ ; and so on.

4. *My Favorite Things:* This activity is the same as item 3. Pages for individual books like these are sometimes available commercially in

teacher supply stores. Typical pages: My favorite pet is _____ ; My favorite color is _____ ; My best friend's name is _____ ; If you want to phone me, call this number _____ ; If you want to send me a letter, here's my name and address _____; My teeth—I've counted them, I have _____ up top and I have _____ downstairs; My hair looks like this; My nose looks like this; My eyes look like this; My favorite song is _____ ; My favorite sport is _____ ; My favorite instrument is _____ ; I go to bed at _____ ; I get up at _____ ; When I grow up, I want to be _____ .

5. *Let's Pretend:* This activity is similar to items 3 and 4; the teacher makes an individual book for each student. Example pages: If I were invisible I would _____ ; If I had a magic carpet I would _____ ; If I had one million dollars I would _____ ; If I were the teacher I would _____ ; If I could have only one wish it would be _____ ; If I met Jack Frost I would _____ ; If I lived under the sea, I would _____ ; Once upon a time there lived an ugly princess who _____ ; A long, long time ago there lived a tiny mouse who _____ ; The wicked witch waved her magic wand and turned the boy into a _____ .

More Ideas

6. *Happiness and Sadness:* This is a two-part book. For the first part, each student draws a picture and then dictates a statement about "Happiness Is." The second part is "Sadness Is." Examples: Happiness is: "Holding a cat and eating ice cream," "Looking at your muscle." Sadness is: "Getting picked on by someone bigger."

7. *A Friend Is:* This is another sentence completer. The student finishes the thought. "A friend is _____ ," and draws a picture. The teacher or other adult takes dictation, collects the pictures, and binds them into a class book. Examples: "A friend is someone who rides bikes with you"; "A friend is someone who celebrates your birthday in a tent with you"; "A friend is my Daddy."

Holiday Specials

8. *Secret Recipe for Witches' Brew:* The teacher writes the word *cauldron* on the chalkboard and discusses it with the children. Each child has a page shaped like a cauldron and draws on it pictures of items to go into the witches' brew. The teacher or other adult then writes down the words that describe the pictures, collects the pages and binds them into a book. Examples from a kindergarten version: *skeleton, fairy godmother, spider, bloodsucker,* and *spider web.*

9. *The Turkey Book:* This is similar to item 8. The students' pages are shaped like a turkey, and the students draw items related to Thanksgiving.

Still More Ideas

10. *Round Is:* This is a concept book. Each student has a circle on which she draws a picture of something that is round. The teacher or other adult writes down each student's words to describe the picture.

11. *Class Fortunes:* An inscription on the first page describes the book. "Before we made this book we pretended that we were fortune tellers. We said some magic words and then looked into our make-believe crystal balls and concentrated very hard. We each drew the name of another person in the class. These are the people whose fortunes we wrote." (Warning: Students must be prohibited from making unpleasant fortunes for their classmates!) Examples (written by second and third graders): (1) "In my crystal ball I see Sherry. She is an astronaut but works in a hospital and at Sir Pizza in her spare time. She lives in Hawaii and is married to a bachelor." (2) "In my crystal ball I see Dennis. He is a truck driver. He lives in Arizona. He is a bachelor and is playing around." (*Bachelor* must have been a popular word that week!)

12. *Riddles from A to Z:* Each student is given a letter of the alphabet. The student writes a riddle, the answer to which begins with the letter. Example: For the letter F—It runs around the house, yet never moves. (A fence.)

13. *Words with Feeling:* Each page in this book has pasted on it an item that students can see or feel. The pages consist of a listing of words that the item makes the students think of. For example, a piece of aluminum foil is pasted on Page 1. The page has written on it: "SHINY makes me think of: diamonds, gold, silver, sun, rings, and clean hair." Other examples: "VELVETY makes me think of my mother's rug, shag carpets, and green moss." "STRETCHY makes me think of rubber bands, elastic, waking up, spaghetti, gum, and silly putty." Other key words are: SILKY, STRIPED, ROUGH, WAVY, FURRY, BUMPY, SMOOTH, SPOTTED, SPONGY, and BRIGHT.

14. *Moody Me:* The inscription on the first page describes the book. "We had a lot of fun writing this book! First, we acted out all the different moods and talked about them. All of the things in the book have happened or could easily happen to us. These are our real joys, sorrows, dreams, and fears." Each student picks one mood or emotion, draws a picture of herself expressing that emotion, and dictates to the teacher or other adult. Examples: "I feel sad because I don't have any friends." "I feel nervous because I saw a ghost." Other key words: *silly, embarrassed, relieved, happy, awful, excited, confused, proud, mean, overjoyed, itchy, pretty, sick, kind, anxious, mad, hot, worried, cold* and *scared.*

15. *Ridiculous Rhymes:* Each student dictates a couplet and draws a picture that the couplet describes. Examples: "I saw an ant who had no pants." "I saw a turtle who wore a girdle."

16. *Whose Eyes:* The all-time favorite. The inscription on the first page describes the book. "One night, as I lay in my bed almost asleep, I heard a loud knock at my door. The door opened slowly and in the doorway I could see two eyes staring in at me. I have never been so scared in all my life! Who or what could those strange eyes be?" On each page, the student sees a door made of black construction paper, with a yellow self-sticking dot for the doorknob. When the door is opened, the student sees two more yellow dots, which are the eyes. The student then draws a picture around the eyes and dictates to the teacher or other adult what the picture is about. Examples: (1) "It was my mother. She came to bring me a glass of water." (2) "It was a vampire. It wanted to suck my blood." (3) "It was my cat. It came to get tuna fish." (4) "It was my Mom. She came to take my money." (5) "It was a ghost. He was looking for potato chips."

17. *How the Elephant Got Its Trunk:* Inspired by the *Just So Stories,* the students dictate or write their own versions of how the elephant got its trunk.

18. *Our Monsters:* This book combines an art activity with language experience. The students make watercolor monsters and dictate stories about them.

19. *Did You Ever See. . . ?* Based on the book of the same name, this is a collection of illustrated couplets. The illustration on the front side of the page corresponds to the first rhyming word of the couplet; the illustration on the back side of the page corresponds to the second rhyming word. Examples: (1) "Did you ever see a lion—" "—Cryin'?" (2) "Did you ever see a pig—" "—Wear a wig?" (3) "Did you ever see a rabbit—" "—Kick the habit?"

20. *Interviews.* This is a series of language experience books created by a small group of students. Here are the directions: (1) The students interview each other in partners. (2) Each student introduces her partner to the members of the small group; (3) The members of the small group write a page about each student in the group. (4) Each student draws a picture about herself. (5) The teacher makes copies of the books for all members of the group. (6) The students then read each other's books.

EFFECTIVE ORAL READING TECHNIQUES

A number of oral reading techniques or methods may be used to help students to begin the process of decoding, to improve their decoding ability, and to correct various fluency problems such as reading rate, accuracy, phrasing, or expression. Among the best known of these techniques are the neurological-impress method, echo reading or imitative reading, repeated readings, and precision reading. Each of these and a number of other techniques will be described in the following sections. We recommend these methods not because oral reading is the goal, but because these techniques often help students to identify and correct specific reading difficulties.

Oral reading is most effective if it is done in a one-to-one fashion or with very small groups, so that students participate as much as possible. Pairing students is a common practice to facilitate oral reading in the classroom. In using these methods, it is important for the teacher to stress to students that oral reading is only one way of reading and that this practice will ultimately lead the student to greater ability in silent reading. Also, oral reading practice is not substituted for silent reading. Rather, it is presented to give students additional experience with the printed word.

The Neurological-Impress Method

The use of the **neurological-impress method (NIM)** was explained some years ago by R. G. Heckelman.[1] It has been extremely successful with many students with reading difficulties and it is easy to use. NIM is, in fact, so easy to use that teachers are often hesitant to use it. A procedure for its use follows.

1. Sit the student slightly in front of you, so you can point to the material the student is reading and read directly into the student's ear.

2. Begin reading material that is at an easy instructional or independent reading level. As you continue to work with the student, you can increase the level of difficulty of the material.

3. Tell the student that you are going to read the material and that she is to read along with you as you point to the words. Then begin to read at a slightly slower than normal rate for you. While reading, be sure to point to each word as you read it. *This part of the procedure is extremely important.* The student may complain, at first, that she is unable to keep up with you. This should not, however, keep you from using the procedure. Explain to the student that she will become a better reader and will probably soon be able to keep up with you.

4. As you work with the student, you are likely to notice a sharp improvement in her ability to read. Begin to increase your rate of reading as the student's reading improves.

5. Read for periods of 5 to 15 minutes two to four times per day. Heckelman suggests that it is common to cover from 10 to 20 pages of material in one session.

6. Heckelman suggests that if periods of approximately 15 minutes are used, then the procedure should be continued until the student has read for an accumulated total of 8 to 12 hours. However, if the student fails to make progress after 4 hours, the method should be discontinued.

Heckelman has emphasized that in using this method, you will probably see a great increase in the student's ability to read. He cautions that one of the teacher's most frequent mistakes is to spend too much time reading material written at low levels of difficulty because the teacher does not expect the student to learn so rapidly. For example, Heckelman says that if a student is started at the first-grade level, she might be expected to be reading materials at the third-grade level after an accumulated total of two hours. After an accumulated total of six hours, the student might be reading materials at the fifth- or sixth-grade level of difficulty.

Heckelman suggests that one of the reasons for the remarkable success that students often experience with NIM is that the student is exposed to many words, many times, in a relatively short period of time. For example, a student reading for approximately 15 minutes may be exposed to from 1,000 to 2,000 words.

A teacher using NIM seldom, if ever, offers specific correction, nor does she ask questions or test students on the content of the material. As the student's ability improves, she may take over the finger movements and the teacher may select more challenging material to be read.

Studies have been conducted in which teachers have tried to duplicate NIM using tape-recorded materials and having students follow along with the tape-recorded reading. However, this has not produced results comparable to those obtained when working with a student in a one-to-one setting. This is probably because when a student is reading in conjunction with a tape recorder, the teacher has no way of ensuring that the student is actually looking at the words being read. If the student is not actually looking at the words being read, then she is not likely to benefit any more than if she were only listening to the passage.

Dyad Reading

Eldredge and Butterfield[2] adapted the neurological-impress method so that it could be used in the classroom by pairs of students; this is known as the **dyad reading** method. The teacher should identify both proficient and struggling readers and pair them up. The capable reader (known as the *lead reader* or *team leader*) assists the less able student (called the *assisted reader* or *team member*). In this method, the difficulty level of the material is not as important as the interest level to the students. The student pairs are encouraged to read extensively from both narrative (stories) and expository (text) materials.

The two students share one book and sit next to each other while reading. The lead reader sets the pace of oral reading and points to each word with her finger while reading, as the assisted reader reads along orally. The reading should be done in a fluent, natural style, not word by word. As the assisted reader's reading ability improves, the lead reader can begin reading silently, allowing the assisted reader to be more assertive. Even in this phase, however, the lead reader should assist the less capable reader with unknown words when necessary.

Group-Assisted Reading

Eldredge[3] modified the dyad reading method so that it could be used with groups of struggling readers in the classroom. He called this technique **group-assisted reading.** To implement this approach, you should follow three steps:

1. The material to be read must be seen by all students who are participating. This can be accomplished by using big books or chart paper, presenting the material on an overhead transparency, having at least one book available for every two students, or having the material printed and duplicated for each child.

2. The teacher and the students read the material out loud together. In this method, the teacher assumes the role of lead reader, while all of the participating students become assisted readers. The teacher should read orally at a slightly slow pace and in a fluent, expressive manner.

3. The teacher touches each word with her finger as it is read. If using this method with big books, a chart, or an overhead transparency, the teacher should be sure that all students can see the simultaneous reading and touching of the words. If one book is used for every two students, then they can take turns touching the words as they are read. If each child has a copy of the material being read, then each child can read and touch along with the teacher.

Echo Reading or Imitative Reading

In **echo reading,** or *imitative reading,* the teacher reads first and the student repeats what the teacher read. Material can be read in either phrases or sentences, and finger pointing is used in this method also. A common variation uses recorded texts; students first listen straight through while following the written text and then read along with the recording. An advantage of this method is that a teacher need not be present. On the other hand, this variation lacks the immediacy and psychological force of the teacher's presence. A number of high-interest, low-vocabulary read-along materials are available in varying formats with accompanying records, tapes, or slides. Students seem to enjoy these, and, if used properly, they can be beneficial. The teacher must be sure that students *can* read the materials and that they stay on task and *do* read when they are supposed to. Whenever possible, encourage students to point to each word as it is read.

Repeated Readings

Repeated readings is a method suggested by S. Jay Samuels.[4] Students are given selections that consist of 50 to 200 words. The student is instructed to practice her selection and then is timed, after which her reading rate and number of errors are recorded on a chart. (See Appendix C-6 for a blank repeated readings chart and an example of a completed chart.)

While the teacher is checking other students, the student rereads the material along with a recording of the text. The rereading may be done over and over. When the student feels ready, another test is given. Comprehension checks may also take place. Graphing the student's results serves as a motivator for continued progress.

We believe that the repeated-readings method is excellent, but we would add one caution. Our experience has led us to conclude that a primary cause of efficiency or fluency difficulties is that disabled readers often try to read too fast. For most students, it is helpful to encourage them first to read accurately and later to work to improve their speed.

Paired Repeated Reading

Koskinen and Blum[5] created **paired repeated readings** (PRR) so that students could work in pairs to achieve the goals of Samuels's method. Each pair of students chooses easy, interesting material that is about 50 words long. Then each student reads the material silently. Next, the students decide who will begin reading orally. The first reader reads the selection out loud three times while the other student listens and provides assistance, if necessary. After each reading, the reader evaluates her effort; after the second and third readings, the student who was listening uses a check sheet to offer positive feedback to the oral reader. Then the roles and the responsibilities that go with them are reversed, so that each student has an opportunity to read orally, self-evaluate, and critique the other reader. The teacher's role is to demonstrate and facilitate the activity, provide a model of fluent reading, and support and encouragement for the students' efforts.

Precision Reading

Precision reading is an oral reading technique that emphasizes accuracy first, then speed. While the student reads, the teacher records the student's accuracy sentence by sentence on the precision reading form. (See Appendix C-7 for a blank precision reading form and instructions for its use.) The form has spaces to indicate the beginning and ending page numbers of the material read, the total number of sentences read, the number of sentences read perfectly, and the number of sentences read with one or more errors. At the beginning, the student is given relatively easy material and reads a set number of sentences, such as 25. The teacher records the student's accuracy on each sentence, so that on completion a fraction of correct sentences out of the total is derived—for example, 20/25. This indicates that the student read 20 sentences perfectly and made one or more errors on 5 of the sentences. The fraction is then changed to a percentage—in this case, 80% accuracy—and the percentage figure is graphed daily. (Appendix C-7 also includes a sample accuracy graph.) Students enjoy seeing their performance graphed, and this serves as a powerful motivator for continued progress.

The material selected should not cause the student's accuracy rate to drop below 75%. Also, the teacher may select different material for the student to read each day. However, it is helpful if the passage is chosen at least one day in advance so that the student can begin practicing the material in advance as part of her homework. As the student improves and begins to read consistently at or near 100% accuracy, the teacher may provide more difficult material or add the factor of speed. To do the latter, you may have the student read as many sentences as possible within a prescribed time, as long as the accuracy does not drop below, say, 90%. Then the *number* of sentences read perfectly is graphed daily. (An example of this type of graph is also presented in Appendix C-7.)

Reader's Theater

Reader's Theater is a strategy that is very popular with most students. It provides students a safe way to read out loud and perform before a group. Unlike a play in which students must memorize a script, Reader's Theater allows students to read their parts from a script while standing or seated (often on step stools) in front of the group. Of course, the students have ample opportunity to practice reading their parts; this enables them to read fluently and confidently. Minimal or no props are required. Sometimes teachers will have students wear hats or masks or use stick figures.

The selection of material to be read for Reader's Theater is critical. The material should not be too difficult for the students doing the reading, but should be highly motivating. Students enjoy selections with a number of characters and lots of dialogue. They also enjoy reading poems and rhymes. In either case, some of the reading can be performed in unison, while other parts are read by individual students. Few rules apply, and teachers should feel free to experiment.

Listed here are some typical steps to be followed in preparing for a Reader's Theater performance.

1. Select the material to be read.
2. Discuss the topic to be read and draw on students' own experiences with the topic, story, or characters.
3. Have the students read the selection silently, or, if this is too difficult, the teacher may read the script to the students while they follow along.
4. Have all students read the script out loud together (choral reading).
5. Have students select or assign parts. It may be helpful to mark or have students mark their own parts on the script.

6. Do more oral rereadings, this time with students reading their own parts and the unison parts.

7. Perform the material in front of other class members or another audience. Often multiple performances are provided.

8. Discuss the performance with the participating students. This is a good opportunity to provide students with praise and encouragement.

Shared Book Experience

The **shared book experience,** often called *shared reading,* was derived from whole-language theory and is designed for beginning readers. It was developed by Holdaway[6] to extend to the classroom many of the nurturing aspects of the "lap method" provided by parents to their young children. Big books are especially appropriate for this method, because they provide big colorful pictures along with large print, both of which can be seen by many children at once. Charts may also be used, and teachers may add illustrations or rebuses to such charts. It is helpful to have a big book stand or easel to hold the book while it is being read to and by the class. In some cases, teachers also provide small, personal copies of the story for children to use in reading along with the big book or for later reading on their own in school or at home.

In the shared book experience, teachers can model many aspects of reading in front of their students. For example, they can point to or move their hands under the words as they are read aloud. By watching and following along, children will begin to identify specific words and discern that reading is a process of identifying symbols from left to right. Teachers can use this method to help children learn many other concepts about print, including word boundaries, reading from top to bottom, the return sweep at the end of each line of print, upper- and lowercase letters, and so forth. When students are ready, teachers can also begin providing specific instruction on aspects of decoding, such as phonics, sight words, or context clues.

Often books are chosen that contain repetitive rhymes, predictable patterns, or other easy-to-learn structures. Students enjoy having favorite books read over and over. As students begin to memorize or recognize words or phrases, they may read out loud along with the teacher. Extension activities may include writing language-experience charts or class books, drama, art, or movement activities.

Other Oral Reading Techniques

The following oral reading activities are also effective and provide variety for students:

1. The teacher and student (or pairs of students) take turns reading the material out loud by alternating paragraphs, sentences, or lines.

2. The student prereads silently first, notes difficult vocabulary, and reviews the vocabulary with the teacher or other helper; then the student and teacher or helper read together.

3. The teacher provides choral reading activities for small groups of students.

4. The teacher provides plays for students to read. A number of kits are available with simple two-, three-, or four-person plays; or teachers and students can write their own plays.

5. Many students enjoy relaxed paired reading. A student and a friend select two copies of a good book and then take turns reading it out loud together.

6. Younger students read selections using puppets.

7. Older remedial readers can be assigned as tutors to help younger students. In the process of assisting the younger student, the older student often learns more about words and reading than the student she is helping.

8. The teacher may provide a reinforcer, such as clicking a counter or putting a chip in a bank, each time the student reads a sentence perfectly.

9. The teacher may use favorite games such as tic-tac-toe, hangman, and dots to score reading accuracy. For example, a student reads while the other draws part of the hangman if the student who is reading makes an error. (Items 8 and 9 are variations of the precision reading method described earlier.)

10. A number of suggestions for using an audio tape recorder to help students practice oral reading are presented in Chapter 3 under item L.

ENDNOTES

1. Heckelman, R. G. (1966). Using the neurological-impress remedial reading technique. *Academic Therapy Quarterly, 1,* 235–239.
2. Eldredge, J. L., & Butterfield, D. D. (1986). Alternatives to traditional reading instruction. *Reading Teacher, 40,* 32–37.
3. Eldredge, J. L. (1990). Increasing the performance of poor readers in the third grade with a group-assisted strategy. *Journal of Educational Research, 84,* 69–77.
4. Samuels, S. J. (1979). The method of repeated readings. *Reading Teacher, 32,* 403–406.
5. Koskinen, P. S., & Blum, I. H. (1986). Paired repeated reading: A classroom strategy for developing fluent reading. *Reading Teacher, 40,* 70–75.
6. Holdaway, D. (1979). *The foundations of literacy.* Sydney, Australia: Ashton Scholastic.

PART TWO

PREREADING ABILITY

CHAPTER 1

Phonemic Awareness and Alphabet Knowledge

RECOGNIZED BY

PHONEMIC AWARENESS: While the child may not have difficulty in speaking or understanding English, he is unable to recognize, identify, and manipulate individual speech sounds.

ALPHABET KNOWLEDGE: The child is unable to recognize the letters of the alphabet when shown the letters, is unable to point to the letters of the alphabet, is unable to match uppercase and lowercase letters, or is unable to match one uppercase or lowercase letter with another letter that looks exactly the same.

DISCUSSION

Phonemic awareness (sometimes called *phoneme awareness, phonological awareness,* or *oral phonemic segmentation*), is the understanding of, and the ability to manipulate, the smallest units of sound (**phonemes**) that make up spoken words. There are approximately 40 different phonemes in English, which are represented by one or more of the 26 letters in our alphabet. For example, in the word *dog,* there are three phonemes, the sounds of which are represented as follows: $/d/$, $/o/$, and $/g/$. While phonemic awareness is not necessary for understanding and speaking the language, research has shown that it is critical to reading success. In fact, phonemic awareness is more highly related to learning to read than are other well-known measures such as alphabet knowledge, intelligence, reading readiness, and listening comprehension. Phonemic awareness has been shown to be the most important causal factor that distinguishes successful and disabled readers. Youngsters who lack phonemic awareness tend to have difficulty in understanding the alphabetical system of English required for changing print into meaningful sound. Phonemic awareness skills are prerequisite for benefiting from phonics instruction. They are also an important factor in learning how to spell.

Experts do not agree on all of the components of phonemic awareness. Some believe that some of the higher-level phonemic awareness skills are more a consequence of reading acquisition than a cause. One helpful sequence of phonemic awareness skills is provided by Eldredge. His examples can be used to quickly assess the child's level of phonemic awareness ability prior to providing instruction in the areas where weaknesses are exhibited. The following examples, from easiest to most difficult, indicate five different levels of phonemic awareness, as presented by Eldredge:[1]

A. Slowly pronounce the three phonemes /m/ /a/ /n/. Ask the child to tell you what the word is. (Answer: *man.*)

B. Say the word *back.* Ask the child to tell you how many sounds can be heard in that word. (Answer: three.)

C. Say the word *box.* Ask the child to tell you the beginning sound of the word. (Answer: /b/.)

D. Say the word *toss.* Ask the child to tell you the ending sound of the word. (Answer: /s/.)

E. Say the word *cat.* Ask the child to say each of the three phonemes in the word. (Answer: /k/ /a/ /t/.)

Children's phonemic awareness ability should be assessed by mid-kindergarten. Children who are not progressing adequately should be provided with intensive phonemic awareness training.

Alphabet knowledge, a child's ability to recognize and name the letters of the alphabet, appears to be the second most important instructional factor in learning to read. Research has consistently shown that alphabet knowledge is highly correlated with, and usually predictive of, later reading success.

Children who, when given an informal reading inventory, know very few words, or children who appear to be severely disabled in reading, should be given a test for letter knowledge. Keep in mind that there are various levels of difficulty in testing for letter knowledge. The materials listed in Appendix B-2 will enable you to determine whether the child has difficulty with the alphabet and, if so, the *level* of difficulty at which the child is weak. For example, it is more difficult for a child to name letters in random order than it is to point to the letters named by the teacher.

RECOMMENDATIONS

Phonemic Awareness

Phonemic awareness can be fostered both through informal language activities that encourage children to explore and manipulate the sounds in words and through formal, systematic instruction. Phonemic awareness activities should begin prior to kindergarten and may include the activities listed here.

To provide informal, language activities that encourage children to explore and manipulate the sounds in words, the teacher might:

A. Read to children throughout the day and engage them in discussions and explanations to enhance oral language development. Use pictures and objects to demonstrate word meanings and associations.

B. Point out to students the separate words as they appear in sentences on charts or in big books. Pronounce the words clearly while doing this.

C. Help young students to hear the syllables in words by clapping them out and pronouncing them in exaggerated ways.

D. Teach and practice rhyming skills using songs, rhymes, and finger plays.

E. Engage children with alliterative language activities, such as listening for or generating words that start with a specific beginning sound.

F. Provide other activities that encourage children to identify and manipulate phonemes, such as:

   1. "What is the beginning sound of . . ."
   2. "What is the ending sound of . . ."
   3. "Do *dog* and *cat* rhyme?"
   4. "How is *bat* different from *sat?*"
   5. "Listen to the word *time.* Can you change that word by giving it a beginning sound of /*d*/?"
   6. "What are all of the sounds you hear in *feet?*"

   Each of these suggestions can be expanded into activities that may consume several instructional sessions. Do not attempt to teach these concepts too quickly; nor should you expect all students to learn them at the same time.

To provide specific instruction in phonemic awareness, the teacher might key the instructional activities to each of the five phonemic awareness skills identified by Eldredge.

A. Select a number of easily discriminated one-syllable words, such as *bat, sit, red, top,* and *cup.* It is better initially to use words with single consonants at the beginning and end, rather than consonant blends.

   1. Begin with the first word, *bat.*
   2. Slowly pronounce each of the phonemes, being careful to clearly separate them from each other initially. Say: "I'm going to tell you a word by first saying each of its parts very slowly. Listen carefully. /b/ (pause) /a/ (pause) /t/. Now, I'm going to blend those parts of the word together. Listen. /b/ (brief pause) /a/ (brief pause) /t/. Now, listen one more time, while I put the whole word together." Say the whole word *bat* slowly, enunciating each phoneme. "Who can tell me what the word is? Good. What is a bat?"
   3. Repeat the previous step with the other one-syllable words.
   4. As students begin to catch on, you can speed up the process of pronouncing each word as described in step 2.

B. Choose more words, such as *fun, rope, me, is,* and *I.*

   1. Begin with the word *fun.*
   2. Say: "This time I want to see what good counters you are." Slowly pronounce the three separate phonemes of the word *fun.* Say: "Listen. /f/ /u/ /n/. How many sounds did you hear in that word? Three? Good for you."
   3. Say: "Now listen for the next word and count again: /r/ /ō/ /p/. How many sounds did you hear? Three? Very good!"
   4. When you get to the word *me,* you can expect that some of the children will guess three again. Those who, in fact, are developing phonemic awareness should get the correct answer of two.
   5. Alternate between one-, two-, and three-phoneme words (all only one syllable) to make sure the students are listening and telling you how many sounds they are hearing rather than guessing.

C. Choose more one-syllable words or repeat some of those already used, such as *top, dog, bus, sit,* and *cup.*

   1. Say: "This time I want to see if you can listen very carefully and tell me the sound you hear at the beginning of the word I say. Listen. /t/ /o/ /p/. Were you listening for the /t/ sound at the beginning of the word? Good for you. Let's try /d/ /o/ /g/. What was the first sound? /d/. Good."
   2. Continue with the rest of the words. Expect that some children may have difficulty with the concept of "beginning sound." You may need to demonstrate several times. It may be helpful to use a hand signal, such as raising your hand, while you are pronouncing the first phoneme.

D. Repeat the process in step C, but this time have the students listen for and identify the ending sound of the words you pronounce. This task may be considerably more difficult than the previous one for some of the students.

E. Choose more words. This time ask the students to listen and identify (repeat) each of the phonemes as you pronounce them.

   1. Say: "This time I am going to say a word and I want you to tell me all of the sounds you hear in the word. Let's try one. Listen. /p/ /a/ /t/. Did you hear all three sounds? Good. Let's say them again together: /p/ /a/ /t/. Very good."
   2. Continue with other two- and three-phoneme words.

In using this approach, do not expect young students to go through all five areas at one sitting. How fast they are able to progress will depend on your skill in providing the instruction, the number of students present (the fewer the better), the literacy backgrounds of the students, and other factors. Do remember that your goal is to *teach* the students to enhance their phonemic awareness, not merely to test them. Therefore you will need to modify your instructions as necessary to help your students understand these concepts. That may mean moving more slowly, providing more repetition, or presenting smaller increments of learning.

Alphabet Knowledge

A. Teach the child the alphabet song. Then, present a copy of the alphabet (in alphabetical order) and as the child sings the song, ask the child to point to each letter.

B. Present a letter and discuss its characteristic shape; for example, that it has an ascender, such as the letter *h,* or a descender, such as the letter *p.* The speed at which children can learn the letters is highly variable. Some children can learn several letters at a time, while some beginning readers can learn only one letter per week.

C. Make a tape recording of the letters of the alphabet to accompany an alphabet book such as *Animalia* by Graeme Base. Children will find this entertaining, and it provides a way for the child to learn the letters in context.

D. Make a list of the first third of the alphabet:

1.	A	5.	E
2.	B	6.	F
3.	C	7.	G
4.	D	8.	H

Then make a recording for the child to take home or work with in the classroom. The tape-recorded script can be as follows: "Look at the letter by number one. This letter is *A.* Point to it and say '*A.*' Look at it very carefully and say '*A*' again. The next letter by number two is *B.* Point to it and say '*B.*' Look at it very carefully and say it again." Continue through the list. You may wish to modify this script to have the child also write the letter. In this case the script would be as follows: "Look at the letter by number one. This letter is *A.* Point to it and say '*A.*' Look at it very carefully and say it again. Now write the letter and say '*A*' as you write it," and so on. This presentation will be successful only with children who are able to learn the letters easily and rapidly. For other children the presentation can be simplified by presenting only one or two letters at a time. Also, you must observe the children when they are learning in this way. Some children, especially younger ones, can not stay on task for long without direct participation or instruction from the teacher.

E. If some letters are reversed, or if the child seems to have a difficult time learning them, prepare letters cut from fine sandpaper and have the child feel the letters as he pronounces them. This can also be done with three-dimensional letters made of felt or similar material. (Do not become overly concerned if children tend to reverse letters. This is a normal part of the learning process with emergent readers and almost always disappears gradually as the children's letter knowledge increases.)

F. Place a thin layer of salt or fine sand in the bottom of a shoebox lid and ask the child to trace letters with his finger in the sand or salt.

G. When teaching the alphabet, be sure that it appears on a chart where children can see it constantly. Using just a few letters at a time, work with children until they can instantly tell you which letter comes before or after any other letter. For example, if you say, "Which letter comes before *G?*" and point to a child, he should instantly say '*F.*' Most adults can instantly give the letter that immediately *follows* another; however, they usually pause a few seconds before they tell which letter *precedes* another. Knowing the order of the letters will save time later when children are using the dictionary.

GAMES AND EXERCISES

Alphabet Race

Purpose: To teach knowledge of the alphabet

Materials: A racetrack (or open-ended game board)
Flash cards containing each letter of the alphabet (or each letter to be learned)
A marker and a die
Procedure:

A child throws the die and can then move that many spaces if he can identify the letter on the flashcard. To provide more practice, modify the rules so that the child must identify one flashcard for each space he moves.

Newspaper Search

Purpose: To teach knowledge of the alphabet

Materials: A newspaper page and a crayon or marker for each child
Procedure:

The teacher or a child names a letter and the remaining children search their newspaper pages to find the letter and circle it with the crayon or marker. Then have them hunt for another letter and continue in the same manner. Additional practice may be provided by having the children search for both uppercase and lowercase examples of the letter named.

Letter Bingo

Purpose: To teach knowledge of the alphabet

Materials: A bingo card filled with alphabet letters
Markers for each child

Procedure:

The caller names a letter and holds up the matching card while the children search for and cover the named letter on their cards. The first player to cover a row calls "Bingo!"

ENDNOTE

1. Eldredge, J. L. (1995). *Teaching decoding in holistic classrooms.* Englewood Cliffs, NJ: Merrill.

PART THREE

ORAL READING

CHAPTER 2

Word-by-Word Reading

RECOGNIZED BY

The student pauses after each word and does not allow the words to flow as they would in smooth or fluent oral reading.

DISCUSSION

Word-by-word reading may be caused by one or more of the following: (1) failure to apply **decoding** skills effectively (these include basic sight vocabulary, phonics, structural analysis, and context clues); (2) lack of adequate **comprehension;** or (3) poor reading **efficiency skills** (lack of *fluency*). Young students who are beginning to read are often word-by-word readers. However, as their sight vocabulary continues to grow and their word-analysis skills are refined, this habit should disappear.

You should determine which of the previously listed factors is causing the word-by-word reading. Make this determination as follows: Give the student something to read at a much lower reading level than she is capable of. If she continues to read poorly, the problem may then be assumed to be poor efficiency skills. If she immediately improves, the problem can generally be considered one of either decoding or comprehension. You must then decide between these two difficulties. Ask the student questions about the more difficult material she was reading word-by-word. If the student can answer approximately 75% or more of the questions correctly, then her problem probably lies in the area of decoding. If she cannot answer approximately 75% of the questions correctly, she may be having trouble with comprehension. You may also take a few of the more difficult words from the reading passage and put them on flash cards to see if the student can recognize these words in isolation.

If the student is unable to decode the words, the recommendations listed under "Recommendations" in items A through G will be helpful. If the difficulty results from poor efficiency skills, the recommendations under items H through Q will be more helpful. However, if the student is having difficulty with comprehension, you should follow the suggestions listed under "Comprehension Inadequate," Chapter 21. Remember that students can read efficiently (fluently) only when they are thoroughly familiar with the vocabulary in the material that they are required to read. Therefore, if a student is having difficulty with the vocabulary in the material, you should not try the types of suggestions listed in items H through Q. You would be treating the symptoms rather than the actual cause of the difficulty.

RECOMMENDATIONS

For students whose word-by-word reading is caused by inadequate decoding ability:

A. Use reading material on a lower level of difficulty.

B. Do not expect students to read material above their meaning-vocabulary level. Generally use easy materials and encourage students to read in great quantity.

C. Have the students dictate or write their own stories and read them aloud. Tape-record their readings of these stories and contrast the recordings with their readings of less familiar stories. Discuss the differences and their need for smooth fluent reading. (This is an adaptation of the language-experience approach.)

D. Use other aspects of the language-experience approach as described in the introductory chapter.

E. If word-by-word reading is caused by an insufficient sight vocabulary, you should follow the suggestions listed in Chapter 3 under "Recommendations," item A, p. 40, and those listed in Chapters 12 and 13.

F. If the student is unable to use phonics or structural analysis sufficiently for decoding, then the recommendations in Chapters 14 through 17 will prove helpful.

G. To help students use their existing decoding skills effectively, teach the word-attack strategy shown in Figure 2.1.

This strategy and effective ways to teach it are described in Chapter 19, which also presents a number of other recommendations for teaching students to use context clues.

For students whose incorrect phrasing is caused by poor efficiency skills:

H. If the student seems unaware of her word-by-word reading, it is often helpful to tape-record the student while she is reading orally. Then play back the recording so she can become aware of the specific problem. If necessary, take time to demonstrate both inappropriate (word-by-word) and fluent reading.

FIGURE 2.1

WHEN YOU COME TO A WORD YOU DON'T KNOW:
1. Say the beginning sound.
2. Read the rest of the sentence. THINK.
3. Say the parts that you know. GUESS.
4. Ask someone or skip it and go on.

I. In item B, we suggested that you urge students to read in great quantity. This suggestion was aimed at readers whose word-by-word reading results from poor decoding skills. This recommendation is equally valuable for students whose word-by-word reading results from poor efficiency skills. The recommendation bears repeating: *Provide abundant opportunities for students to practice the act of reading, both orally and silently.*

J. Use one or more of the oral reading techniques described in detail in the introductory chapter. These procedures are highly effective with a variety of oral reading difficulties.

K. Allow students to preread material silently before asking them to read it orally. You might allow students to ask you for assistance with difficult words during the silent reading phase. If they ask for help on more than 10% of the words, then the material is too difficult for them and should be replaced with easier material.

L. Using an audio tape recorder may also serve as an excellent way for students to practice oral reading. The teacher might set up a "recording studio," providing a tape recorder, microphone, and cassette tapes for the students. The following activities are effective:

   1. The student reads orally into the tape recorder, plays back the tape, and
      a. listens to the recording noting errors,
      b. reads along silently, or
      c. reads along orally.
   2. The teacher or another person reads a selection into the tape recorder and the student plays it back as in item 1. The teacher may make purposeful errors or exhibit poor efficiency skills, such as word-by-word reading. The student evaluates the teacher's performance and tries to apply this to her own reading.
   3. Two or more students read into a tape recorder together, using some of the techniques in items 1 and 2.

M. Provide experience in choral reading. This activity may be done with as few as two students or with the entire class.

N. Give a series of timed silent-reading exercises. The addition of the time factor will often make the student aware of the word-by-word reading.

O. Allow students to choose stories that they feel are exciting and then let them read their selections aloud.

P. Have the children read poetry. They should reread it until it becomes easy for them.

Q. Use commercial materials, such as *Plays for Echo Reading* (published by Harcourt Brace Jovanovich), that are designed to develop expressive, fluent oral reading.

CHAPTER 3

Incorrect Phrasing

RECOGNIZED BY

The student fails to read fluently, that is, in natural phrasing or linguistic units. He may fail to take a breath at the proper place and will often ignore punctuation, especially commas.

DISCUSSION

The causes of incorrect phrasing may be inadequate decoding ability, insufficient comprehension, or poor efficiency skills. You should first determine the cause. Select a passage of 100 words that is at a reading level at which the student is experiencing difficulty. Give the student a disorganized list of the 100 words that appear in that passage.

If he does not recognize approximately 95 of the words on the list, you can assume that inadequate decoding ability is contributing to the problem of incorrect phrasing.

If the student does recognize at least 95 of the words on the list, then have him read the story from which the words came and answer at least six questions about that story. If the student phrases incorrectly and fails to answer at least 75% of the questions (but knows 95 or more of the words), then insufficient comprehension is probably a major contributor to the problem. Reading material is probably not too difficult for a student if he can correctly decode 95% or more of the words and can answer at least 75% of the questions about the passage. So, if the material is not too difficult in terms of decoding and comprehension, *and* a student continues to phrase incorrectly, you may assume that he has poor efficiency skills.

If inadequate decoding ability is a contributing factor in incorrect phrasing, then the suggestions under "Recommendations" in items A through G should be beneficial. If the cause of incorrect phrasing is a lack of comprehension, consult item H and refer to the appropriate chapter. Poor efficiency skills include a failure to understand the meaning of certain punctuation marks. If this is the student's problem, then the suggestions listed in items I through O are appropriate. If incorrect phrasing is caused by other poor efficiency skills, then consult items P through X.

If the incorrect phrasing is caused by either a lack of decoding ability or a lack of comprehension, you would be treating only the symptom and not the cause by using the recommendations listed in items I through X.

RECOMMENDATIONS

For students whose incorrect phrasing is caused by inadequate decoding ability:

A. If the cause of incorrect phrasing is a lack of knowledge of basic sight vocabulary or a limited number of other words in the student's sight vocabulary, then the suggestions recommended in Chapters 12 and 13 will be helpful. A word becomes a sight word after it has been read many times. Some writers and researchers have estimated that it takes from 20 to 70 exposures to a word before it actually becomes a sight word. A student who has not built up a sight vocabulary equivalent to his grade level must do an enormous amount of reading to expose himself to as many new words as many times as possible.

B. Have the student practice reading sight phrase cards such as those described for testing basic sight word phrases in Appendix B-4.

C. Compile lists of common prepositional phrases and have the student practice reading these phrases. (See Appendix C-4.) Follow this practice, and that described in item B, with timed tests of the student's ability to read the phrases off flash cards. Such tests can be administered by the teacher, another adult, or other students. Be sure to mix up the phrases or sentences before flashing them. Provide a penalty for missed phrases. After the test, graph and display the student's performance, so that he can see his improvement. It is important to emphasize to all students who participate in the timed tests that they are competing only against themselves, not against each other.

D. Have the student read the basic sight word sentences presented in Appendix C-1, with appropriate phrasing.

E. Use one or more of the tape recorder activities described in Chapter 2 under "Recommendations," item L.

F. If the cause of incorrect phrasing is weakness in other decoding skills (phonics, structural analysis, or context clues), then the suggestions recommended in Chapters 14 through 19 will be helpful.

G. Use low-level material that presents no decoding problems, allowing the student to concentrate on phrasing without experiencing difficulty in word attack.

For students whose incorrect phrasing is caused by insufficient comprehension:

H. The recommendations in Chapter 20, "Word Meaning/Vocabulary Knowledge Inadequate," or Chapter 21, "Comprehension Inadequate," will be helpful if incorrect phrasing is caused by a lack of comprehension.

For students whose incorrect phrasing is caused by a failure to understand the meaning of certain punctuation marks:

I. Review the meanings of various punctuation marks and discuss how these help the students to phrase properly. It often helps to draw an analogy between traffic signs and punctuation marks; that is, commas are likened to yield signs and periods are likened to stop signs. Another option is to use guides: three counts for periods, two for commas.

J. Prepare a paragraph with no punctuation marks. Have the student try to read it. Then you and the student together punctuate and read the selection.

K. Use short written paragraphs to demonstrate how punctuation affects the pitch and stress of your voice. Have the student repeat and then reread the paragraphs.

L. Use an overhead projector with paragraphs without punctuation. Together with the student, fill in appropriate marks and read.

M. Dictate simple paragraphs. Have the student provide the punctuation, in part by listening to the inflections of your voice.

N. Use the language-experience approach (see the introductory chapter) and leave out all punctuation marks from the student's dictated story. Then have the student fill them in.

O. Provide cards with words or phrases and cards with punctuation marks. Have the student arrange them properly.

For students whose incorrect phrasing is caused by other poor efficiency skills:

P. Demonstrate proper phrasing by reading to the class.

Q. Reproduce certain reading passages divided into phrases as in the following sentence:

Fred and Mary   *were on their way*   *to the movies.*

In doing this, you may find that there is more carryover if a space is left between the phrases rather than using a dash (—) or a slash (/) to separate the phrases.

R. An alternative to the previous suggestion is to write the sentences using crayons or markers. Make each phrase a different color. After they read sentences in color, have the students read them in black-and-white print. In the following example, the different styles of type represent different colors.

Fred and Mary   *were on their way*   to the movies.

S. Have the students read and dramatize conversation.

T. Provide choral reading with several readers who phrase properly.

U. Photocopy songs. Have the students read these without the music.

V. Have students read orally phrases that extend only to the end of the line. After practicing with these phrases, have students read phrases that carry over onto the next line (however, leave more than the normal amount of space between each phrase). Gradually go from this style to normal writing.

W. Use commercial materials, such as *Plays for Echo Reading* (published by Harcourt Brace Jovanovich), that are designed to promote fluent oral reading.

X. Use one or more of the oral reading techniques described in detail in the introductory chapter. These procedures are highly effective with a variety of oral reading difficulties.

GAMES AND EXERCISES

Bouncing for Words

Purpose: To provide practice on basic sight words, other sight words, or sight phrases

Materials: Group-size (6″ × 3″) cards for the basic sight words, sight words in general, or sight phrases to be learned
A chair for each child
A basketball or volleyball

Procedure:

Each child is given one phrase card. He stands behind a chair and places his card face up on the seat of the chair. The leader, one of the children in the group, bounces the ball to the first child. As the child catches the ball, he says the phrase. If the student says it correctly, he then picks up the card. If the student misses the phrase, the card remains on the chair. Play continues until all the children have had a turn at their phrases. At the end of the game, the children exchange cards and play continues. Any child who could not say the phrase when he caught the ball is told the phrase and keeps the phrase card until all the cards are exchanged at the end of the next game.

As variations, use sight word cards or even sight word sentence cards instead of phrase cards, or use two teams. Instead of beginning with the children in a circle, have opposite teams face each other with 8 or 10 feet between each team. The leader then rotates the bounces between teams. The team with the least number of cards on its chairs after a certain number of sets or games is the winner.

Search

Purpose: To provide practice on the basic sight words or on phrasing

Materials: Three or more identical packs of sight word cards or three or more identical packs of sight phrase cards

Procedure:

Three or more children sit around a table, each with a pack of phrase or word cards that are identical to those of the rest of the players. One child looks at his pack and calls a phrase. The remaining players then see who can find the same phrase. The child who finds the phrase first places the card face up in the middle of the table and scores a point for himself. Play continues until a certain number of points are scored by an individual.

Pony Express

Purpose: To provide practice on phrasing

Materials: Pocket chart
Sight phrase cards

Procedure:

Fill a pocket chart with sight phrase cards. Each word may represent a letter in the Pony Express saddlebag. The children come one at a time to claim their letters and read them to the rest of the class. After all cards have been removed from the chart, the children exchange cards (letters) and begin again by mailing their letters (placing them back in the pocket chart).

A Phrasing Scope

Purpose: To provide practice in proper phrasing

Materials: Pieces of paper about 5″ wide
A piece of cardboard a little larger than the strips of paper
Two dowel pins about 1/2″ in diameter and 7″ long

Procedure:

Paste the pieces of paper into a long strip. Type a story, either original or from a book, on the strip. Type only one phrase on a line and double-space the lines. Next, fold the piece of cardboard and seal the sides, leaving the top and bottom open. Cut a window near the top of the cardboard. Slide the strip of paper through the cardboard and attach a 1/2″ dowel at each end of the strip of paper. The student rolls the paper from the bottom to the top and reads the story as each phrase passes through the window's opening. (See Figure 3.1.)

Sets

Purpose: To learn new phrases and to provide practice on reading those already known

Materials: Two decks of identical phrase cards (the number of cards used depends on the number of players; use four phrase cards for each player)

Procedure:

Deal one deck of phrase cards, so each player has four different phrases. Place all duplicate phrases from the second deck face up in several rows on the table. Begin by pointing to a phrase and saying it. The student who has the matching phrase picks it up and says it as he places it in his hand to make a matching "set." Play continues until one player has a complete set of four matches. The student must then read all of the phrases in his hand as they are

FIGURE 3.1

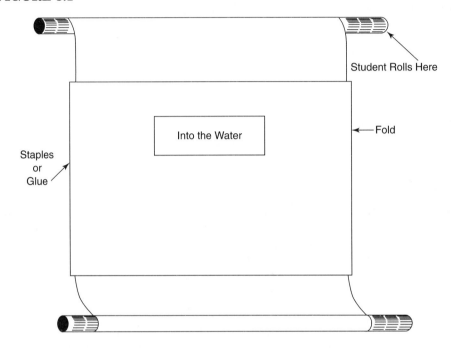

Student Rolls Here

Into the Water

Fold

Staples
or
Glue

placed on the desk or table. If the student cannot read them, play continues until another student has a complete matching set and *can* read them without help. The winner is the first student who obtains a complete matching set and is able to read all phrases from the set in his hand.

Drawing for Phrases

Purpose: To provide practice in reading basic sight words and phrases

Materials: Three small boxes
            1″ squares of tagboard

Procedure:

In this game it is beneficial to have a disabled reader work with a good reader. Write a number of different prepositions on 1″ squares of tagboard and place them in box 1. Use words such as *with, in, under,* and *over* that would fit with almost any noun. In box 2, place 1″ tagboard squares with the words *the* and *a.* In box 3, place a few 1″ tagboard squares with nouns on them such as *house* and *chair.* Ask students to draw one square from each box to form a phrase. After all squares have been drawn and the phrases read, the squares may then be rearranged to form more phrases. You may wish to have the students write down the phrases to see who can create the most phrases. The written list is also useful for reviewing the phrases at a later date.

CHAPTER 4

Poor Pronunciation

RECOGNIZED BY

The student fails to pronounce a word correctly.

DISCUSSION

Mispronunciation of words is one of the most serious reading problems of disabled readers. The problem may be caused by one or a combination of the following factors: (1) the student is weak in knowledge of phonics or structural analysis;[1] (2) the student possesses, but does not use, knowledge of phonics or structural analysis; (3) the student has poor efficiency skills; or (4) the student has a hearing, speech, or language difficulty. In any case, a careful diagnosis is needed before a program of correction is started. The following paragraphs suggest ways to diagnose the various reasons for poor pronunciation.

The student lacks the ability to use phonics when decoding. If the student fails to correctly pronounce one-syllable words that are not basic sight words, then this student probably lacks the ability to use **phonics** to decode unknown words. The Phonics Assessment found in Appendix B-6 can be used to quickly spot those areas of weakness in the student's knowledge of phonics. Teachers should be especially careful in selecting a phonics test to use. Research has shown that group phonics tests simply do not measure what a student actually does in applying phonic word-attack skills in the act of reading. Therefore, such tests do not aid diagnostic teaching. This inadequacy is also true of some individual phonics tests. The Phonics Assessment in Appendix B-6 includes test situations that require the student to respond in a way that is similar to or the same as the application of these skills in the act of reading.

The student lacks the ability to use structural analysis when decoding. If the student fails to correctly pronounce words of more than one syllable, then this student probably lacks the ability to use **structural analysis** to decode unknown words. The Structural Analysis Assessment found in Appendix B-7 will enable you to identify the student's specific weaknesses in this area. The teacher may want to supplement test results by observing the ways in which the student attacks or fails to attack words of one or more syllables.

Poor efficiency skills. You should stop the reader at a mispronounced word and ask for the correct pronunciation. If the student usually says it

45

correctly, she may lack reading fluency (poor efficiency skills). This would still not exclude the possibility that training in various forms of **word analysis** might be beneficial.

Hearing, speech, or language differences. An auditory discrimination test is easy to administer and will determine whether a student has difficulty discriminating between somewhat similar sounds. The inability to discriminate between certain sounds can lead to the mispronunciation of words. This knowledge, supplemented with informal hearing tests, such as determining whether the student hears a normal voice at the distance most students hear it, will help you decide whether a hearing defect is contributing to the reading difficulty. Students indicating difficulty in any of these areas should be examined further by a specialist. To determine whether the student has a speech difficulty, ask the student to repeat sentences that are given orally. Use words that were mispronounced in previous reading. Words read incorrectly, but spoken correctly, are not speech problems. Some students may mispronounce words because their first language is not English. This may also occur if the student speaks a nonstandard dialect of English. This need not be cause for concern. If the mispronunciation does not cause loss of meaning (comprehension), then it is not necessary to remediate this difficulty. You can determine whether meaning is affected by using the procedure described in the previous chapter to check comprehension. Teachers of students who are limited-English speakers or speakers of nonstandard dialects should become familiar with the differences in pronunciations that will occur in the language or dialect spoken. With this knowledge and some experience, you will have little difficulty in determining whether problems in mispronunciation of words affect reading comprehension.

If the student lacks the ability to use phonics in decoding, then the suggestions listed under "Recommendations" in items A through D and in Appendix C-2 should be beneficial. If the student lacks the ability to use structural analysis in decoding multisyllable words, consult items E through I and Appendix C-3. If the pronunciation difficulties are caused by poor efficiency skills, the suggestions listed in items J through L are appropriate. Finally, if poor pronunciation is caused by hearing, speech, or language differences, then consult items M through P.

RECOMMENDATIONS

For students who need help with phonics:

A. Teach the phonics skills in which a weakness is indicated by the Phonics Assessment in Appendix B-6. Then refer to the appropriate chapters (14 through 16) for corrective procedures.

B. Have the students make word cards or lists and build their own file of words that they habitually mispronounce. Allow for periodic independent study of these words. (A shoebox makes an excellent file box for indexing word cards.)

C. Have students make their own lists of common letter combinations that are generally phonetically regular, such as *-tion, -ance,* and *-edge,* as they are encountered and learned.

D. Use the phonogram list in Appendix C-2 as suggested under "Using the Phonogram List to Teach Phonics." If the student continues to have difficulties with phonics, use the phonogram list as follows:

   1. Have the student first pronounce *sent;* then give her a number of other words and nonsense words to pronounce that end in *-ent,* such as *dent, pent,* and *bent.* This exercise will give the student practice in using various consonant sounds in conjunction with various word endings.

   2. Do the same as in item 1, using consonant blends with various combinations; for example, pronounce *slash,* then give a number of other words and nonsense words ending in *-ash,* such as *crash, flash,* and *scash.* As the student reads, ask her to try to pronounce difficult words aloud. You should determine which sounds she knows but is not using. Use these sounds to construct exercises similar to the two shown previously or others appropriate for improving the particular phonic elements not being used correctly.

For students who need help with structural analysis:

E. Teach the structural analysis skills in which a weakness is indicated by the Structural Analysis Assessment found in Appendix B-7. Then refer to Chapter 17 for corrective procedures.

F. Make lists of prefixes and suffixes; however, do not expect the students to learn the *meaning* of many of these. Focus only on the students' correct pronunciation of these affixes. (See the list of prefixes and suffixes in Appendix C-5.)

G. To help students use their existing decoding skills effectively, teach them to use the word-attack strategy. This strategy and effective ways to teach it are described in Chapter 19, which also presents a number of other recommendations for teaching students to use context clues.

H. For longer, more difficult words, first teach the student to use structural analysis, then teach the student the word-attack strategy, which will enable her to use the various word-attack skills together when she meets unfamiliar words in the act of reading. For structural analysis, the student must learn to identify word parts, visually separate word parts, pronounce word parts, and blend the parts together to form the whole word. Procedures for doing this are presented in Chapter 17.

I. Use the materials in Appendix C-3. These have been designed specifically to remediate difficulties in structural analysis.

For students who have poor efficiency skills:

J. When the student mispronounces a word in oral reading, call attention to the correct pronunciation with as little fuss as possible. Ignoring the mistake tends to reinforce the wrong pronunciation with the student as well as with any other members of the class who are listening. If the student misses the same word more than once, reinforce the student's pronunciation as follows:

   1. After you pronounce the word for the student for the second time, ask her to focus her eyes on the word and repeat it five times, then say it loudly.

   2. A few minutes later, come back to the word, point to it, and have the student pronounce it. If she says it correctly, lavish the student with praise. If she has again forgotten the word, have her write it carefully on two flash cards or slips of paper. Have her keep one of the cards or slips of paper to use for practice while you keep the other. Later that day or the next, show her your copy of the flash card or slip of paper. If she says it correctly this time, praise the student emphatically. (This procedure will work with only a few words at a time. If the student is missing more than a few words of the material being read, then the material is probably too difficult and should be replaced by easier reading material.)

K. Use commercial materials designed to promote fluent oral reading, such as *Plays for Echo Reading,* published by Harcourt Brace Jovanovich.

L. Use one or more of the oral reading techniques described in detail in the introductory chapter. These procedures are highly effective with a variety of oral reading difficulties.

For students whose pronunciation difficulties are caused by hearing, speech, or language differences:

M. To teach certain sounds with which students are having difficulty:

   1. Set up pairs with only one different sound, such as *hit—heat.*
   2. Make sure the students can hear the sound differences.
   3. Make sure the students can say the words.
   4. Use each word in a sentence and then have the students say the single sound following that sentence.

N. Have students hold their throats with their hands to feel the difference in vibration from one word to another or from one letter to another.

O. Play games that deal with sounds. For example, the first student says, "I am a *ch.*" The rest of the students then guess whether she is a chicken, chipmunk, and so on. This gives all students many exposures to word beginnings.

P. Consult a speech, hearing, or language specialist, if available, for suggestions or direct services to the student.

ENDNOTE

1. If the student has difficulty pronouncing one-syllable words, then she is likely to have a problem with phonics. If the student has difficulty pronouncing words of two or more syllables, then she is likely to have a problem with structural analysis. These are analogous decoding skills. When using *phonics,* the student visually divides a one-syllable word into the letters (*graphemes*) that represent the individual sounds (*phonemes*), pronounces each sound, and blends the sounds together. When using *structural analysis,* the student visually divides a word of two or more syllables into pronounceable parts (*morphemes*), pronounces each part, and blends the parts together. In using both skills, the student must perform the three acts quickly. A third decoding skill, using *context clues,* enables the student to use the meaning of other words in a sentence to help in figuring out the unknown word. Skilled readers use all of these skills together, along with sight word recognition, to decode effectively.

CHAPTER 5

Omissions

RECOGNIZED BY

The student omits words, phrases, or both while reading orally.

DISCUSSION

Omissions in reading are usually caused by inadequate decoding skills. The student encounters a word or phrase he cannot pronounce and skips over it. The student may or may not pause before omitting the word or phrase. Often such a student is fearful of mispronouncing a word when reading orally. In some cases, omissions result from poor efficiency skills. The student may read too rapidly or carelessly and omit words for this reason. In either case, the omissions are likely to lead to reduced comprehension, which is a serious problem. Occasionally, omissions result when students purposely skip over unknown words because they have been taught to do so. (This is an appropriate decoding strategy in some circumstances. See the section in Chapter 19 that describes the word-attack strategy. When students do this, they should return to the omitted word and attempt to decode it using context or other clues.) Omissions are the second most common type of miscue.

Before beginning a program of help, you should determine the cause. To determine whether the omission of words is caused by decoding difficulties or poor efficiency skills, ask the student to pronounce any words omitted after he has read a passage. If the student still does not know the word or words, then the problem is likely to be lack of decoding skills. If the student now knows the word or words, assume that the problem is one of poor efficiency skills. You might also have the student read the material at the level in which he is making omissions and note the percentage of words omitted. Then have the student read an easier passage, and note whether omissions still occur. If the percentage of omissions decreases markedly, assume that the student has insufficient decoding skills. If, however, the omissions continue with approximately the same percentage of occurrence, assume that they are a result of poor efficiency skills.

The student may lack decoding skills in sight vocabulary, phonics, structural analysis, or context clues, or he may lack comprehension to some extent. If the problem stems from one of these difficulties, the suggestions in items A through I under "Recommendations" will probably be of little or no value, since the omissions are actually only symptoms of a larger problem with decoding or comprehension. It is then necessary to determine in which of these areas the student is deficient. The procedures and suggestions recommended for each area are given in the following chapters:

Sight vocabulary—Chapters 12 and 13

Phonics—Chapters 14, 15, and 16

Structural analysis—Chapters 17 and 18

Context clues—Chapter 19

Comprehension—Chapter 21.

The word-attack strategy presented in Chapter 19 will prove especially useful to students whose omissions result from inadequate word-analysis skills.

If the student is able to analyze new words but does not have instant recognition of words that, for his grade level, should have become sight words, he probably lacks word-recognition skills. It would then be necessary to help the student build a sight vocabulary. To improve this area, see Chapter 13. If the student's problem is determined to be one of poor efficiency skills, the suggestions listed in items A through I should be helpful. Also keep in mind that unless the student's errors are rather frequent and affect comprehension to some extent, they may not be worth worrying about.

Some of the recommendations that follow may encourage the student to substitute temporarily one symptom for another. For example, in item D, the student is encouraged to use finger pointing to eliminate omissions. The use of such crutches should not be a problem. As the student's reading ability improves, the new behavior (in this case, finger pointing) will no longer be necessary.

RECOMMENDATIONS

A. Call the reader's attention to omissions when they occur. Making an immediate correction is the first step toward breaking the habit.

B. Allow students to preread material silently before asking them to read it orally. You might allow students to ask you for assistance with difficult words during the silent reading phase. If they ask for help on more than 10% of the words, then the material is too difficult and should be replaced with easier material.

C. Use one or more of the oral reading techniques described in detail in the introductory chapter. These procedures are highly effective with a variety of oral reading difficulties. After calling the student's attention to the problem as mentioned in item A, you may find that these methods are extremely effective.

D. If whole words or phrases are consistently skipped, you might require the student to point to each word as he reads it. It is helpful to ask the student to pick up his finger and then bring it down on each word as it is read. This keeps the student from pointing to words that are ahead of the actual word being read. This technique also should be stopped when the student no longer needs it.

E. Have several students choral-read.

F. Use commercial materials, such as *Plays for Echo Reading,* published by Harcourt Brace Jovanovich, that are designed to promote fluent oral reading. Participation in the reading of a play or a Reader's Theater activity will strongly encourage students to read each word that is written.

G. Ask detailed questions that require thorough reading. Ask about only one sentence or paragraph at a time. Students often will omit adjectives. In this case, it is often helpful to give the student a list of questions such as, "Was the bear big or little?" and "What color were the flowers?" The student will be forced to focus on adjectives that could otherwise easily be omitted.

H. To focus attention on words omitted by the reader, tape-record a passage and then give the student a copy of the material as it is played back to him. Have the student follow along and point to each word as it is read. Have him circle all words omitted. After the reading, discuss possible reasons for his omitting the words and the importance of not doing so. Suggestions for additional tape recorder activities appear in Chapter 2 under "Recommendations," item L.

I. As the student reads, ask him to outline the first letter of each word read, as shown in Figure 5.1.

FIGURE 5.1

Sam plays baseball in the park.

This will be helpful for students who make many omissions. You will, of course, want to discontinue this as soon as the student stops making omissions. Another variation of the previous procedure is to have the student underline the first letters of words, as shown in Figure 5.2.

FIGURE 5.2

Mary went with her mother to the store.

Following this, you may wish to have the student draw lines over or below words in phrases or natural linguistic units as he reads, as shown in Figure 5.3.

FIGURE 5.3

Fred has a large brown cat.

CHAPTER 6

Repetitions

RECOGNIZED BY

The student rereads words or phrases.

DISCUSSION

The most common causes of repetitions in a student's reading are similar to the causes of omissions in reading; that is, poor word-recognition skills, poor word-analysis skills, or poor efficiency skills. Of these, a problem with **word-recognition skills** (sight vocabulary) occurs most often. It should be pointed out, however, that sometimes a student repeats certain words in order to correct a reading error or to gain time so as to avoid making an error. This may be a stalling tactic the student uses while she mentally works on the upcoming word. If this happens only on certain words that you know are new or difficult for the student, you should, in most cases, ignore it. If the words the student does not recognize are ones that normally should be sight words for that student, you can assume that she is deficient in word-recognition skills. In this case, the recommendations in Chapters 12 and 13 should be beneficial.

The problem of word-analysis difficulties may be in any of the following areas: (1) phonics, (2) structural analysis, or (3) use of context clues. Occasionally the student will need assistance with dictionary skills. If the problem is in one of these areas, some of the recommendations that follow will probably be of little or no value, since the repetitions are only a symptom of the larger problems of word-recognition or word-analysis difficulties. You would need to determine in which area of word analysis the student is deficient. These procedures and the suggestions recommended in each case are given in the following chapters:

Phonics—Chapters 14, 15, and 16

Structural analysis—Chapters 17 and 18

Context clues—Chapter 19

Dictionary skills—Chapter 27

The word-attack strategy presented in Chapter 19 will also prove useful to students whose repetitions result from inadequate word-analysis skills.

You can determine, to some extent, whether poor word-recognition or word-analysis skills are the cause of repetitions by having the student read material at the level in which she is making repetitions. Note the percentage of words or phrases repeated. Then give the student a much easier passage and note whether there is a definite decrease in the percentage of repetitions. If there is, the problem is probably insufficient word-recognition or word-analysis skills. If, on the other hand, a student continues to make as many repetitions as she did on the more difficult passage, then the problem is probably poor efficiency skills.

If you determine that the problem results from poor efficiency skills, then the suggestions listed under "Recommendations" in items A through F should prove beneficial. Of these, the simple suggestion given in item A is often all that is needed. Also, the suggestions listed in items G and H are very important and may give the student the confidence she needs to begin reading fluently.

RECOMMENDATIONS

A. Call the repetitions to the student's attention. This is often the most important step in breaking the bad habit.

B. Use one or more of the oral reading techniques described in detail in the introductory chapter. These procedures are highly effective with a variety of oral reading difficulties.

C. Have the students choral-read.

D. Have the student set a certain pace with her hand and keep up with this pace as she reads. Do not let the eyes pace the hand.

E. To focus attention on words repeated by the reader, tape-record a passage that she reads and then give the student a copy of the written material as it is played back to her. Have the student follow along, pointing to each word and underlining any words as they are repeated. After completing the passage, discuss any reasons that the student believes are causing her to repeat words or phrases.

F. Follow the other suggestions for using the tape recorder, as listed in Chapter 2 under "Recommendations," item L.

G. Provide easier or more familiar material in which the vocabulary presents no problem.

H. Let the students read the material silently before they attempt to read orally.

CHAPTER 7

Inversions or Reversals

RECOGNIZED BY

The student appears to read words from right to left instead of the normal left-to-right sequence, for example, *was* for *saw,* or *pot* for *top.*

The student reads letters in reverse, for example, *d* for *b,* or *p* for *g.* The student makes partial reversals in words (the letters within words), for example, *ant* for *nat.*

The student reverses words within sentences, for example, "the *rat* chased the *cat*" instead of "the *cat* chased the *rat.*"

DISCUSSION

It is important to recognize that reversals are a normal symptom of poor decoding skills regardless of the age of the reader. An adult who reads at a first-grade level is likely to make the same reversal errors as a 6-year-old reading at a first-grade level, especially when reading words in isolation. As decoding ability improves, reversals almost always disappear.

In nearly all cases, the student has simply not developed a strong enough visual image for the word and miscalls the word because he simply cannot remember what it is. (For an instant the child may ponder: "Is the word *was* or is it *saw?*") When a student is first learning how to decode, the task of correctly pronouncing printed words is quite a struggle and demands most or all of the student's mental energy. At this early stage the student may pay little or no attention to the context of what he is reading. Gradually, as reading ability develops, context clues help the student pronounce the word correctly. ("The boy *was* the dog" doesn't make sense, but "The boy *saw* the dog" does.) With practice and success over time, the student learns to recognize instantly the many little, easily confusable words in English, such as *on* and *no, that* and *what, big* and *dig, come* and *came, went* and *want,* and so on. With this in mind, the teacher should be careful not to fuss too much about these problems with beginning readers. Sometimes too much focus on these errors makes matters worse instead of better.

Some experts claim that reversals occur because the student has failed to develop a left-to-right eye movement or a left-to-right reading pattern. (This problem, if and when it exists, is difficult to determine.) Others believe that a student who reverses letters or words may suffer from some neurological impairment, or he may not realize that the order or position in which letters appear make a difference.

Regardless of the cause, the recommendations for solving this problem are the same. Most children who make reversals tend to outgrow the behavior after a few months of school. However, if the difficulty persists after several weeks of instruction and the student is making normal progress otherwise, the suggestions listed in this chapter, along with a little patience, should solve the problem.

For many years, reading teachers believed that students who made many reversals or inversions tended to have more severe difficulties than students who made other types of errors. More recent research has tended to refute this belief. We now believe that, if you check carefully, you are likely to find that children who make numerous reversals will also make just as high a percentage of other types of errors.

RECOMMENDATIONS

The suggestions in items A through H can be used effectively with groups of students. The recommendations listed under items I through Q are designed for use with individual students.

A. Use Big Books for beginning readers to point out left-to-right progression (as well as other skills, such as sequencing of words and common sight words). The larger print and the high interest level of most of these books enhance motivation for learning these skills. The *shared book experience* is an instructional technique in which the teacher attempts to duplicate some of the best features of the "lap method" that parents use when reading to their young children. When the teacher glides his hand under the words as they are read (some teachers prefer pointers), he is emphasizing not only left-to-right progression and the return sweep at the end of a line of print, but also the separation of the individual words in the story. When you use this technique with students, be sure to read slowly and with expression. Big Books or language-experience stories that the students have dictated (see the introductory chapter) should be read many times and the children should be encouraged to participate by reading along orally as much as possible.

B. Poetry, songs, and rap music can also be used effectively for shared reading experiences as described in item A. When teachers engage students in reading (or singing) words as they see them, they are using a powerful technique to help students decode words. Remember to insist that the students look at (focus on) the words as you and they pronounce them slowly and clearly.

C. After discussing the problem with the student, give him sentences in which words that he tends to reverse are covered by a small piece of paper. Allow him to read to the end of the sentence, using the context to determine the word he thinks should be in the sentence. Then allow him to uncover the word and check the accuracy of his use of context.

D. Provide students with their own copies of the simple sentences, stories, songs, and so on that are being read; have the students underline the words, phrases, or sentences, pronouncing each word as it is underlined or reading the phrases or sentences as they are underlined.

E. Teach students to pace their reading with their hands, practicing a left-to-right movement.

F. Draw arrows pointing from left to right under troublesome words or phrases.

G. Write in pairs the words sometimes reversed (*was/saw, net/ten, war/raw, trap/part*). Use one word in a sentence and ask students to point to or write the word used.

H. Use a colored letter at the beginning of words commonly confused. Discontinue this practice as soon as these words no longer present any difficulty.

I. As mentioned in the "Discussion" section, one of the most effective things you can do to help a student correct the problem of reversals is to call his attention to the context in which the word is used. If the student is made aware of the context, then he will have a tendency to correct the problem on his own. To do this, give the student a number of simple sentences in which the word or words being reversed could only logically be used in one context. It may be helpful to have the student work at the sentence level, rather than at the paragraph or passage level, so he can focus more on the context. Also, try not to put other difficult words in the sentences you prepare. The following is an example:

Bob *was* going with Tom to the store.
Mary *saw* a big dog on the way home.

J. Emphasize left-to-right in all reading activities. The following method may be helpful: Cover words or sentences with your hand or a card and read the word or sentence as you uncover it. Then have the student do the same. The student may find it helpful to make a window marker as shown in Figure 7.1. The student uses it as he would a regular marker but lets the line of print show through the slot.

FIGURE 7.1

K. Let the child use a typewriter or computer to practice words with which he has difficulty. This will enable him to see the word formed from left to right as he types.

L. Pair the letters that are causing difficulty (such as p and q). Have the student trace the letters with his index and middle fingers, sounding each letter as it is traced. Or, place a thin layer of salt or fine sand in the bottom of a shoebox lid and ask the student to trace letters with his fingers in the sand or salt.

M. If whole words are reversed, you can have the student trace the word and then attempt to write it from memory. It is often helpful to have the student say the word slowly as he writes it, and to repeat this procedure several times. (It is important for the teacher to provide motivation for this type of activity. It is hoped that the student will view this as a game or a fun activity rather than punishment or drudgery.)

N. Use a magnetic board with 3-dimensional letters. Have the student manipulate letters to form words commonly reversed. The use of magnetic letters has become very popular in recent years as an outgrow of their use in practices associated with **Reading Recovery.**

O. Blindfold the student, then form letters or words with which he is having difficulty, using 3-dimensional letters. Have the student trace the letter and say it as you trace it on his back, making sure that your finger follows the same part of the letter on the student's back that his finger does in tracing the 3-dimensional letter.

P. To help make the student aware of the importance of the sequence of words commonly reversed, place one word commonly reversed above itself. Then have the student draw lines from the first letter of the top word to the first letter of the bottom word, as shown in Figure 7.2.

FIGURE 7.2

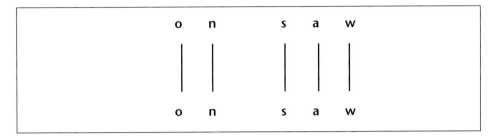

Have the student say each letter as he begins to draw the line from it and each letter as the line reaches it.

Q. Write two words commonly reversed side by side. Ask the student to number the letters in the first word by placing a number under each letter. Then ask him to assign the same numbers to the letters in the second word:

saw was
on no
123 321 12 21

CHAPTER 8

Insertions

RECOGNIZED BY

The student adds words that are not present in the sentence. For example, in the sentence, "The dog chased the little boy," the student may add *big* to make the sentence read, "The *big* dog chased the little boy."

DISCUSSION

Insertions are the third most common type of miscue made by students in oral reading. They are often not as serious as other types of errors. A possible cause of insertions is that the student's oral language development may surpass her reading level or that she may anticipate what is coming next and read that instead of what actually is written. Insertions that make sense within the context of the sentence indicate the student's awareness or comprehension of the material being read. In this case, you may assume the insertions are caused by either poor efficiency skills or oral language development beyond the reading level of the student. When insertions do not make sense within the context of the sentence, you may assume that comprehension problems are involved. The suggestions listed under "Recommendations" in items A through I are appropriate when the problem is poor efficiency skills or when the oral language development of the student surpasses her reading ability. If students make these types of insertion errors, you should first determine whether they appear often enough, or are serious enough, to cause concern. If they seldom appear, it may be best to ignore them. If the cause of the insertions is a lack of comprehension, then the suggestions in Chapter 21, "Comprehension Inadequate," are recommended.

RECOMMENDATIONS

A. Call the student's attention to the insertion. Sometimes she is not aware of the habit. Allowing the student to continue only provides reinforcement for the mistakes.

B. Encourage the student to read more slowly. Students often believe erroneously that good reading is fast reading. When students try to read more quickly than they are able, insertions may result.

C. Use commercial materials, such as *Plays for Echo Reading,* published by Harcourt Brace Jovanovich, that are designed to promote fluent oral reading.

D. Use one or more of the oral reading techniques described in detail in the introductory chapter. These procedures are highly effective with a variety of oral reading difficulties.

E. Ask questions that require an exact answer. If the student usually follows a certain pattern in making insertions (such as adding adjectives), you may wish to provide questions for the student to review before reading the story. These questions can focus on the objects in the story described by the adjectives that are often inserted. This will cause the student to read more carefully. Use questions such as: "Does it say how big the frog was?" and "Was it a sunny, warm day, a sunny, cold day, or just a sunny day?"

F. Have students choral-read.

G. Play a tape recording in which the student made insertions. Ask the student to follow the written passage, stopping the tape recorder as often as necessary. Have the student write on the written passage the insertions that she made on the oral reading of the material. Use the student-corrected passages as a basis for discussing the problem.

H. Have the student read along with a passage that has been tape-recorded. See Chapter 2 under "Recommendations," item L, for additional activities using the audio tape recorder.

I. If the student makes many insertions, have her point to each word as she reads it. Have the student lift her finger up and bring it down on each word as it is read. Do not allow the student to continue this technique after the habit has disappeared.

CHAPTER 9

Substitutions

RECOGNIZED BY

The student substitutes one word for another when reading orally.

DISCUSSION

Substitutions are the most common type of miscue or oral reading error. The student who substitutes one word for another is either a reader who has not developed adequate decoding skills or one with poor efficiency skills. Some readers make substitutions that are nearly correct within the context of the material being read; for example, "The man drove the *automobile*" might be read, "The man drove the *car*." If these minor mistakes appear rarely, it may be best to ignore the problem. If, however, they occur frequently or consistently, then some steps should be taken. These errors do matter. As students grow older and read increasingly difficult materials, even contextually appropriate substitutions can result in lowered comprehension.

Substitutions that are not in the proper context of the sentence usually are caused by decoding difficulty. When help is given with decoding skills, the problem of substitutions usually disappears. You should determine whether substitutions are caused by inadequate decoding skills or inefficient reading and plan help accordingly.

The suggestions listed under "Recommendations" in items A through H should be helpful for students whose substitutions are caused by decoding difficulties. If, however, the substitutions are caused by poor efficiency skills, then the suggestions in items I through S should be helpful.

RECOMMENDATIONS

For students whose substitutions are caused by inadequate decoding ability:

A. Use reading material on a lower level of difficulty.

B. Do not expect students to read material above their meaning-vocabulary level. Generally, use easy materials and encourage students to read in great quantity.

C. If many words are not known, the suggestions listed in Chapters 12 and 13 should be used. When the student's sight vocabulary is increased, the problem of making substitutions will probably decrease.

D. If the student is unable to use phonics or structural analysis sufficiently for decoding, the recommendations in Chapters 14 through 18 will prove helpful.

E. To help students use their existing decoding skills effectively, teach the word-attack strategy shown in Figure 9.1.

FIGURE 9.1

WHEN YOU COME TO A WORD YOU DON'T KNOW:
1. Say the beginning sound.
2. Read the rest of the sentence. THINK.
3. Say the parts that you know. GUESS.
4. Ask someone or skip it and go on.

This strategy and effective ways to teach it are described in Chapter 19, which also presents a number of other recommendations for teaching students to use context clues.

F. Sometimes students feel they must make a continual response while they are reading. When such students do not know a strange word, they are likely to substitute whatever word comes into their minds rather than take the time to use the word-attack strategy. Assure these students that they will be given ample time to attack a word before someone tells them the word.

G. Use the difficult words in multiple-choice sentences, such as in the following examples:

1. John's father gave him a (watch, witch, water) for his birthday.
2. He (though, thought, through) he would be the tallest boy in the class.
3. He asked his father (what, where, when) they would leave.
4. She said, "The books belong to (them, that, this)."

H. Use the words in sentences where the student must complete the word to make the sentence sensible:

1. Can you tell me wh____ they will be home?
2. Does th____ book belong to Lori?

3. The stunt driver drove his car thr____ the wall of fire.
4. Jamie said, "That funny I_____ dog belongs to me."

For students whose substitutions are caused by poor efficiency skills:

I. Call attention to the mistake and correct it when it occurs.

J. In item B, we recommended that you urge students to read in great quantity. This suggestion was aimed at readers whose substitutions result from poor decoding skills. The suggestion is equally valuable for students whose substitutions result from poor efficiency skills. Thus, the recommendation bears repeating: Provide abundant opportunities for students to receive practice in the act of reading, both orally and silently.

K. Allow students to preread material silently before asking them to read it orally. You might allow students to ask you for assistance with difficult words during the silent reading phase. If they ask for help on more than 10% of the words, then the material is too difficult and should be replaced with easier material.

L. Use commercial materials that are designed to promote fluent oral reading.

M. Use one or more of the oral reading techniques described in detail in the introductory chapter. These procedures are highly effective with a variety of oral reading difficulties.

N. Have the student trace over the first letter or underline the first letter of each word in the sentence, as shown in Figure 9.2.

FIGURE 9.2

Debbie went with Tom to the movies.

Debbie went with Tom to the movies.

Do not ask the student to continue this practice for a long period of time. Use it only to break the habit and then stop using it.

O. Have the students choral-read.

P. Have the students follow a printed copy of what they have read as it is played on a tape recorder. As they listen, have them circle words for which substitutions were made. Use this student-corrected material when discussing the problem.

Q. Have the students read along with a passage that has been tape-recorded. Suggestions for additional tape-recorder activities appear in Chapter 2 under "Recommendations," item L.

R. Ask questions about the subject matter that will reflect the student's mistakes. Have him read to make corrections.

S. Some students, especially when they are under pressure during a test or in a situation somewhat different from their normal environment, will feel pressure to read rather rapidly. If you sense that a student is reading more rapidly than he should or normally does, stop him and explain that it is not necessary to read faster than usual.

CHAPTER 10

Guesses at Words

RECOGNIZED BY

The student guesses at new words instead of analyzing the correct pronunciation.

DISCUSSION

Guessing at words is similar to, and often difficult to distinguish from, substitutions (Chapter 9). Accordingly, the suggestions offered in the previous chapter should also be effective for correcting this problem. Guessing at words may be the result of one or several factors. The student may not possess a knowledge of the decoding skills of phonics, structural analysis, or context clues. Before attempting to help the student, you should determine which of the factors are responsible for her guessing at words. An effective way of determining why a student guesses at words is to ask her. You should ask whether she knows the sound of the first letter, the blend, the first syllable, and so forth. Also, you should check to see whether the student knows how to blend sounds together rapidly. Finally, ask questions to determine whether she is aware of the context in which the word is used. If you are unsure about the student's ability to use phonics, structural analysis, or context clues, follow the suggestions listed under "Recommendations" in item A. If she has some knowledge of these decoding skills but does not use them effectively when decoding, the remaining suggestions should prove useful.

RECOMMENDATIONS

A. If the student guesses at phonetically regular one-syllable words, administer the Phonics Assessment (Appendix B-6) and provide help where needed according to the results of the test. If the student guesses at words of more than one syllable, administer the Structural Analysis Assessment (Appendix B-7) and, again, give the student instruction on those aspects of structural analysis in which she is weak. Because an inability to use context clues can cause the student to guess at both one-syllable and multisyllable words, testing for the student's ability to use context clues (Appendix B-9) is also recommended. Recommendations for correcting difficulties in the areas of phonics, structural analysis, and context clues are found in the following chapters:

Phonics—Chapters 14, 15, and 16

Structural analysis—Chapters 17 and 18

Context clues—Chapter 19

B. While the student is reading orally, the teacher should call attention to the words at which she guesses. At the same time, the student should be taught how to systematically attack unknown words. The most effective way to do this is by teaching the student to use the word-attack strategy presented in Chapter 9 and described in more detail in Chapter 19 (see item A).

C. The word-attack strategy teaches students to examine the words that both precede and follow a difficult or unknown word and sound out at least the first one or two sounds of the unknown word. This strategy teaches students to use both the context of the sentence and the letter sounds (or structural parts) of the unknown word. Thus students learn to use more than just the first letter or syllable of the unknown word as the need arises. For example: "The large black dog was ch _____ on the bone." If the student continues past the unknown word and reads *on the bone* after decoding the sound of *ch,* she will in most cases correctly pronounce the unknown word *chewing.*

D. Give the student sentences in which there is one difficult word that she has guessed in her oral reading (or a word that you suspect she will be unable to decode in isolation). Have her work independently, using the method described in item C, to correctly decode the difficult words.

E. As the student reads, circle or underline the words that she guesses. Replace these words with blank lines and have the student reread the material. Ask her to fill in the correct words from context.

F. Do not expect the student to read material above her meaning-vocabulary level. Generally, use easy materials and encourage the student to read in great quantity, both orally and silently.

G. Use one or more of the oral reading techniques described in detail in the introductory chapter. These procedures are highly effective with a variety of oral reading difficulties.

H. Allow the student to preread material silently before asking her to read it orally. Encourage the student to ask you for assistance with difficult words during the silent reading phase. If the student asks for help on more than 10% of the words, then the material is too difficult and should be replaced with easier material.

I. Have the student trace over or underline the first and last letters and middle vowel or vowels of words at which she pauses, as shown in Figure 10.1.

FIGURE 10.1

> It was a very **humid** day.

> It was a very humid day.

J. Teach the student that there are a number of types of context clues. The student does not have to categorize them; however, working with several different kinds of context clues will enable her to become more adept in their use. For example:

1. Definition context clues:

   The word *mongrel* sometimes refers to a *dog* of mixed breeds.

2. Synonym context clues:

   The team was *gleeful* and the coach was also *jubilant* because they had won the game.

3. Contrasting words:

   He was *antisocial* but she was *friendly*.

4. Common sayings or expressions:

   It was *dark* as *pitch*.

K. Use commercially prepared materials designed to improve use of context clues.

Voicing, Lip Movements, Finger Pointing, and Head Movements

RECOGNIZED BY

When reading silently, the student voices words or reads with visible lip movements; when reading orally or silently, the student points to words with his finger or moves his head while reading.

DISCUSSION

A student who continually voices words or moves his lips while reading silently is not likely to gain any speed until he can be taught that it is not necessary to pronounce each word as it is read. Many people unconsciously pronounce words to themselves even though they do not actually move their lips. Often voicing and lip movement can be detected by watching for visible signs that are apparent when someone speaks. Other students may voice words and yet show no visible signs of doing so. One way to determine whether students are voicing words is to ask them. Very slow silent reading is also a sign that a student may be voicing words. That in itself, however, is not enough evidence to support such a diagnosis. Remember that voicing or lip movement is often an indication that a student is reading material that is too difficult for him. By giving him material that is considerably easier and then noting whether the voicing and lip movement continue or stop, you can determine whether they are caused by habit or indicate that the student has been reading at or near his frustration level.

Finger pointing and head movements can also reduce a student's reading speed and interfere with comprehension. All of these behaviors are normal for beginning and severely remedial readers. Usually, they disappear as reading ability improves. When these habits continue in spite of the student's improving reading ability, they can usually be extinguished rather easily. Occasionally, teachers will temporarily encourage a student to finger-point to remediate another problem, such as excessive omissions (see Chapter 6 under "Recommendations," item D).

RECOMMENDATIONS

For students with a habit of lip movements and/or voicing of words:

A. As strange as the technique may seem, a most effective way to alleviate these problems is to ask the student to hum a familiar tune as he reads. While doing this, the student can neither subconsciously nor consciously voice the words he is reading. The student may at first find it distracting and complain about a lack of comprehension. However, if he continues, the student will soon find that his reading speed is not only considerably faster in most cases, but that his comprehension has also improved. The methods that follow are also effective but will usually not work as well as this method.

B. As the student reads, have him hold his mouth shut with the teeth firmly together. Tell the student to hold his tongue against the roof of his mouth.

C. Have the student place a finger against his lips when reading silently.

D. Have the student place a small piece of paper between his lips when reading silently.

E. Discuss with the student the importance of forming mental images when reading silently. Explain that it is not necessary to say each word.

F. Temporarily reduce the amount of oral reading.

G. Have the student pace his reading with his hands. Make sure the rate he uses is faster than his normal speaking rate. This technique may not be effective with children in first, second, or third grade.

For students with a habit of finger pointing:

H. If you suspect a vision problem, have the student's eyes checked by an appropriate professional.

I. Have the student use a marker *temporarily*.

J. Provide practice in phrase reading.

K. Provide practice in reading from big books, charts, and the chalk-board.

L. Have the student use both hands to hold the book.

M. Use material with large, clear print.

For students with a habit of head movements:

N. Have the student place his elbows on the table and his index fingers against his temples.

O. Demonstrate how to use the eyes to scan a page while the head remains stationary.

DECODING ABILITIES

CHAPTER 12

Basic Sight Words Not Known

RECOGNIZED BY

The student is unable to read some or all of the **basic sight words,** those words of high utility that make up from 50% to 70% of the words in most reading material. The percentage is, of course, higher in materials written at a lower reading level.

DISCUSSION

There are several lists of the common or basic sight words. One is provided in Appendix B-4. Since, by definition, these are the words that appear most frequently, it is essential that students recognize them instantly. If students do not have these words in their sight vocabulary, or cannot recognize them instantly, they cannot become fluent readers. Students often confuse certain basic sight words, especially those with similar beginnings, such as *when, where,* and *what,* or *this, that,* and *those.*

If you observe your students when they read orally, you can determine whether they usually pronounce basic sight words accurately. With some experience you will have little difficulty recognizing which words are basic sight words. (Just by glancing at the words listed in Appendix B-4, you will see that most of the words you would think of as most common do in fact appear on the basic sight word list.)

A first grader is generally expected to master about one-third of the basic sight word list by the end of the year, a second grader is expected to master another third, and a third grader should master the final third of the list by the end of the school year. Mastery means that the student can pronounce the basic sight words instantly on viewing them. Also, the student should pronounce the words correctly *each time* they appear. If a student mispronounces or even hesitates on the pronunciation of a basic sight word, or if the student pronounces the word correctly only some of the time, then the student has not mastered this basic sight word.

Many children older than third graders and most illiterate adults have significant problems with basic sight words. These individuals, along with primary-grade children who are not progressing satisfactorily, need systematic and thorough instruction on basic sight words.

A test of the basic sight words often is given by having the student look at four or five different words on a page while the teacher pronounces one of the words and asks the student to circle or underline the word pronounced. The task required to *distinguish* a word from a choice of four or five words is not, however, the same as the task required to *pronounce* the word after seeing it in print. You frequently will find that students can score 100% on a basic sight word test if it is given in the manner described, but these same students may not be able to pronounce the same words when they are asked to read them.

When you are testing for students' knowledge of basic sight words, you should present each word for approximately one-half to one second. If you give the student more time than this to look at the word, then, to some extent, the test becomes a measure of word-analysis skills rather than of knowledge of sight words. You can have the student read words from a list; however, it is difficult to control the time each word is exposed to the student. If you do have the student read basic sight words from a list, remember to count as wrong any word at which the student pauses for more than about one second. Having students read the basic sight words from a list is a quick way to check those students who you think, but are not quite sure, know most of the words. The Quick Check for Basic Sight Words, which appears in Appendix B-3, may be used for this purpose.

The best way to test basic sight words is to use flash cards with a tape recorder. Specific instructions for doing this are presented along with the lists of basic sight words and phrases that appear in Appendix B-4. This procedure should be used to test both the individual basic sight words and the **basic sight word phrases.** Each sight word test takes approximately 6 minutes per student to administer and score.

When the testing is completed, you can examine the prepared lists and determine specifically which basic sight words and phrases the student has not mastered. These can then be taught without having to misuse instructional time teaching words or phrases that are already known.

RECOMMENDATIONS

The suggestions listed in items A through J and the games and exercises will be helpful in teaching the words. Most students will learn basic sight words quickly and easily when they are simply shown the word, hear it used in a sentence, repeat it, and practice reading it. Immediate reinforcement (lots of practice) is essential for students to *master* new words. The best way to provide this reinforcement is to have students read over and over simple student-or teacher-constructed sentences or stories that contain the new words and to do lots of reading in easy books.

The suggestions listed in items A through F and the games and exercises in this chapter can be used to have students learn and practice the sight word *phrases* as well as the individual words. Many teachers will have students practice the phrases after a set number, say 20, of the words have been mastered. The sight word phrases that appear on the list in Appendix B-4 are compiled so that each word from the isolated word list is presented in a phrase without adding a lot of new words for the student to master. In addition, a comprehensive list of prepositional phrases is provided in Appendix C-4. You may wish to have students practice reading these phrases after all the basic sight words have been learned. A list of basic sight word *sentences* is provided in Appendix C-1. These sentences are derived from the basic sight word phrases presented in Appendix B-4.

The language-experience approach and the various oral reading procedures presented in the introductory chapter are also effective. In using these methods, you will not be focusing on any particular basic sight word. However, since the words appear so often, most students will be successful in learning them because of their repeated appearance in the stories that the student writes using the language-experience approach and in the passages she reads during oral reading.

When teaching children individually or in small groups, introduce the words a few at a time. The number of words to be learned per week will vary from student to student. Success, however, is critical. *It is better to learn fewer words well.* The students should see mastery as a challenging goal. Often the students themselves can best determine the number of new words to be learned at a time. If in doubt, begin with five words.

When presenting sight words, always be sure that the student is looking *at the word,* not at you. If possible, you should try to spend a few minutes with the student individually when presenting the words for the first time.

   A. The following dialogue presents a thorough approach to the initial teaching of basic sight words. Usually not all of the steps noted are necessary.

Teacher:	(Hold up a flash card.) "Look at this word. The word is *the.*" (Use it in a sentence.) "I am *the* teacher. Say the word."
Student:	"The."
T:	"Good. Now say it five times."
S:	"The, the, the, the, the."
T:	"Outstanding. Now say it really loud."
S:	"The."
T:	"No, that's not loud enough. Let me hear you say it really loud."
S:	"The."
T:	"Here, I'll show you. THE!"
S:	(chuckle) "THE!"
T:	"Fantastic. Now let me hear you whisper it."
S:	(whispering) "The."
T:	"Excellent. Now close your eyes. Can you see the word on your eyelids?"
S:	"Yup."

T:	"Spell it."
S:	"T-h-e."
T:	"Good. Now describe the word. What does it look like?"
S:	"Well, it's kinda small."
T:	"How are you going to remember it?"
S:	"Uh, it has two letters that stick up."
T:	"Terrific!"

Present each new word using the "overlearning" procedure: 1, 2; 1, 2, 3; 1, 2, 3, 4; 1, 2, 3, 4, 5. For example: *the, to; the, to, and; the, to, and, he;* and so on. If, after all the new words have been presented, the student still has difficulty pronouncing them quickly, you may take the following steps:

1. Have the student trace the word, write it on paper, or use chalk or a magic slate.
2. Have the student repeat the word each time it is written.
3. Have the student write the word without looking at the flash card; then compare the two.

B. Create "study buddies." Match learners in the classroom with fellow students who have mastered the words. Take time to teach the "tutors" how to reinforce new words. Provide a reward to both tutor and learner once the learner has attained the goal.

C. Provide reinforcement games for students to use on their own or with their study buddies. (See the suggestions under "Games and Exercises" later in this chapter.)

D. Provide charts, graphs, and other devices for students to display their progress. These serve as excellent motivators, especially since students are competing with themselves rather than with one another.

E. Pass out a few basic sight words on cards to students. Each student in turn goes to the board and writes her word. The other students participating should try to say it aloud. After it is pronounced correctly, have them write it in a notebook. On some days, have students select words from their notebooks and write them on the chalkboard. Then ask various members of the group to say these words.

F. Have the students use the words from their notebooks to create simple sentences or stories. It is fine for these stories to be silly; students can also be encouraged to include their own names and names of fellow students in the stories. During free time, students may illustrate or decorate these sentences and stories. As often as possible, students can practice reading their own and fellow students' sentences and stories over and over again.

G. Have the student write troublesome words on cards. Use the cards to form sentences. Also, provide sentences with the sight words omitted.

Have the student fill in the blanks with the appropriate word from her cards.

H. Use the sight words that cause difficulty in sentences. Underline the words that cause difficulty, as in the following examples:

1. I thought it was you.
2. I could not go even though I have time.
3. She ran right through the stop sign.

A list of basic sight word sentences, derived from the sight word phrases, is provided in Appendix C-1.

I. Have the student read the entire sentence, look at the beginning and end of the word, and then try to pronounce it on the basis of its context and configuration.

J. Use commercially prepared games or computer software designed for teaching basic sight words.

For students who have particular difficulty with certain words:

K. Cut letters from fine sandpaper or velvet so that the student can "feel" the word as she pronounces it. For certain students it may be helpful to put a thin layer of salt or fine sand in a shoebox lid and let them practice writing the word in the salt or sand.

L. Place a piece of paper over a piece of screen wire such as the wire used for screen doors. It is a good idea to cover the edges of the screen wire with bookbinding tape, so the rough edges do not cut anyone. Writing on the paper over the screen with a crayon will leave a series of raised dots. Have the student write basic sight words in this manner, and then have her trace over the words, saying them as they are traced.

GAMES AND EXERCISES

Note: For the games and exercises to be most effective, the students must receive lots of practice in *looking at and quickly saying* the sight words. (See also the games and exercises in Chapter 13, "General Sight Vocabulary Not up to Grade Level." Many of these are appropriate for improving knowledge of basic sight words.)

Guess the Word

Purpose: To provide practice in recognizing basic sight words.

Materials: Basic sight words written on an overhead transparency, large flashcards, or sentence strips, OR flashcards placed in a pocket chart, as shown in the examples in Figure 12.1.

FIGURE 12.1

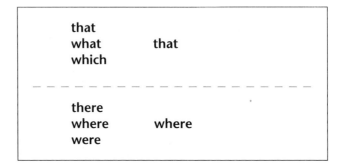

Procedure:

Show only the three words on the left to the students while you cover the word on the right. Have the students pronounce each of the exposed words while you point to them one at a time. Then give the students a moment to guess which one of the three words will appear when you reveal the word on the right. Then uncover the mystery word so the students can see if they guessed correctly. Before going on to the next set of words, have the students again pronounce all four words while you point to them in varying orders. (Note that the examples shown for this activity require the students to pronounce easily confused basic sight words. For many students such words are especially challenging and require considerable practice, using both isolated activities such as this one and frequent practice in the act of reading easy contextual materials.)

Dominoes

Purpose: To provide practice in word discrimination

Materials: Flash cards, divided in half by a line, with a different word on each side of the line. (See Figure 12.2.) Make sure that the words are repeated several times on different cards.

FIGURE 12.2

the	what		and	the
a	and		go	a

Procedure:

After mixing the cards, the game proceeds the same as dominoes. The student pronounces the word as she matches it.

Word Order

Purpose: To provide practice on basic sight words, on general sight words, or in recognition of phonic elements

Materials: Dittoed sheets of words arranged in the same manner as shown here:

A. why	_____	B. c	_____
what	_____	d	_____
when	_____	g	_____
where	_____	b	_____
which	_____	f	_____

C. cat	_____	D. sound	_____
mule	_____	frog	_____
cage	_____	wolf	_____
pill	_____	rabbit	_____
duck	_____	pass	_____

Procedure:

Play a recording or read words or sounds to the students who have the dittoed sheets. Each set of words should, however, concentrate on practice in only one area. The directions for the preceding sets would be similar to the following example:

Set A: Number the words in the order in which they are read.

Set B: Number the letters that match the beginning sound that you hear in the following words (in the order they are given): *book, food, good, can, dog.*

Set C: Put numeral *1* in front of the word with a long /a/ sound.

Put *2* in front of the word with a short /u/ sound.

Put *3* in front of the word with a short /a/ sound.

Put *4* in front of the word with a long /u/ sound.

Put *5* in front of the word with a short /i/ sound.

Set D: Number the words, in the order they are given, that have ending letter sounds. Give the following sounds: /f/, /t/, /g/, /d/, /s/.

Passport

Purpose: To provide practice on the basic sight words or general sight words

Materials: Use either group-size (6″ × 3″) or individual-size cards (3″ × 1½″). One set is given to the group of students and one is kept by the captain, who is usually a student who knows the words well.

Procedure:

Each student is given one or several words (passports). In order to get aboard the boat, she must show her passports to the captain. When the captain calls the port (the word or words) from her deck of cards, the person who has a card matching the captain's must show it to her to get off the boat.

Variation in Procedure:

The same game can be played with the sounds of the consonants and vowels to practice phonics skills. In this case, the captain has word cards, and the student who has a letter matching the sound of the first letter in the word called by the captain shows her passport (letter) and is allowed to leave the boat.

Word in the Box

Purpose: To provide review and reinforcement of words that present problems to students

Materials: A large box
Word cards with words on them that have given the students trouble in their reading

Procedure:

The students sit in a circle around the box. You either read or play a tape recording of a story. Before hearing the story, each student is given a card on which there is a word from the story. When that word is read in the story, the student says, "_____ goes in the box," and throws the word in the box. The student then is given another word, so she may continue in the game.

Word Football

Purpose: To provide practice on recognizing basic sight words or general sight words

Materials: A large sheet of drawing paper
A small replica of a football
Word cards

Procedure:

Draw a football field on a large piece of paper. The game begins at the 50-yard line, where the football is placed. The word cards are placed face up on the table, and two students, or two teams, take turns reading them. If a student reads a word correctly, she moves the ball 10 yards toward the opponent's goal. If she reads the word incorrectly, it is considered a fumble, and the ball goes 10 yards toward her own goal. Each time the ball crosses into the end zone, 6 points are scored. The scoring side then gets to read one more word to try for the extra point.

Word Checkers

Purpose: To provide practice in word recognition or phonic sounds

Materials: Checkerboard
              Small squares of paper with sight words or phonic sounds on them
Procedure:

You or the student covers the black squares with the words. The game is played the same as regular checkers, but the player must say the word that appears on the square before a checker is placed on that space. (To give the students extra practice, have them say the words three times before moving the checkers.)

Variation in Procedure:

Phonic sounds may be used instead of words.

Pack of Trouble

Purpose: To discover which children do not know certain words and to provide special help in such cases

Materials: Word cards using the vocabulary currently being studied
              Blank cards on which you can print words
Procedure:

You flash word cards to individual students and ask them to pronounce the words as quickly as possible. Whenever a student misses a word, she is given that word and makes a copy of it to keep. The student then can give the original back to you. Each student develops her own pack of trouble, which she can use for study with another individual or with a small group. As soon as the student masters a word, she may give it back to you. The idea is, of course, for students to keep their packs of trouble as small as possible.

Climbing the Word Ladder

Purpose: To provide practice on basic sight words, on general sight words, or on sight phrases

Materials: A number of card packs of 10 words. On the cards can be basic sight words, other sight words, or sight phrases.
              A small ladder that will hold 10 cards. The rungs of the ladder may be made from wooden dowels ¾″ round and the vertical poles from wood of 1″ × 2″. See Figure 12.3.

FIGURE 12.3

Procedure:

Each student receives a pack of cards and tries to climb the ladder with them. Cards are laid on each rung of the ladder. The student then tries to climb it by saying the words. After the student has mastered her own words, she exchanges packs and begins again with new words.

Hands Up (Words)

Purpose: To provide practice on recognition of basic sight words or general sight words

Materials: Group-size cards (6″ × 3″)
Procedure:

Quickly flash a word card around the group, allowing each student to see it. The student whose turn it is to pronounce the word then has a chance to do so. If the student pronounces the word correctly, she is given the word card. If the student does not pronounce the word correctly, then she is required to raise her hand. When the next card is flashed, the second student has a chance to say it. If, however, the student who has her hand up can pronounce the word before the second student, she gets the card and may put her hand down. The second student then receives a chance at another word. If she misses that word, then that student must hold up her hand, and so on. The object is to get the most cards. There may also be a number of children with their hands up at any one time. If this is the case, the one who pronounces the word first gets the card.

Surprise Words

Purpose: To reinforce knowledge of the basic sight words or general sight words

Materials: Word cards to fit a pocket chart
            Pocket chart
Procedure:

Fill the pocket chart with words that are currently being studied. Turn the cards so only the backs are showing. The students take turns coming up to the chart and taking a surprise word. If they can pronounce the word, they get to keep it; if they cannot, they must leave it in the chart. The student with the most words at the end of a certain time period wins the game.

Gamble for Words

Purpose: To provide practice on either basic sight words or general sight words

Materials: Pocket chart
Cards with either the basic sight words or any sight word on them
A die

Procedure:

Place the words to be worked on in the pocket chart. One student then rolls a die. She may pick up the same number of cards from the chart as the number indicated on the die. She must, however, be able to say each word as she picks it up. The turn then passes to another student. The object is to see who can get the most words. This game may be played using either a student-versus-student approach or a team-versus-team approach. You may set a time limit for the game or limit the game to a certain number of refills of the pocket chart.

Word Match

Purpose: To provide practice on word recognition

Materials: A pack of word cards in which every card has a word on it that is duplicated; that is, there should be two cards for each word to be used. The number of cards will depend on the number of players involved.

Procedure:

The players are each dealt four cards, which are placed face up in front of each player. Five cards are then placed face up in the middle of the table. The remainder of the pack is placed face down in the middle of the table. If the first player has a card that matches any of the five face-up cards in the middle of the table, she picks it up, pronounces the word, and keeps the pair, placing them face down in front of her. The student may continue playing until she can make no more pairs. The student then draws to fill her hand to four cards and replaces the five face-up cards on the table. If, in this process, cards that match are drawn and placed on the table, they are left for the individual who has the next turn. Play continues to the first player on the left. If a player can match a card in the middle of the table but cannot pronounce the word, she must place her card in the middle and leave it. If the following player can pronounce the word, she receives the pair. The winner is the person with the most cards when all of the cards are paired.

Rolling for Words

Purpose: To teach and provide practice on basic sight words

Materials: Three colors of construction paper
             A die
             Three small boxes

Procedure:

Cut the colored construction paper into 1″ squares. Print a basic sight word on each square. Put the squares into separate boxes according to the color of the paper. The players throw the die to see who starts the game. The student with the highest number starts by selecting as many words from any one box as the number on the die. If she fails to say any one of the words, she loses all the words from that turn. After being told the missed word by the teacher, the student returns the words to the appropriate box. Play continues to the first player's left. The winner is the one with the most words when all three boxes are empty, and the game ends.

Finding Rhyming Words

Purpose: To teach and reinforce basic sight words

Materials: Flash cards of basic sight words from which rhyming words can be
               made
             Pocket chart

Procedure:

Place the flash cards in the pocket chart. You then say, "I want a word that rhymes with fat." Students take turns looking for a word to rhyme with the one you give. If the student cannot find the word, she is given a word to hold by you or by another student who knows it. The winners are those students who are holding no words at the end of the game.

Finding Phrases

Purpose: To reinforce knowledge of the basic sight words

Materials: Pocket chart
             Basic sight word cards (3″ × 8½″)

Procedure:

Place the words in the pocket chart to make four or five phrases (for example, *is in* and *wants to go*). Then say a sentence such as, "The boy wants to go." Students take turns going to the pocket chart and placing their hands on the phrase from the sentence and reading it. If a student fails to read it correctly, she must take the cards from that phrase to be studied. The object is to have no cards at the end of the game.

The Password

Purpose: To provide practice on especially difficult basic sight words

Materials: Straight or safety pins
$3'' \times 8\frac{1}{2}''$ cards

Procedure:

Take a group of students who are having trouble with the same basic sight words. Write one of the basic sight words on each card, and go over the words thoroughly with the students. Then pin one card on each student. Throughout the day, whenever one student must deal with another or whenever you wish to get a response from that student, call the basic sight word written on the student's card rather than her name before that student is to respond. This can be done daily with different groups of words and students.

Concentration

Purpose: To develop the ability to recognize basic sight words

Materials: Basic sight word flash cards in which each card has a duplicate
Procedure:

Find 10 to 12 cards and their duplicate cards (for a total of 20 to 24). Shuffle the cards and lay them face down on the table. The first student turns up a card and says the word. She then turns up another card, trying to find the duplicate of the first one turned up. If the second card is not a duplicate of the first or if the student does not know the word, she turns them face down, and the next student takes her turn. If a student is able to turn up one card, say the word, and then turn up the duplicate of that card, she gets to keep the pair. As play continues, students will, of course, find it easier to find matching pairs. The person with the most pairs at the end of the game wins. (*Note:* Be sure to have each student *pronounce* each word as it is turned over. This is where the practice and learning takes place. Often, in a game of Concentration, the students are interested only in matching pairs quickly and will prefer not to say each word.)

CHAPTER 13

General Sight Vocabulary Not up to Grade Level

RECOGNIZED BY

The student fails to instantly recognize words thought to be common at or below his grade level. (Failure is not limited to basic sight words.)

DISCUSSION

In advancing from grade to grade, the student should increase his sight vocabulary at each grade level. A student's sight vocabulary is not up to grade level unless he can correctly pronounce 95% of the words in a book written at his grade level. The student who has not developed an adequate number of sight words is greatly handicapped since he must analyze many more words than a normal reader. This student is more likely to encounter reading material at his frustration level.

You should not determine whether a book is at a certain grade level using the publisher's recommendation unless that recommendation is based on one of the better readability formulas. Unfortunately, even many of the popular basal readers are prepared with stories at a variety of levels. That is, you cannot be sure that all stories in a basal reader that is designated at, say, a fourth-grade level are actually written at that level.

RECOMMENDATIONS

The first and most important recommendation to help a student increase the size of his sight vocabulary is to have the student read widely on many subjects. If the student has adequate word-attack skills and is pronouncing the words correctly, then he will automatically learn many new sight words by seeing them a number of times. However, if the student does not have adequate word-attack skills for his grade level, then the appropriate procedures in Chapters 12 through 19 should be used as needed to improve the student's ability with phonics, structural analysis, or context clues. The various methods described in the introductory chapter will also improve the student's overall sight vocabulary.

A. Have the student read as widely as possible at his independent or low-instructional level. In doing so, he will learn new words from their context.

B. Have the student start a card file of new words. Write the word (or have the student write the word) and the definition on the front of the card. On the back, write the word in its proper context in a sentence. (Never write just the word and the dictionary definition alone.)

C. Build on the student's background of experience as much as possible. Use discussions, demonstrations, computer software, videotapes, tape recordings, or anything that will build his listening/speaking vocabulary. This will make it easier for the student to acquire new words through context clues.

D. Use picture word cards on which the unknown word appears under a picture illustrating that word. When making these, it is important to use the word in a sentence as well as by itself. Have students work in pairs or small groups to learn these new words from the word cards. Have the students work cooperatively to build a file of pictures representing scenes, action events, and so forth in stories. Before the students begin to read the new stories, discuss these picture files with them. Pictures may also be put in scrapbooks, and pages may be divided into sections (represented by letters) on numbered pages. You can then make a tape recording to go along with the scrapbook. The script for the tape recording might read as follows:

> **On page 3 of the scrapbook, in picture A, you see a picture of a waterfall. In the story you are going to read today, a man goes over a waterfall in a boat. The boat probably looks like the one in picture B. The men have been camping in the woods and probably look like the men in picture C.**

Put the students at listening stations and have them prepare for reading a story by listening to these tapes and looking at the scrapbooks.

E. Have the students pantomime certain words such as *write, hear,* and *walk.* Make sure the students see the words immediately before, during, and after the pantomime.

F. Allow the student to preread material silently before asking him to read it orally. Encourage the student to ask you for assistance with difficult words during the silent reading phase. Remember, if the student asks for help on more than 10% of the words, the material is too difficult and should be replaced with easier material.

G. Teach the word-attack strategy described in Chapter 19.

GAMES AND EXERCISES

Sight Words in Context

Purpose: To provide practice on sight words and context clues

Materials: Pocket chart
Group-size word cards
Tape recorder

Procedure:

Place 8 to 10 words in the bottom pockets of the pocket chart. These should be new words on which you wish to provide practice. Play a tape recording of a short story that uses the words in the bottom rows of the pocket chart. Say the word and at the same time ring a bell or sound a buzzer. At the signal, the student picks the correct card from the 8 to 10 choices in the bottom rows and places it in the top row of the pocket chart. Be sure to pause briefly after the word to give the student a chance to look for it. You will need to allow for longer pauses at the beginning of the story when there are more words at the bottom of the pocket chart. The cards should be placed in order from left to right beginning with row 1. When the top row is full, the cards begin the left-to-right sequence in row 2, and so on until all cards have been transferred from the bottom to the top of the chart. After all the words are transferred from the bottom to the top of the chart, you can check the words with the students in the following manner: "In row 1, the first word is _____ , the next word is _____ ," and so on. This makes the exercise self-correcting when it is programmed on the tape along with the rest of the exercise.

Variation in Procedure:

Instead of saying the word as a bell or buzzer rings, ring the buzzer and let the student find the word from context.

Zingo

Purpose: To provide practice in the recognition of the basic sight words or general sight words

Materials: A number of word cards (7″ × 7″) with 25 squares, each of which has a different sight word on it
A list of each of the sight words
A number of kernels of corn, buttons, or beans

Procedure:

This game is played like bingo. Read a word from the word list and ask the students to hunt for that word on their word (zingo) cards. When they find the word pronounced, they place a kernel of corn or some other marker on it. The first student to get five spaces filled in any direction is the winner. After a student has won, he should pronounce the words covered by the markers. This will ensure that the students not only recognize words by sight but that they also can say them.

Construct your word list so that you can allow various individuals to win if you so desire, e.g., zingo card 3 may win by saying words 2, 8, 10, 12, and 15. Although this is a prearranged game, it will enable you to allow the students who need motivation to win.

Racetrack

Purpose: To provide practice in recognition of basic sight words or general sight words

Materials: A large sheet of drawing paper
Two duplicate sets of individual-size word cards (3″ × 1½″)
Two toy automobiles

Procedure:

Draw an oval track on the drawing paper to resemble a racetrack, as shown in Figure 13.1. Be sure to put in a start and finish line. Divide the track into sections in which there are printed drill words. Each of the two players has a toy automobile, placed on the starting line of the track. Each player has a set of small word cards that are duplicates of those of the opposing player and are the same as the words on the racetrack. Each player places his pile of cards face up. One player then reads the word on his top card. If the word is the same as the one in the first space of the racetrack, he moves his auto to that space. If it is not the same, he may not move. His card is placed on the bottom

FIGURE 13.1

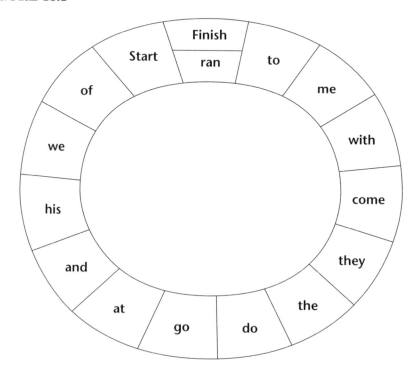

of the deck, and the other player takes a turn. The winner is the first player to go around the racetrack to the finish line. Be sure cards are shuffled well before each game.

Treasure Hunt

Purpose: To provide practice on the basic sight words or general sight words.

Materials: Sight word cards with a word on one side and a direction on the back such as "Go to a word that starts with *c*," or "Go to a word that starts with *w*."

Procedure:

A number of word cards are placed on the top of the students' desks with sight words showing. To begin the hunt, give two or three students different cards with the directions face up. The students immediately start to hunt for words with the beginning letters as indicated. When they find a word that starts with one of the letters, they say it. They may then turn the card over and get directions for the next step in the treasure hunt. The last card should have a picture of a treasure chest on the back of it instead of directions to look further. You will need to arrange the card sets so that each student goes through the same number of steps.

Donkey

Purpose: To provide practice on basic sight words or general sight words

Materials: Make a deck of cards using one new word causing difficulty on each card. You may use any number of players. In the deck you should include three to five cards with the word *donkey* written on them.

Procedure:

Deal all cards to the players face down. The players then take turns turning up a card, pronouncing it, and placing it in a pool in the middle of the table. When the donkey card appears, the player drawing it says "donkey" and throws it in the center of the table. All the players try to grab the donkey card. The one who gets it may keep it and all cards that have been thrown into the pool. The winner of the game is the player who ends up with all of the cards or the most cards when all donkey cards have been drawn.

The Head Chair

Purpose: To provide practice in recognizing basic sight words or general sight words

Materials: Group-size word cards (6″ × 3″)

Procedure:

Arrange students' chairs in a circle and mark one as the head chair. Begin play by flashing a card to the person in the head chair. If the student says the word correctly, he stays in his chair. If the student misses the word, he goes to the end chair; and all the students from this student to the end move over one chair. Continue around the circle from the head chair to the end chair. The object is to try to end up in the head chair.

Variation in Procedure:

If you are working with a relatively small group, have all of the chairs facing you. This will enable all of the students to see all of the words.

Cops and Robbers

Purpose: To provide practice in recognizing basic sight words or general sight words

Materials: Tagboard
             Word cards

Procedure:

On a piece of tagboard construct an irregular course of dots and then connect the dots with lines. At points along the course place hideouts, dried-up water holes, deserts, and so on. The game is played with two students—one a bank robber, one a police officer. The bank robber will place his marker on the course as far from the officer's marker as possible. The game begins with each player turning over a word card from a pack placed face down on the table. The student reads the word on the card and then moves the number of dots denoted by a number appearing in one of the corners of the word card. The robber tries to avoid the officer. The game ends when the robber is captured (that is, when the police officer catches up with the robber). A more difficult game can be made by increasing the number of moves allowed according to the difficulty of the word given.

Team Sight Word Race

Purpose: To provide drill on basic sight words or general sight words

Materials: A group-size (6″ × 3″) set of basic sight word cards or sight words on which you want to provide practice

Procedure:

The students are divided into two teams. Each team member takes a turn attempting to pronounce a word turned up from a pile of sight words. If one team member misses, the opposite team then receives a chance to pronounce that word, in addition to the team member's regular turn. Score is kept on the number of words each team pronounces correctly. Do not have the members sit down when they miss a word, but have each team member go to the back of the line after each try, whether successful or not. This enables all members of each team to gain equal practice and does not eliminate those people who need practice most.

Variation in Procedure:

Instead of using single or isolated words, use phrase cards or sentence cards in which the word being emphasized is underlined. Allow the students to make the cards with a final check by you. You can use a number of smaller teams and have several races going at one time.

Stand Up

Purpose: To provide practice in recognizing the basic sight words or general sight words

Materials: Group-size word cards (6" × 3")
Procedure:

The students are seated in a group around you. One student stands behind the chair of another student who is sitting with his chair facing you. You then flash a card. If the student who is standing pronounces the word before the student in the chair, then the student who was sitting must stand up behind someone else.

Word Hunt

Purpose: To provide practice on the basic sight words or general sight words

Materials: Blindfolds
Group-size word cards (6" × 3")
Procedure:

Have several students cover their eyes. The rest of the group hides the cards where they can be found easily. When all the cards are hidden, the students who are "it" are given a signal to immediately take off their blindfolds and begin hunting for the cards. A student may pick up a card if he knows the word on it. No cards may be picked up unless the word is known. The student who finds the most words is the winner.

Seven Up

Purpose: To provide practice on word recognition and word meaning

Materials: Group-size word cards (6" × 3"). Be sure there are seven times as many cards as students playing.
Procedure:

The students sit in a circle, with the flash cards in a pile face down in the center of the group. Each student takes a turn by turning over a card and reading it. If the student reads it correctly, he keeps it. When a student has seven correct cards, he stands up. The game continues until all the students are standing. The students then sit down and see how fast they can make a sentence with some or all of their seven cards. Be sure both nouns and verbs are included in the stack. As soon as a student has made a sentence, he stands. This play continues until all the students who can make sentences of their words have done so.

Noun Label

Purpose: To teach nouns to non- or limited-English-speaking students and to improve the vocabulary of those students who have insufficient vocabulary knowledge. It may, of course, be used in the early stages of reading in the regular developmental program.

Materials: Group-size word cards (6″ × 3″) with the names of common nouns written on them
8½″ × 11″ tagboard sheets with a picture of one of the common nouns on the top half of the sheet
Chalkboard

Procedure:

The pictures on the tagboard sheets are placed on the tray of the chalkboard. The students are then given words that correspond to the pictures. They come up to the chalkboard and place their words under the appropriate pictures. See the example in Figure 13.2.

Word Golf

Purpose: To provide practice on the basic sight words or general sight words

Materials: Nine packs of word cards. Each pack should have 10 sight words in it.
A player and a scorekeeper

FIGURE 13.2

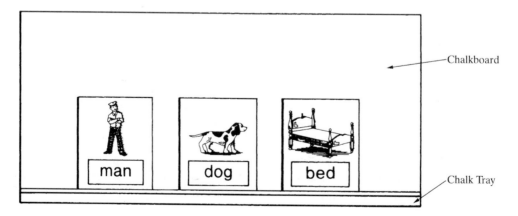

Procedure:

The player takes the first pack, shuffles the cards, and places them face down in front of him. He takes a card from the top of the pack, turns it face up, and reads it. If he misses a word, the scorekeeper makes one mark on the scoring sheet. The number incorrect for the first pack is the player's score for the first hole. The student continues in this manner through the nine packs, trying to receive as low a score as possible.

What Word Am I?

Purpose: To provide practice with sight words

Materials: Two duplicate sets of cards with sight words printed on them

Procedure:

Divide the class into two groups. Each student has a word card pinned on his back. The duplicates of the cards are spread out on a table. The object of the game is to see which group can guess all their words first. The students take turns going to the table, picking up a word card, and asking, "Am I _____?" saying the word on the card. If the student chooses the card that matches the word on his back and pronounces it correctly, he keeps the card. If the student selects a card that doesn't match, he puts the card down on the table and takes his seat. The game continues until one group guesses all its words.

Jumping the Fence

Purpose: To provide practice on the basic sight words or general sight words

Materials: Flash cards with sight words on them
             White tape

Procedure:

Place the flash cards on the floor in a row leading to the fence (white tape on the floor). A student who reads a word correctly jumps over the card and advances toward the fence. He may jump the fence when he reaches it. If he misses a word, he sits down and another student has a turn.

The Witch

Purpose: To provide practice with sight words. This game works well with four players if 20 cards are used.

Materials: Use a deck containing about 20 cards with one additional card that has a witch on it. Print one set of words on half of the cards. Duplicate the first set of words on the other half of the cards.

Procedure:

One person deals out all the cards; players pick them up and look at them. Beginning with the person at the dealer's left, the players take turns drawing cards—each player draws from the person on his right. As students form pairs, they pronounce the words and place their cards on the table. Play continues until all cards are matched. The player left with the witch is the loser and receives a *w*. The next time he loses, he has *wi*, and so on. The object is to try to avoid losing enough times to spell *witch*.

Silly Sentences

Purpose: To teach or reinforce sight words

Materials: Plain flash cards and a pocket chart, OR flash cards with flannel backing and a flannel board

Procedure:

Lay out sentences in mixed-up order on the pocket chart or flannel board. Have students take turns coming up and unscrambling the sentences and reading them after they are placed in a sensible order. Make sure all students get a chance to read each logically ordered sentence.

CHAPTER 14

Phonics Difficulties: Consonants

RECOGNIZED BY

The student is unable to use consonants to decode one-syllable words because the student is unable to give the correct sounds and variant sounds of the consonants. The letter-sound associations for the consonants are presented in Appendix A-2.

DISCUSSION

An enormous body of research over many years has clearly established the fact that effective phonics instruction can be a crucial aid in unlocking the puzzle of reading for the beginning reader. However, phonics is only one of the tools that readers use in decoding. Millions of people have learned to read English without receiving instruction in phonics. These individuals learned to read by relying on a substantial sight vocabulary combined with skill in using context clues. Indeed, the reading progress of many students may be hampered by too much emphasis on phonics, particularly if the focus is on the phonic elements that are least critical for successful decoding.

Phonics instruction tends to be most helpful to students reading at or below the second-grade reading level. Students who can read at or above a third-grade reading level rarely profit from an emphasis on phonics. That is because phonics is a useful tool for decoding one-syllable words that happen to be phonetically regular. Unphonetic words (such as many of those on basic sight vocabulary lists) should be learned as sight words; that is, by memorizing them. Words of more than one syllable are decoded most efficiently through the combined use of structural analysis and context clues.

For the student who is unable to decode regular, one-syllable words, some phonics skills are more helpful than others. Research and experience have shown that beginning letter sounds are most useful. Generalizations about ending sounds and vowel sounds are less helpful. Students who struggle to read materials written at or below the second-grade level should be taught to recognize and apply the letter-sound associations for single consonants, **consonant blends,** and consonant **digraphs.** In addition, instruction on vowels should be provided as described in Chapter 15.

The application of phonics skills is really quite simple. The beginning reader is taught to do the following when she encounters an unfamiliar one-syllable word: first, identify and separate the letters; then, pronounce and blend the individual letter sounds, or phonemes, to decode the word. For example, in the word *cat,* the reader identifies and separates the three letters *c, a,* and *t.* Then she thinks of the sound that each letter represents, and pronounces and blends the three sounds together to make the whole word. (When reading in context, the student is encouraged to use other words in the sentence to assist with decoding unknown words.) Not all one-syllable words are composed of three letters, of course; however, the process remains the same. To decode the word *shine,* for example, the reader identifies and separates the letters—*sh, i, ne,*—then pronounces and blends the three letter sounds together to make the whole word. These examples are illustrated in Figure 14.1.

Note that the decoding of these words requires a considerable amount of phonics knowledge for a young child. In the word *cat,* the reader must know the hard *c* sound, the short *a* sound, and the *t* sound. To decode the word *shine,* the reader must know the sound of the consonant digraph *sh,* the long *i* sound, and the *n* sound.

Before beginning phonics instruction, you should determine whether the student needs instruction in some or all areas of phonics. To do this, administer a phonics test such as the Phonics Assessment found in Appendix B-6 (Subtests 1, 2, 3, 6, 7, and 9). If a student is deficient in nearly all

FIGURE 14.1

Phonics

	cat	shine
Step 1	c |a |t	sh |i |he
Step 2	c+a+t	sh+i+ne
	cat	**shine**

Step 1: Identify and separate
phonemes.

Step 2: Pronounce and blend
letter sounds.

areas—initial consonants, consonant blends and digraphs, and so on—you may need to start from the beginning with the teaching of phonics. In this case you will find that, for many disabled readers, instruction using the phonogram list as described in Appendix C-2 will enable the student to quickly learn a great many initial consonants, consonant blends, and consonant digraphs in a relatively short time.

RECOMMENDATIONS

Many of these suggestions provide effective ways to teach students to recognize and pronounce consonants in isolation or in single words. However, for phonics instruction to be effective, students must transfer their knowledge of consonant letter sounds to the act of decoding. The best way to help students do this is to first provide direct instruction on the consonant letter sounds to be learned, then give the student substantial practice in the act of reading. As each consonant sound is taught, you should provide short, easy sentences and/or stories for the students to read. You may create these sentences or stories yourself, have the students assist you in their development through language-experience activities (see the introductory chapter), or use commercial materials that have been designed for this purpose. The students may need to read these sentences and stories over and over to master their phonics skills. The use of contextual material is essential because you want students to rely on context clues as they are learning phonics. You also want to be sure that students understand that the purpose of your instruction is to aid them in decoding so that they can obtain *meaning* from printed words.

There are many methods of teaching phonic elements. One typical procedure for teaching a consonant letter sound follows:

1. Develop awareness of hearing the sound:
    Say, "Listen to these words. Each of them begins with the *b* sound. Circle the *b* on each word on your paper as you hear the sound. *Ball . . . bat . . . base . . . banana. . . .*"

2. Develop awareness of seeing the sound:
    Tell the student to circle all of the words in a passage that begin with *b*.

3. Provide practice in saying words with the *b* sound:
    Pronounce each word and have the students pronounce it after you: "*Big, bad, baseball, basket, beach. . . .*"

4. Provide practice in blending the *b* sound with common word families or phonograms:
    Teach or use several phonograms with which students are already familiar, such as *-ake* and *-and*. Put the *b* in one column, the phonogram in a second column, and the two combined in a third column as follows:

b	ake	bake
b	and	band
b	at	bat
b	ig	big
b	ike	bike

and so on. Instruct the students to say *b* (either the letter name or the sound /b/), then the phonogram (the sound represented by the letters in the phonogram, such as /at/), and then the word formed by the two, /bat/.

5. Ask the students to help you make a list of some words that begin with *b*. Ask the students to say each word with you as you write it. You may then have the students themselves write the same words (on paper, small chalkboards, white boards, or magic slates) and say them as they write them.

6. Provide practice in reading *b* words. Present sentences, paragraphs, or simple stories that have a number of *b* words in them for the students to read. If the students are able to read only a few words, then you can use illustrations (or rebuses) if necessary instead of the other words.

The following activities will also assist students in learning the consonant sounds:

A. If the student does not know a great many of the initial consonants, consonant clusters, vowels, vowel teams, and special letter combinations, use the phonogram list as described in Appendix C-2.

B. Construct flash cards on which the consonant is shown along with a picture illustrating a word that uses that consonant, such as *b* in *b*all, or *c* in *c*at. On the opposite side of the flash card print the letter only. This can be used as the student progresses in ability. See Figure 14.2.

FIGURE 14.2

Ball

Front of Card

b

Back of Card

C. Put the consonant letters on 3″ × 3″ cards. Divide these cards into groups of 10 each. Lay out separate groups of letters, so the student can see all 10 at once. As you call the sounds of letters, or as they are played from a tape recording, have the student pick up the correct card to match the sound of the letter. As there are fewer words to observe—that is, after some have already been picked up—you will need to speed up the rate at which you pronounce the remaining words. The following timing seems to work well: pronounce the first word, wait 7 seconds; pronounce the second word and wait 7 seconds again; then 6, 6, 5, 5, 4, 4, and 3 seconds. Many students are unable to manipulate the cards in less time than this.

D. Tape-record words and have the students write the letter that stands for the beginning, ending, or both beginning and ending sounds of these words. See the following example:

Directions: As you hear a word called on the tape, write the letter that begins the word. (Tape script says, "Number one is *come*, number two is *dog*," and so on.)

1. c
2. d
3.
4.
5.

E. Use the same system as in item D. Instead of having the students write letters they hear, have them pick up the card that matches the beginning or ending letter they hear in the words.

F. Put various consonant letters on the board or in a pocket chart and have the students make lists of the words that begin with these letters.

G. Record the consonant letters with their sounds and let the students hear these as many times as is necessary. They should, however, have a chart they can follow to see the letters as they hear the sound.

H. Use commercial charts that are available for teaching consonants. Tapes that give the proper pronunciation of the consonant sounds are also available.

I. Use commercially prepared games or computer software designed to teach consonants and the application of consonant sounds in decoding.

GAMES AND EXERCISES

Phonics Posters

Purpose: To develop an awareness of related sounds

Materials: Tagboard
            Old magazines or old textbooks

Procedure:

At the top of a piece of tagboard, place a letter or combination of letters. Have the students find pictures of objects in the old magazines or textbooks that start with the sound or sounds displayed in the heading. These object pictures should be cut out and mounted on the tagboard to provide practice for individuals who need special help.

Poet Play

Purpose: To help students develop an awareness of sound similarities through the use of rhyming words

Materials: Pocket chart
             Word cards
             Envelopes

Procedure:

Give the students envelopes containing a number of word cards. Place a master word in the pocket chart and have the students locate in their envelopes a word that rhymes with the one posted. Number the envelopes and allow the students to exchange them after each round, so they will become familiar with a great many words and their sound similarities.

Line Up

Purpose: To provide practice in discriminating between like and unlike sounds

Procedure:

When there is extra time before lunch or dismissal, you might use this game. It is both interesting and beneficial. You call, "All those whose names start like *meat* may line up and get their coats." Repeat as many times as needed to dismiss the students. As a variation, use letters that are in the middle or end of students' names. The students also might use this method to choose groups or sides in other games.

Rhyme Time

Purpose: To discover which students are having auditory discrimination problems and to provide practice through the use of related phonic sounds

Materials: Tagboard
             Word cards

Procedure:

Write sentences on the tagboard. On the word cards print a variety of words that will rhyme with selected words given in the sentences. Have the students locate and match their cards with the rhyming words in the sentences. Place each set of cards in an envelope and number the envelopes, so the students can keep a record of the sets on which they have worked. See the following example:

1. **The dog bit the mailperson. (log, hog)**
2. **The candy tasted sweet. (treat, beat)**
3. **Look out the window. (took, book)**
4. **The wall had a large crack. (back, sack)**
5. **She cut down the apple tree. (see, flee)**

Making and Exchanging Picture Dictionaries

Purpose: To learn initial consonant sounds

Materials: Old notebooks or paper to be bound together
             Crayons and/or paints
             Magazines and other materials containing pictures

Procedure:

Have students cut out or draw pictures representing various initial consonant sounds. Under the picture write the letter or letters of the initial sound and the word that stands for the picture. Also under each picture use the word in a sentence. After the students have finished their books, have them exchange dictionaries, so each student learns to read every other student's dictionary.

I'm Thinking of a Word

Purpose: To provide practice in auditory discrimination and the recognition of beginning, ending, or both beginning and ending sounds

Materials: Pocket chart
             Cards with words that begin with various consonants
             Cards with words that end with various consonants

Procedure:

Fill the pocket chart with about 10 cards, each of which has a different beginning sound. The first student says, "I'm thinking of a word that begins like /d/." (The student says the *d* sound.) The student draws a card, trying to get the word beginning with that sound. She gets to keep the card as long as she matches a sound and word. She may thus take all of the cards from the pocket chart. If the student gives a sound and draws a word that does not begin with that sound, play then passes to the next student. If the student gets all of the cards, another student then follows the same procedure. The same procedure can also be used with ending sounds.

Variation in Procedure:

There are many possible variations of this game. You may have students come to the front and say, "I'm thinking . . ," and call on someone to guess the word.

Another game might have a student put letters in the pocket chart and say, "My word is *dog*." The other students then have to find a *d* or *g* depending on whether you are working with beginning or ending sounds. The students also may play the same game and be required to find both the beginning and ending sounds.

Catch the Stick

Purpose: To improve auditory discrimination and to improve the students' ability to make the connection between sounds and letters

Materials: A number of group-size cards (6″ × 3″) with the beginning consonant sounds on them
            A yardstick

Procedure:

Seat the students in as small a circle as possible for the number of students you wish to have play the game. Ten to 12 students are optimum. The students are all given a different beginning consonant sound on a group-size card. One student stands in the center of the circle and holds the yardstick in an upright position with one end on the floor and the top end held in place by the tip of her finger. The student in the center then pronounces a word that begins with a consonant. At the same time the student pronounces the word, she takes the tip of her finger off the top of the yardstick. The student who has the beginning letter of the word named by the student in the center of the circle must catch the yardstick before it falls on the floor. If the student who had the consonant letter catches the stick, she returns to her seat and the person in the center must say another word. However, if she does not catch the stick, then she must change places with the student in the center and give her card to the student she is replacing.

Phonic Rummy

Purpose: To provide practice in various phonic elements. This game works well with two to four players when using 36 cards, or up to six players when using 48 or 52 cards.

Materials: A deck of cards with phonic elements that you wish to teach. On each card will appear one phonic element and four words that use that particular phonic element. One of the four words will be underlined. The deck may consist of 36, 40, 44, 48, or 52 cards. For each phonic element there will be 4 cards, each of which has a different word underlined. A deck of 36 cards would involve 9 phonic elements; 40 cards would involve 10 phonic elements. See the following example:

i	*ay*	*gr*
did	stay	green
pit	may	grass
if	play	grow
fish	clay	grab

Procedure:

The dealer shuffles the cards and deals eight cards face down to each player. The rest of the cards are placed face down in the center of the table. The first player to the left of the dealer calls for a word using a certain phonic element on which she wishes to build. (See the examples.) For example, the student might say, "I want Sam to give me *fish* from the *i* group" and would pronounce the short /i/ sound. If Sam had that card, she would give it to the caller. The player (caller) then continues to call for certain cards from specific people. If the person called upon does not have the card, the caller takes a card from the center pile, and the next player to the left takes her turn. When a player completes a "book" (that is, when she has all four cards from a certain phonic element), she lays it down. Players can only lay down books when it is their turn to draw. The object is to get the most books before someone empties her hand.

Think

Purpose: To provide practice with initial vowels, consonants, and initial consonant blends. This game works well with four players.

Materials: Enough small cards so that each letter of the alphabet and each initial blend can be printed on a separate card. There may be more than one card for each vowel.

Procedure:

Place the cards face down on the table. The players take turns selecting a card and naming a word that begins with the same letter or blend. If someone cannot name a word within 5 seconds, she puts the card back. The winner is the person who has the greatest number of cards after the entire pile has been drawn.

Word Trail

Purpose: To provide practice on consonants, consonant blends, vowels, digraphs, and diphthongs

Materials: A piece of tagboard
A list of phonic elements to be taught
A die

Procedure:

Draw a margin (approximately 2″) around the sheet of tagboard. Divide the margin into spaces large enough for inserting the phonic elements for practice. On the corners and in several spaces between corners, insert penalties and rewards, such as "Take another turn" or "Move back three spaces." The players then take turns rolling the die and moving their markers along the spaces, saying each phonic element as they move. If they cannot say a certain phonic element, they must stop on the space behind it and wait for another turn. The first player around the word trail is the winner.

Any Card

Purpose: To provide practice with consonants, consonant digraphs, consonant blends, and rhyming sounds. This game can be played with two to four players.

Materials: A deck of 36–52 cards with words such as the following:

pan	fun	sock	mill	call	harm
man	bun	knock	still	fall	charm
can	run	shock	kill	ball	farm

Also include four cards with "any card" written on them.

Procedure:

A player deals out five cards. The player to the left of the dealer plays any one of her cards and names it. The next player plays a card that either rhymes with or begins with the same letter as the first card. For example, if *sun* has been played, *bun* (rhyming with *sun*) or *sock* (with the same first letter) could be played. If a student cannot play, she draws from the pile in the center until she can play or has drawn three times. If the student has the card with "any card" written on it, she may play this card and name any appropriate word. The first player who runs out of cards wins the game.

Blending Wheel

Purpose: To provide practice on blending beginning consonants, consonant blends, or beginning consonant digraphs

Materials: Two cardboard circles, one of which is approximately 2″ smaller in diameter (convenient sizes are 8″ and 10″)

Procedure:

Fasten the two circles together with a paper fastener, as shown in Figure 14.3. The outside circle should have word roots or major parts of a word on it, and the inside circle should have a specific consonant, consonant blend, or consonant digraph on which you wish to provide practice. Have the student

FIGURE 14.3

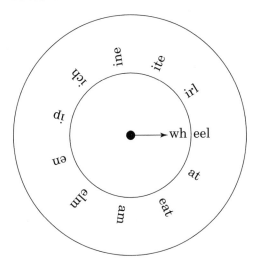

rotate one of the circles and practice blending the root or word part with the consonant, consonant blend, or consonant digraph.

Word Puzzles

Purpose: To provide practice in recognizing blend sounds and to provide practice in blending

Materials: Envelopes
Word cards

Procedure:

Cut out a few word cards of equal size. Print a word containing a blend that has been taught—for example, *gl*ad or *st*and—on each card. Cut each word in two between the blend and the remainder of the word. Place about 8 to 10 of these in each envelope and pass out the envelopes to the students. The students then assemble the blends and word parts to make words. After you check them, have students exchange the envelopes so that each student eventually assembles the words in each envelope.

Hard and Soft C and G

Purpose: To teach the rules for hard and soft *c* and *g*

Materials: Rule chart with pockets
Flash cards with various *c* and *g* words on them

FIGURE 14.4

G followed by *e, i,* or *y* usually has a soft sound. If *g* is followed by any other letter, it usually has a hard sound.	
Hard *g* (game)	Soft *g* (gentle)

Procedure:

Construct a large chart about 8½″ × 11″, like the chart shown in Figure 14.4. The bottom half should contain two large pockets marked as shown. The top half should contain the rule for soft and hard *c* and *g*. Students are then given a number of flash cards with soft and hard *g* words on them. They put each card into the appropriate pocket according to the rule stated on the chart. Students may check their own work if the words *hard* or *soft* are written on the back of each flash card. (Do the same for *c*.)

CHAPTER 15

Phonics Difficulties: Vowels

RECOGNIZED BY

The student is unable to use vowels to decode one-syllable words because the student is unable to give the correct sounds and variant sounds of the vowels and vowel teams. The letter-sound associations for the various vowels and vowel teams are presented in Appendix A-2.

DISCUSSION

To check the student's knowledge of vowels, use the Phonics Assessment in Appendix B-6 (subtests 4, 5, 7, 8, and 9).

In the past, students who were learning phonics were often taught a great many rules that would supposedly help them to decode. Some programs taught students well over 100 different symbol-sound correspondences. However, research studies over many years have shown that some of the rules formerly taught had little utility. Most of the unreliable rules related to the teaching of vowel sounds. Listed here are 10 generalizations that appear to be the most reliable of the vowel rules. However, even these rules are not helpful to many struggling readers:

1. If there is only one vowel letter and it appears at the end of a word, the letter usually has a long sound. Note that this is true only for one-syllable words. (Examples include: *go* and *be.*)

2. A single vowel in a syllable usually has a short sound if it is not the last letter in a syllable or is not followed by *r.* (Examples include: *cat* and *sit.*)

3. A vowel followed by *r* usually has a sound that is neither long nor short. (Examples include: *star* and *work.*)

4. When *y* is preceded by a consonant in a one-syllable word, the *y* usually has the sound of long *i.* (Examples include: *by* and *my.*) But in words of two or more syllables, the final *y* usually has the sound of long *e.* (Examples include: *baby* and *funny.*)

5. In words ending in vowel-consonant-*e,* the *e* is silent, and the vowel may be either long or short. Try the long sound first. (Examples include: *cave* or *have* and *dome* and *come.*) As you can see, this generalization is not particularly helpful.

6. In *ai, ay, ea, oa,* and *ee,* the first vowel is usually long and the second is silent. A common mnemonic that is used to help students remem-

ber this generalization is: "M*ai*ds m*ay eat oak* trees." (Note, however, that *ea* has many exceptions, including *head, great,* and *heard.*)

7. The vowel pair *ow* may have either the long *o* sound as in *low* or the diphthong heard in *owl.* (In a **diphthong,** the two vowel letters, in this case *o* and *w,* are both heard and make a gliding sound.)

8. In *au, aw, ou, oi,* and *oy,* the vowels usually blend or form a diphthong.

9. The *oo* sound is either long as in *moon* or short as in *book.*

10. If *a* is the only vowel in a syllable and it is followed by *l* or *w* then the *a* will usually be neither long nor short, but will have the *aw* sound heard in *ball* and *awl.* (When one of the letters *r, w,* or *l* comes immediately after a vowel, it usually distorts the sound of the previous vowel, making it neither long nor short. *R*eally *W*eird *L*etters is a good mnemonic to help you remember this.)

If you study these rules for a while, you will have little difficulty coming up with exceptions to all of them. In fact, every one of these so-called reliable rules uses words such as *either, or, usually,* or *may,* and many of the rules also include alternative examples. It is important to recognize that the vowel rules are the *least* consistent phonics generalizations in English. It would probably be accurate to say that these rules are best understood by those students who least need them: the students who are already capable decoders. Thus, forcing students to learn many inconsistent phonics rules often proves fruitless.

For students who have difficulty learning the symbol-sound associations for vowels, the phonogram approach is often more effective. A **phonogram,** as defined here, is a common word family beginning with a vowel or vowel pair followed by a consonant or consonants, and sometimes ending in *e.* Examples of phonograms are: *ake, at, ed, ime, old,* and *up.* These word endings, and many others, almost always are pronounced the same way in the many different words in which they appear. Because of this consistency in pronunciation, students often find it much easier to learn to decode when they are taught using phonograms.

RECOMMENDATIONS

A. It is helpful to teach the most common vowel sounds (long and short) using the following types of phonograms: words that end with the vowel-consonant-*e* configuration (as in *cake*) for long vowel sounds, and words that have the CVC configuration (as in *hit*) or the CVCC configuration (as in *mask*) for the short vowel sounds. The complete procedure for using the phonogram approach presented in this book appears in Appendix C-2. A brief review of this method is presented here.

If you wish to teach the long and short vowel sounds for *a,* choose the following words:

mat   hat   rat   fat

Discuss the sound represented by short *a.* Then present the previously listed words. If the student cannot pronounce them, help him to do so. Then present the following words:

mate   hate   rate   fate

Discuss the fact that when the *e* is added, the first vowel takes on its long sound; when the *e* is removed, the vowel takes on its short sound. Review the long vowel sound as you did the short vowel sound. Then present other words, such as those that follow, from Appendix C-2. Cover up the final *e* in each word and ask the student to pronounce the word. Then expose the final *e* and ask him to say the word with the long sound.

pale   gale

Use the words in Appendix C-2 to teach each of the short and long vowel sounds in the same manner. The advantage of this method of teaching the vowel sounds is that students learn these two fundamental rules at the same time.

B. Construct flash cards in which the vowel is shown along with both the word and a picture illustrating a word that uses that vowel, for example, short *a* in *hat* or long *a* in *rake.* On the opposite side print only the vowel letter, marked long or short, to be used as the student progresses in ability. When using this method with a large group, you can substitute transparencies for the overhead projector for flash cards. See Figure 15.1.

FIGURE 15.1

Front of Card

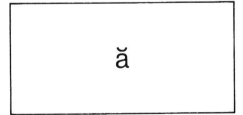

Back of Card

C. Have the students circle or underline the words that have vowels with the same sound as the first word in the line. See the following examples:

 1. **lot**   lone, dog, of, to
 2. **rat**   car, bear, sad, same
 3. **line**   with, win, bike, is

D. Record the vowel letters with their sounds and variant sounds and play them to the students as many times as necessary to learn them. They should, however, have a chart they can follow to see the letter as they hear the sound. Many commercial programs exist to achieve this objective in fun or clever ways.

E. Put the vowel letters on cards (3″ × 3″). Use the breve (˘) and the macron (¯) to indicate the short and long sounds. Divide these cards into groups of 10 each. Lay out separate groups of letters, so the student can see 10 at once. As you call the sounds of the vowel letters, or as they are played from a tape recording, have the student pick up the correct card to match the sound of the letter. (See Chapter 14, "Phonics Difficulties: Consonants," under "Recommendations," item C.

F. Use the same system as in item E. Instead of having the students match letters they hear, have them write the letter matching the letter sound (phoneme) they hear in words.

G. Use commercial charts that are available for teaching vowels. Records to accompany the sounds are also available.

H. Use commercially prepared games or computer software designed for teaching the vowels and the application of vowel sounds in decoding.

GAMES AND EXERCISES

Note: Much of the material listed under "Games and Exercises" in Chapter 14 can also be adapted for teaching the vowel sounds.

Game Board for Sorting Vowel Sounds

Purpose: To learn to hear various vowel sounds

Materials: Word cards containing pictures or words with various vowel sounds in them
            Tagboard

Procedure:

Construct a board as shown in Figure 15.2. Have students sort the pictures or words into the correct intersecting squares (pictures must be used with beginning readers) according to the sound in the name of the object in the

FIGURE 15.2

	A	E	I	O	U
Long					
Short					
R-Controlled					

picture. For example, *hen* would go under the square under the *e* column and the row across from *short*. The pictures from some commercially sold games such as Vowel Lotto work well with this game board.

Vowel Tic-Tac-Toe

Purpose: To learn vowel sounds

Materials: Flash cards with the following written on them:

Short *a*	Long *a*	R-controlled *a*
Short *e*	Long *e*	R-controlled *e*
Short *i*	Long *i*	R-controlled *i*
Short *o*	Long *o*	R-controlled *o*
Short *u*	Long *u*	R-controlled *u*

Procedure:

Have the two students who are playing tic-tac-toe draw a vowel card. Then, instead of marking each square with *X* or *O,* the student writes words that have the sound on his card. If, for example, one student gets short *o* and the other gets long *a,* then each person must write a word with that sound when it is his turn to play instead of making the traditional *X* or *O.* An example of a partially finished game is shown in Figure 15.3.

Variation in Procedure:

This is also a good learning device if the two participants have to draw a new card before each move. When playing the game this way, use two different colors of chalk or pencil to help remember which words belong to each player.

Sorting Pictures According to Matching Vowel Sounds

Purpose: To teach short and long vowel sounds

Materials: Use a pocket chart OR construct a large chart using all 10 of the short and long vowel sounds on pictures placed on pockets as

FIGURE 15.3

FIGURE 15.4

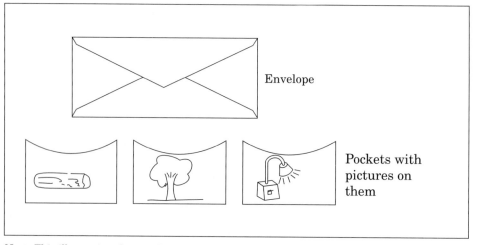

NOTE: This illustration shows only 3 pictures: a log, a tree, and a light. There should, of course, be 10 pictures, each representing a short or long vowel sound.

shown in Figure 15.4. On the top half of the chart, glue a large envelope in place. Find many pictures representing various short and long vowel sounds and place them in the large envelope.

Procedure:

Have students take pictures from the large envelope and say the word related to the picture. Remind them to listen for the vowel sound they hear in that word. Then have them find the corresponding vowel sound from the picture on the pockets below and place the picture from the large envelope in the proper pocket. This activity can be made self-checking by numbering the pockets and the backs of the pictures from the large envelope to correspond with the small pocket it should go in. After students have placed all of the pictures from the large envelope in the small pockets, they can turn the pictures over to see if they match the numbers on the small pockets.

Sorting Vowel Sounds

Purpose: To learn to hear various vowel sounds

Materials: Ten shoeboxes for each group
About 100 word cards, each using the sound of only one vowel

Procedure:

You or a team captain draws a card. Students read it and listen for a specific vowel sound. They then analyze the word and place it into the correctly marked short or long *a, e, i, o,* or *u* shoebox.

Vowel Relay

Purpose: To give practice in blending and learning sight words

Materials: Chalkboard
Flash cards with various sounds (graphemes) such as the following:

Long *a*	Short *a*	R-controlled *a*	L-controlled *a*
Long *e*	Short *e*	R-controlled *e*	W-controlled *a*
Long *i*	Short *i*	R-controlled *i*	W-controlled *o*
Long *o*	Short *o*	R-controlled *o*	W-controlled *e*
Long *u*	Short *u*	R-controlled *u*	

Procedure:

Divide the students into two groups and the chalkboard into two parts. Each group lines up in front of its half of the chalkboard. The pile of cards is divided in half and placed in the chalk tray below each of the two divisions of the chalkboard. When you say "Go," the two front players each move up and turn over a card. Each player must write a word using his designated vowel sound in a period of 10 seconds. However, new players cannot move up until you again say "Go" in 10 seconds. If the student cannot think of a word, he draws a line. The next player moves up and turns over another card when you say "Go." The team that has all of its cards turned over with the most correct words is the winner.

CHAPTER 16

Phonics Difficulties: Blends, Digraphs, or Diphthongs

RECOGNIZED BY

The student is unable to give the correct sounds of the blends, digraphs, or diphthongs (see Appendix A-2), unable to use these phonic elements to decode, or both.

DISCUSSION

As with the consonant and vowel sounds, it is important that the student know the consonant blends and consonant digraphs to analyze certain words. The vowel digraphs and diphthong sounds, however, are much less important. If the student has mastered phonics in the areas of single consonants, consonant blends, consonant digraphs and long and short vowels, then it may not be necessary to teach the vowel digraphs and diphthongs. Instead, remediation efforts to assist decoding might more wisely be spent on the areas of structural analysis, context clues, and basic sight words.

The Phonics Assessment in Appendix B-6 will help you determine which phonics areas are causing the most difficulty for the student. Administer the test before beginning a program of help in this area.

RECOMMENDATIONS

A. As with the initial consonant sounds, if a student does not know a number of consonant blends, use the phonogram list as explained in Appendix C-2. You are likely to find that the student learns most of these in a relatively short time. You can then retest the student and teach those that are still not known.

B. For teaching vowel digraphs and diphthongs, use the phonogram list to find words with the digraphs or diphthongs not known. Use the tape recorder to provide practice on those combinations, as explained in Appendix C-2. For example, give students who do not know the *ai* sounds words such as *aid, braid, laid, maid,* and *paid,* as well as *ail, hail, nail, pail, quail,* and so on.

C. Construct flash cards in which the blend, digraph, or diphthong is shown along with a picture that illustrates a word using that letter combination. See Appendix A-2 for suggested words. On the opposite side of the card, print only the blend, digraph, or diphthong, to be used as the student progresses in ability. When using this method with a large group of students, you can substitute 2″ × 2″ slides or transparencies for the overhead projector instead of flash cards. (See the illustration of a sample card in Figure 15.1, Chapter 15.)

D. Record the letter combinations with their sounds and let the students hear these as many times as necessary to learn them. They should, however, have a chart they can follow to see the letter combinations as they hear the sounds. Ask each student to point to the letters as she hears them on the tape.

E. Put diphthongs, digraphs, and blends on 3″ × 3″ cards. Divide these cards into groups of 10 each. Lay out separate groups of diphthongs, digraphs, and blends and allow the student to see all 10 at once. As you call the sounds of these various letter combinations, or as they are played from a tape recording, have the student pick up the correct card to match the sound of the letter combinations. (See Chapter 14, "Phonics Difficulties: Consonants," under "Recommendations," item C.)

F. Use the same system described in item E, only tape-record words and have the student pick up the letter combinations she hears in these words.

G. Use commercial charts that are available for teaching various letter combinations. Recordings to accompany these sounds are also available.

H. Use commercially prepared games or computer software designed for teaching blends, digraphs, and diphthongs. Often such materials can be used by students either individually or in small groups.

I. Immediately after using any of these procedures to teach the symbol-sound correspondences (phonics) for blends, digraphs, or diphthongs, it is *extremely important* that students be provided with sentences, passages, or stories that enable them to apply the newly-learned phonics skills in the act of reading contextual materials. Many commercial materials are available for this purpose. Also the teacher, or the teacher and student, may create sentences or stories (including silly ones) that emphasize the blends, digraphs, or diphthongs just taught.

GAMES AND EXERCISES

See "Games and Exercises" in Chapters 14 and 15. Much of the material listed in these two sections can be adapted to the teaching of blends, digraphs, and diphthongs.

Structural Analysis Difficulties

RECOGNIZED BY

The student is unable to pronounce multisyllabic words.

DISCUSSION

Structural analysis, often referred to as *morphology,* is concerned with the study of meaning-bearing units such as root words, prefixes, suffixes, possessives, plurals, and syllables. As a decoding skill it is analogous to phonics but is used to decode words of more than one syllable. This relationship is illustrated in Figure 17.1.

As described in Chapter 14, in using phonics, the reader identifies, separates, pronounces, and blends individual sounds, or *phonemes,* to decode one-syllable words. In the word *cat,* for example, the reader identifies and separates the three letters *c, a,* and *t.* He then thinks of the sound that each letter represents, and pronounces and blends the three sounds together to make the whole word. (Context clues provided by other words in the sentence simultaneously assist the reader in decoding this or any other unknown words.)

Let us assume the student does not immediately recognize the word *refinement.* This word has too many phonemes (eight to be exact) for phonics to be an efficient decoding tool. So instead, the reader uses structural analysis to decode *refinement.* To do so, the reader first identifies and separates the units or parts of the word: *re, fine,* and *ment.* He then pronounces each of the parts and blends them together. As you can see from Figure 17.1, phonics and structural analysis are very similar decoding processes. They differ primarily in the sizes of the parts of the words used in decoding.

For purposes of decoding multisyllable words, it is not necessary for the student to know the meaning of structural parts. In our example word, *refinement,* the student may not know that the prefix *re-* means *back* or *again,* and that the suffix *-ment* means *the act, fact, process, art, state, condition,* or *degree.* Usually the context of the passage provides better clues to the meaning of the word than the meanings of the small structural parts. In this case, the context clues provided in the following sentence will likely assist the student in understanding the meaning of *refinement: She was a woman of refinement.* One of the reasons we teach students to use context clues along with the other decoding skills (basic sight words, phonics, and structural analysis) is that they are helpful in both decoding and obtaining word meanings.

FIGURE 17.1

Step 1: Identify and separate
phonemes or morphemes.

Step 2: Pronounce and blend
letter sounds or word parts.

Structural analysis begins when the student is able to recognize the root word in words with *-s, -ed,* or similar endings; for example, *run* in *runs* and *look* in *looked.* From this beginning, the student learns to recognize the parts that make up compound words, such as *tooth* and *ache* in *toothache,* and *green* and *house* in *greenhouse.* He should also begin to recognize common roots, suffixes, and prefixes. Most authorities in the field of reading believe it is not good, however, to look for little words within bigger words since the smaller words may not have their usual pronunciation. (For example, the words *go, over,* and *me* are not helpful in decoding the word *government.*)

One of the best ways to determine whether a student is having difficulty with structural analysis is to ask him to read orally. While the student reads orally, you can note the types of errors he makes. The student with structural analysis difficulties will often decode basic sight words and most one-syllable words successfully but fail to pronounce accurately words of more than one syllable. This is a common and serious problem among students with reading difficulties. Such students are often unable to read materials with readability levels above grade 3 or 4. As the difficulty of the material increases, the student's ability to read it decreases. Another way to determine whether a student is having difficulty with structural analysis is to administer the Structural Analysis Assessment, which may be found in Appendix B-7. This series of tests measures the student's ability to use structural analysis skills both in isolation and in context and provides a blueprint for instruction on the specific aspects of structural analysis in which the student is weak.

Fortunately, structural analysis difficulties can be overcome if several conditions are present. First, the student must master the prerequisite decoding skills (basic sight vocabulary, phonics, and context clues) required to read up to about the third-grade level. (See Chapters 12–16 and 19.) Second, the teacher must provide adequate direct instruction designed to teach the student strategic ways to decode multisyllable words. Third, the student must receive sufficient practice decoding multisyllable words both in isolation and in context.

Students are often taught five or six syllabication rules or generalizations to assist them in dividing long words. This approach is *not* helpful to most remedial readers for two reasons: (1) the rules are not very reliable—that is, there are many exceptions to these rules; and (2) some of the rules or generalizations are quite complicated and difficult to remember. Fortunately, it is not necessary for a student to memorize the syllabication principles if he is taught how to attack multisyllable words as described under "Recommendations."

RECOMMENDATIONS

A. Teach the students to apply the five-step strategy to decode multisyllabic words shown in Figure 17.2. (This strategy is similar to the word-attack strategy presented in Chapter 19.)

FIGURE 17.2

WHEN YOU COME TO A HARD WORD

1. Look for prefixes or suffixes.

2. Look for a base or root word that you know.

3. Read to the end of the sentence. Think of a word with those parts (from steps 1 and 2) that makes sense.

4. Try other sounds, syllables, and accents until you can form a word that makes sense.

5. If you still cannot figure the word out, skip it, ask someone, or use the dictionary.

To teach the strategy you should model its use, then provide the students with guided and independent practice as follows:

1. Present the steps, using a written chart that students can remember and refer to.

2. Choose a difficult word and put it into a sentence.

3. Demonstrate how you would use the steps, one at a time, to figure out the hard word.

4. Use enough examples to show how a student may use a different number of steps each time to get the correct pronunciation (always go through the steps in order).

5. Provide students with sentences that they may use to apply the steps as you provide guidance.

6. Reassure students that the strategy works and encourage them to read a lot until the strategy becomes automatic.

Listed here are 10 sentences that you may use to teach and give students practice in the five-step strategy. They are difficult because most include more than one long word. If they seem too difficult for your students at first, prepare more sentences like numbers 1 and 2.

1. The amplifier made the music louder.
2. Sara is a kind, compassionate person.
3. The archaeologist studied the bones of the dinosaur and the other artifacts found near the caves.
4. The twelve contributors contributed five hundred dollars to the charity.
5. That delicatessen has delicious potato salad.
6. After the explosion there was an evacuation of the building.
7. The horizontal lines on the television screen make it impossible to see the picture.
8. The intricate puzzle is very frustrating.
9. The hurricane did substantial damage to our neighborhood.
10. The barometric pressure is falling rapidly.

B. Refer to Appendix C-3, "Words, Sentences, and Stories for Teaching Structural Analysis." These materials will be helpful to you in teaching and having students practice structural analysis skills.

C. Make lists of the common word endings and have the students underline these endings and pronounce their sounds.

D. Use multiple-choice questions that require the student to put the proper endings on words. (See the following examples.)

1. The boy was (looked, looks, looking) in the window.
2. That is (John, John's, Johns) ball and bat.
3. The boys came (early, earlier, earliest) than the girls.

E. Make lists or flash cards of the common roots and **affixes** (prefixes and suffixes). Use these in forming new words. You may have students practice these sounds, but do not require memorization of the meanings of affixes. (See Appendix C-5 for a list of suffixes and prefixes.)

F. Make lists or flash cards of common letter combinations such as *tion* and *ult*. Practice with these may be helpful; however, avoid listing letter combinations that have sounds that may vary according to the word in which they are used. Make lists on transparencies for the overhead projector or on large pieces of cardboard.

G. Make lists of and discuss compound words as the student encounters them in his reading lessons.

H. Make lists of all the words that can be made from certain roots. For example:

1. work—works, working, worked
2. carry—carrying, carrier, carried, carries
3. faith—faithful, faithless
4. lodge—lodger, lodging, lodged, lodgement

GAMES AND EXERCISES

Prefix and Suffix Baseball

Purpose: To provide practice in recognizing prefixes, suffixes, and their meanings

Materials: Make cards with a prefix such as *un* _____ or a suffix such as _____ *ly* on them. Be sure to include the line to indicate whether it is a prefix or a suffix.

Procedure:

This game is not to be used until considerable work has been done with affixes. Native English-speaking students have less trouble with the game than nonnative speakers since they already have a large vocabulary and need only to realize that these words contain prefixes and suffixes.

Each of the two teams chooses a pitcher who will "pitch" a word to the "batter." The batter will think of a word to go with the prefix or suffix and then pronounce it. If the student does this much but cannot use it in a sentence, he has hit a single. If the student can think of a word, pronounce it, and use it in a sentence, he hits a double. After the students become more adept at the game, you may wish to confine the hits to singles to slow down the game.

Caution: Remember that only a few suffix and prefix meanings are consistent enough to warrant memorizing their meanings.

Dig Up the Root

Purpose: To develop recognition of word roots and attached affixes

Materials: Pocket chart
Word cards

Procedure:

Divide the pocket chart into two columns. In the left-hand column list a number of root words. In the right-hand column, randomly list words composed of the root words plus an affix. Have the students match the root word in the first column with the root and its affix in the second column.

1. finish	undecided
2. reach	finishing
3. determine	replace
4. decided	nationality
5. place	reached
6. nation	predetermine

Prefix and Suffix Chart

Purpose: To teach the meanings and uses of suffixes and prefixes

Materials: Chart similar to the one shown in Figure 17.3
Procedure:

Have the students fill in the blank spaces in the chart. Place an X in the spaces that are not applicable.

Spinning for Suffixes

Purpose: To give practice in recognizing and attaching suffixes. This game will also help the student to learn the meanings of certain suffixes. This game is intended for small groups of two to five students.

Materials: A heavy piece of cardboard or a piece of plywood cut in a circle about 2–3 feet in diameter. Around the edge of the board, write a few suffixes, so they occupy the same positions as the numbers

FIGURE 17.3

Prefix	Prefix Meaning	Root	Whole Word	Suffix	Suffix Meaning
un	—	do	undo	x	x
x	x	soft	softly	—	in a way
x	x	play	playful	ful	—
—	from	port	—	x	x
pre	—	—	—	x	x
x	x	care	—	—	without
re	—	gain	—	x	x

on the face of a clock. (You don't need 12 suffixes. See Figure 17.4.)

Extra overlays of paper to attach to the face of the circle. These overlays will enable you to readily change the suffixes with which you are working.

A pointer in the center of the circle that can be spun

A number of word cards that can be used with each overlay. For example, for the suffixes *-ed, -ing,* and *-tion* on the overlay, you might use the word *direct* on a word card.

A shoebox

Procedure:

Pass out an equal number of word cards to each member of the group. You or a student then spins the pointer, which stops on a certain suffix. You call on each member of the group, and ask him to take his top card and try to attach the suffix at which the pointer stopped. The student may be asked to spell and pronounce the word. When a student has done this correctly, he puts his card in the box. The student who has all his cards in the box first is the winner.

Variation in Procedure:

Make overlays that contain prefixes to fit on the face of the circle and play the game in the same manner as with the suffixes.

Endings

Purpose: To provide practice in structural analysis

Materials: A number of cards with suffixes or word endings printed on them

FIGURE 17.4

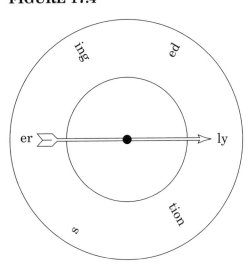

Procedure:

Divide the class into two equal teams. On the chalkboard, list a number of familiar root words such as *run, sleep, help, rain, ask,* and *splash.* In a circle on the floor, place cards of suffixes such as *-ed, -d, -ing,* and *-y.* In the center of the circle, a blindfolded team member is turned around. The student points to a card and the blindfold is removed. He goes to the chalkboard, chooses a word, and adds the ending to it, writing the new word on the board. He then pronounces the word. If the word is written correctly, he scores a point. If the word is pronounced correctly, he scores another point. If the word is written incorrectly, the next member of the rival team gets a chance to write and pronounce the word. If he writes it correctly, the rival team scores a point. The first team to receive 25 points wins.

CHAPTER 18

Contractions Not Known

RECOGNIZED BY

The student is unable to pronounce contractions when she encounters them in print. For comprehension and writing purposes, it is also useful to know what two words each contraction stands for and to be able to make contractions from various words. A test for students' knowledge of contractions may be found in Appendix B-8.

DISCUSSION

For some students, a part of poor oral reading is the student's lack of knowledge of contractions. This is usually a minor reading problem.

When testing for student's knowledge of contractions, you should show the student the contraction and ask her to pronounce it. If she can pronounce the word, it will suffice for decoding purposes. (For example, for decoding purposes the student must pronounce *can't,* but she does not necessarily need to know that it means *cannot.*) You may wish to have the student tell what two words the contraction stands for, so you know if she understands the meaning of the contraction and will be able to use it in her written work. You may refer to the list of 47 common contractions (see Figure 18.1) which was drawn from Appendix A-1, "Scope and Sequence of Reading Skills."

RECOMMENDATIONS

A. For any contraction not known, write the two words it stands for and then the contraction on the chalkboard. Have students make up sentences using both the contracted and noncontracted form. See the example.

> let us   let's
> 1. Let us go with Mother and Father.
> 2. Let's go with Mother and Father.

B. Give students a matching exercise by placing a few contractions on slips of paper in an envelope. Number each contraction. In the same envelope, place slips that name the two words each contraction stands for and write the matching number of the contraction on the back. Students should then try to match the contractions with the correct words by placing them side by side, as illustrated in Figure 18.2.

FIGURE 18.1

anybody'd	I'd	weren't
aren't	I'll	we'd
can't	I'm	we'll
couldn't	I've	we're
didn't	let's	we've
doesn't	she'd	what's
don't	she'll	where's
hadn't	she's	who'd
hasn't	that's	who'll
haven't	there'll	won't
he'd	there's	wouldn't
he'll	they'd	you'd
he's	they'll	you'll
here's	they're	you're
isn't	they've	you've
it's	wasn't	

FIGURE 18.2

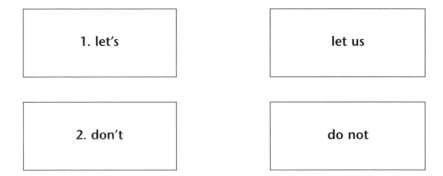

After the student has completed the exercise, she can turn the cards in the right-hand column over to see if the numbers on the back match the numbers on the slips in the left-hand column. (Be aware that whenever you use a self-checking format as described here, some students may not be able to prevent themselves from peeking at the answers on the back of the cards. Because of this, some teachers do not prepare games or exercises that are self-checking in this manner.)

C. Give students paragraphs to read in which several words could be contracted. Underline these words. Instruct students to change these words to a contraction as they read. See the following example.

> Frank said to Jim, "**We have** only two days before **you are** going to leave." "Yes," said Jim, "**I am** waiting to go, and **I have** already packed my suitcase."

After doing this type of exercise, discuss why contractions are used and which form, long or short, sounds more natural in common speech.

D. Conduct contraction races between two students. Tell the students two words and see who can call out the contraction first. Also give contractions and have students call out the words that are contracted.

E. Give students newspaper articles and have them underline all contractions and words that could have been contracted.

F. As students talk, call attention to the contractions they use by writing them down. Discuss why they used the contracted form.

CHAPTER 19

Inadequate Ability to Use Context Clues

RECOGNIZED BY

The student is unable to derive meaning or pronunciation of a word from the way it is used in a sentence.

DISCUSSION

The use of **context clues** can be one of the student's greatest helps in determining the pronunciation and meaning of unfamiliar words. It is not a difficult reading skill to teach; however, many teachers incorrectly assume that all students will learn to use context clues on their own. Capable readers usually do, but disabled readers often need a considerable amount of instruction and a great deal of practice to learn this skill.

A test for determining whether a student is able to use context clues effectively is found in Appendix B-9. When using this test, it is important that the student read at his **independent reading level** or at an easy **instructional reading level.** Do not expect students who are reading at a difficult instructional level or at their **frustration reading level** to be able to use context clues effectively. (An explanation of each of these three levels is found in the section entitled "Definition of Terms" at the beginning of this book.)

You can also determine whether a student is having difficulty using context clues by listening to him read orally from material on which he will make 5 to 10 errors per page. (This material could well be at the student's frustration level, but such reading is justified because you will not have the student read such difficult material for long and because you are doing this for diagnostic purposes.) While the student reads, note whether miscalled words are logical replacements; that is, does the student rely on context clues when other decoding skills are inadequate? You may also question the student about the meaning of certain words where that meaning is evident from the context.

Bear in mind that students' difficulties with context clues may be reflected in two opposite behaviors. Many students fail to use context clues adequately and appear to read word by word. A classic example of this type of problem is the student who reads the sentence *The boy went into the house* as *The . . . boy . . . went . . . into . . . the . . . horse.* This student apparently overrelied on graphic information at the expense of meaning clues, thus substituting the word *horse* for *house.* The two words are similar in appearance but quite dissimilar in meaning. At the other extreme are students who overrely on context. These students may appear to be reading fluently, but what they read may not be what was written. Such a student might read the sample sentence as: *The boy went into the garage.* While the first type of problem is more common and often more difficult to remediate, both forms of context-clue difficulties are detrimental to reading ability.

RECOMMENDATIONS

A. The best way to teach students to use context clues when they are reading independently is to teach them the word-attack strategy shown in Figure 19.1.

FIGURE 19.1

WHEN YOU COME TO A WORD YOU DON'T KNOW:

1. Say the beginning sound.

2. Read the rest of the sentence. THINK.

3. Say the parts that you know. GUESS.

4. Ask someone or skip it and go on.

When encountering an unknown word, step 1, "Say the beginning sound" (phonics), is the one most students will do automatically if they have had any phonics training at all. This is fortunate because beginning sounds are often the most helpful clue in decoding an unknown word. (Students who have had no phonics training at all may guess wildly and insert any word that might make sense.)

Step 2, "Read the rest of the sentence," requires the student to use context clues before applying additional phonics or structural analysis. In most cases the combination of initial letter sounds and context will result in correct identification of the unknown word. Step 2 requires the student to read to the end of the sentence to take advantage of the context clues that may come after the unknown word. (Words that come *after* are often more helpful than those that come *before* unknown words.) If the student still has not decoded the word, step 3, "Say the parts that you know," has him use other word-analysis clues, such as ending sounds, vowel sounds, and structural analysis. The student is encouraged to guess, if necessary, so as not to spend too much time trying to decode a single unknown word. The last step, "Ask someone or skip it and go on," encourages the student to ask for help or continue reading if all else fails. It is quite possible that context clues picked up in reading further will permit the student to identify the unknown word.

If students must resort to step 4 often, they should be given easier material to read. Similarly, if students encounter more than one unknown word in a single sentence, this word-attack strategy is likely to break down, indicating that the material is too difficult.

To teach the strategy, you should use the following steps:

1. Present the steps, using a written chart that students can remember and refer to.
2. Model use of the steps yourself with sample sentences.
3. Reassure students that the strategy works.
4. Provide students with sentences that they may use to apply the steps as you provide guidance.
5. Ensure that students use the steps as they practice in the act of reading.

At the end of this paragraph is a list of sentences that you may use to teach and give students practice in the four-step word-attack strategy. The numbers after each sentence indicate which steps are likely to assist students. It is not possible to determine exactly which steps will help students. Some students will recognize unknown words at sight. Others will use only one or two steps. Some may not succeed at all. You will need to provide other examples for students based on their specific needs.

1. The *light* is red. (1, 2)
2. I will *take* you there. (1, 2)
3. I cannot *remember* your name. (1, 2, 3)
4. I like *chocolate* cake. (1, 2, 3)
5. The *cat* is my pet. (1, 2)
6. The *hamster* is my pet. (1, 2, 3)
7. The *armadillo* is my pet. (1, 2, 3, 4?)

B. Encourage practice in the act of reading. Such practice is essential for students to learn to read for meaning. Provide time, appropriate (*easy!*) materials, the proper setting, and encouragement for sustained silent reading.

C. Show (demonstrate to) the student that it is possible to derive the meaning of words from their context. Provide specific examples.

1. The careless boy did his work in a *haphazard* manner.
2. He felt that although his work was *imperfect,* it was still good.
3. When he tried to *insert* the letter in the mailbox, the mailbox was too full.
4. They called in a *mediator* to help settle the problems between labor and management.

D. Have students preread material silently before reading orally. Discuss troublesome vocabulary.

E. Set purposes for reading. Stress accuracy in reading, not speed.

F. Use short, easy selections. Have students stop frequently to explain what they have read in their own words.

G. Use high-interest material, including student-authored language-experience stories.

H. Have students scan for important words. Have them guess the content and then read to see if the guess was accurate.

I. Construct sentences or short paragraphs, omitting selected words that students should be able to determine by their context. In place of each key word, insert an initial consonant and then x's for the rest of the letters in the words. See the following example:

When Jack ix in a hurry, he always rxxx home from school.

When students have become proficient at this, advance to the next step, which is to replace key words with x's for *each* letter.

When Jack xx in a hurry, he always xxxx home from school.

After students are able to get most of the omitted words by replacing the x's with letters, leave blank lines to replace entire omitted words.

When Jack _____ in a hurry, he always _____ home from school.

J. Use multiple-choice questions in which the student fills in blanks: "Jack _____ a black pony (rock, rode, rod)." Using words that look alike also will give the student practice in phonic and structural analysis.

K. Make tape recordings in which key words are omitted. Give the student a copy of the script and have him fill in the blank spaces as the tape is played.

L. Create a series of sentences using words that are spelled alike but may have different pronunciations or meanings, such as read and lead. Have the student read sentences using these words in proper context.

He **read** the book.
He will **read** the story.
It was made out of **lead**.
He had the **lead** in the play.

PART FIVE

COMPREHENSION ABILITIES

Word Meaning/Vocabulary Knowledge Inadequate

RECOGNIZED BY

The student does not understand the meaning of words commonly understood by students of her age level. The student's weakness may be reflected in poor performance on tests of vocabulary knowledge. Inadequate vocabulary causes reduced reading comprehension.

DISCUSSION

A strong relationship exists between vocabulary knowledge and comprehension. Authorities have differing notions about what it means to know the meaning of a word. Part of the problem is that one may know the meaning of a word at five different levels or stages. These stages are listed here from lowest to highest level of vocabulary knowledge.

1. A student has no recognition of a word. Indeed, she may have never seen it before.
2. A student has heard of the word (that is, recognizes that it is a word), but has no knowledge of its meaning.
3. A student recognizes the word in context and has a vague understanding of its meaning.
4. A student knows well the meaning of the word in the context in which it appears.
5. A student knows the multiple meanings of the word (if they exist), and can actually use the word in thinking, speaking, or writing.

Knowledge at level 2 is usually required for a student to decode a difficult word, while knowledge at levels 3 or 4 is required for the student to comprehend what she reads. Thus, one of the important reasons that teachers teach vocabulary is to enable students to understand written material. Adequate decoding ability alone will not enable a student to understand material in either a narrative or subject-matter book.

The most common method of testing students' knowledge of words or overall vocabulary is the use of standardized achievement tests. The most widely used format is the multiple-choice measure in which the student chooses, from among several choices, a short definition or a synonym for a target word. Such tests usually measure vocabulary knowledge at level 3, rather than the student's full continuum of word knowledge. If you use such a test, examine the students' raw scores to see if they are above that which could have been made by chance guessing. A number of standardized reading achievement tests will allow a student who may essentially not read at all to score well into the norms and to have a vocabulary achievement score well above her actual vocabulary ability. Some students do poorly on standardized tests of vocabulary knowledge because they lack sufficient decoding ability. If a student does much better on an individually administered oral vocabulary test, you may then assume that a lack of proper word-attack skills is contributing to her low score on the standardized test.

Another method of testing students' knowledge of vocabulary is to ask them the meaning of several words that appear in their textbooks (at their grade level). This will give you a general feel for their vocabulary knowledge; however, it will not allow you to compare the vocabulary achievement of your students with those in the country as a whole. If you are a teacher in a school with a large group of students from a low socioeconomic level, this method of testing vocabulary knowledge within the class may give you "tunnel vision," since students with only a normal vocabulary may appear very good in comparison to other students in the class.

RECOMMENDATIONS

Since the meanings of many words can be learned through context and repeated exposure, it is not necessary to teach every new word. Only a very small percentage of the total meaning vocabulary of adults is achieved through specific vocabulary instruction or through the use of the dictionary. Unfortunately, research has shown that students in remedial reading programs usually get little practice in the act of reading. For students with a limited English vocabulary, much practice in oral language is essential. For students who come from an English-speaking background, the single best way of increasing their vocabulary is to encourage them to read widely about a number of subjects. The importance of this cannot be overemphasized.

Direct instruction is also very important. The most effective instructional activities tap into students' prior knowledge and involve the students actively in learning new vocabulary. Often it is best for students to practice these strategies while working in small cooperative groups, so that students can learn from each other as well as from the teacher.

A thorough discussion of the meaning of only a few words is more worthwhile than having students look up many words in the dictionary, write the definitions of the words, and then use them in sentences. Eldon E. Ekwall and an elementary principal once checked students' knowledge of 20 words that they had just completed writing the meaning of and using in a sentence during a one-hour period. The average number of words known by each student was 2 out of the 20, or 10% of the words. And this was immediately after completing the lesson! This indicates that a little more time spent in discussing several words and making sure that they are well known by each student would be more productive than attempting to introduce many words, in a less thorough manner. In addition, the "look it up, write the definition, use it in a sentence" approach tends to be boring for most students.

You will find that the following recommendations are motivating and effective for most students, all the more so when the teacher participates in or directs the activities.

A. Students of all grades can benefit from the use of ***semantic feature analysis.*** (The word *semantic* means "of or based on the various meanings of words.") To use this technique, pick a theme somewhat familiar to a number of students, such as speech communication. First, discuss various ways in which we communicate through speech and list them; for example, *seminar, congress, forum, debate, dialogue, conversation, symposium, lecture, homily, testimony, caucus, interview, sermon, and hearing* (used as a noun). If students are at an age where they are familiar with the use of a thesaurus, they can quickly find synonyms for words first mentioned.

After the list has been completed, discuss characteristics of several of the items on it. Commenting on the list in the preceding paragraph, students may note such characteristics as one-way, two-way, no control over who speaks, one person controls who speaks, anyone can speak, formal, and informal. After a logical set of characteristics has been developed, construct a matrix (on an overhead transparency or on the chalkboard), such as the one shown in Figure 20.1.

When the matrix is complete, ask students to decide whether to place a plus (+) or a minus (−) in each blank space of the matrix, depending on the characteristic of the item in the column. For example, for *seminar* one would be likely to place a plus in the blanks for two-way, one person controls who speaks, anyone can speak, and, perhaps, informal. On the other hand, a minus would be likely to appear after one-way, no control over who speaks, and formal.

Semantic feature analysis provides students with a much better understanding of terms than definitions from a dictionary. Encourage students to discuss the merits of placing a plus or a minus after various items. Also, allow them to place both a plus and a minus in certain blanks. For example, a seminar might be formal or informal, depending on who is conducting it as well as on its purpose.

After students have completed marking each item with a plus or a minus, have them ask each other questions such as, "Arturo, what is

FIGURE 20.1

Semantic Feature Analysis for Speech Communication

	One-Way	Two-Way	No Control Over Who Speaks	One Person Controls Who Speaks	Anyone Can Speak	Formal	Informal
Seminar	-----	-----	-----	-----	-----	-----	-----
Congress	-----	-----	-----	-----	-----	-----	-----
Forum	-----	-----	-----	-----	-----	-----	-----
Debate	-----	-----	-----	-----	-----	-----	-----
Dialogue	-----	-----	-----	-----	-----	-----	-----
Conversation	-----	-----	-----	-----	-----	-----	-----
Symposium	-----	-----	-----	-----	-----	-----	-----
Lecture	-----	-----	-----	-----	-----	-----	-----
Homily	-----	-----	-----	-----	-----	-----	-----
Testimony	-----	-----	-----	-----	-----	-----	-----
Caucus	-----	-----	-----	-----	-----	-----	-----
Interview	-----	-----	-----	-----	-----	-----	-----
Sermon	-----	-----	-----	-----	-----	-----	-----
Hearing	-----	-----	-----	-----	-----	-----	-----

the difference between a debate and a dialogue?" This will, of course, make students more active participants, and they will be much less likely to forget the meanings of various words. The discussion following the completion of the matrix should be considered an essential part of the use of this technique for vocabulary development.

B. **Semantic mapping** also can be fun and challenging to students. Using semantic word maps together with a dictionary and a thesaurus will enable students to learn words that are not in the listening-speaking vocabularies of the students involved in making the map. In using this technique, first pick a word familiar to students, such as *house*. Then ask the students simply to list a number of things that come to mind when hearing this word. Examples might include *stone, wood, ice, concrete, electricity, dishwasher, carpenter, mason, skins,* and *concrete*.

After a fairly comprehensive list has been developed, ask students if they see logical categories into which they could fit each of the items. For example, logical categories for this list might be as follows: *equipment* (electricity, dishwasher, garbage disposal), *building materials* (stone, wood, ice, concrete, skins), and *workers* (painter, carpenter, mason).

Show the development of the semantic map as shown in Figure 20.2.

FIGURE 20.2

In doing a topic as common as a house, there would, of course, be more categories than those shown in the example. After the map has been developed, draw lines beside each word in the various categories, as shown. Then have students use a thesaurus to find a word or, preferably, more than one word, that could possibly be a synonym for each listed word. Also, depending on the ages of the students involved, you may wish to use words that are synonyms of the roots of words used in each category. Place these words in the blanks. Examples of words that might be used in Figure 20.2 would be *painter* (tint, dye, pigment, stain); *carpenter* (cabinetmaker, builder, producer); *mason* (bricklayer, plasterer, cement worker); *electricity* (current, juice, power); *dishwasher* (cleaner, cleanse, filter, purify); *garbage disposal* (dirt, filth, muck, slime); *stone* (boulder, gravel, pebble, rock); *wood* (forest, lumber); *ice* (freeze, chill, refrigerate); and *concrete* (cement).

C. The *four-square strategy* will help students use prior knowledge to increase vocabulary.[1] First, select four important words from an assignment students are about to read and have the students fold four papers into quarters. Have the students write the first word in square 1, for example, *salubrious*.

Use the word in appropriate context so that the students will have some clues to its meaning; for example, *Joggers lead a salubrious lifestyle by engaging in regular exercise.* Ask, "Is there anything you do that you believe is *salubrious?*" Label these student examples as *salubrious*.

Have students write in the second square something they personally find to be *salubrious*. In the third square, have students write a non-example—something that is not *salubrious*, for example, smoking. Finally, in the fourth square, have students write a definition of the word in their own words. See the completed example in Figure 20.3.

D. The *context redefinition* strategy[2] encourages students to predict word meanings, then use oncoming context to confirm their predictions. This strategy is used unconsciously by all good readers and consists of five steps:

1. **Select** about four key words from a story or text chapter (try to pick at least one that students may know).
2. **List** these on the chalkboard or overhead projector with a blank space for the students' predictions.
3. Have students **predict** what they think each word means, write their predictions verbatim, then vote on the most plausible prediction.
4. Have students read to **verify** their predictions.
5. After reading, have the students edit or **redefine** their initial predictions to reflect contextual meaning. (Students can copy these definitions in their own glossaries.)

FIGURE 20.3

salubrious 1	surfing 2
4 any aspect of life that is healthful	3 smog

An example of context redefinition follows.

Write a definition or synonym for the two words that follow:

1. eggrails:
2. mushburgers:

Now read the following selection to see if you need to modify your initial hypotheses:

She preferred a surfboard with *eggrails* for slow, sloppy waves. A board with rounded edges was ideally suited to this afternoon's conditions. The wind was blowing straight onshore, creating bumpy *mushburgers.*[3]

E. Whenever new words come up in lessons, stop and discuss them in sufficient detail so that all students develop a concept of their meaning.

F. When reading stories or books aloud to students, stop occasionally to discuss the meanings of new or unfamiliar words. With practice, teachers can learn to do this without spoiling the flow of the story. For example, when reading books to younger children, vocabulary can be discussed while you are showing the students the illustrations in the book.

G. Appoint a vocabulary committee to preview each new lesson and to identify all words for which they do not know the meaning. Use these words as a guide to the new vocabulary in addition to the vocabulary given in the textbook. You might also have members of this committee find out the meanings of these words and introduce them to the rest of the class. Of course, it is a good idea to rotate membership on this committee.

H. Develop picture files for each unit in the students' textbook. Use the pictures to show the meaning of new words and concepts. These pictures may be placed on a bulletin board or shown and discussed as you introduce each new unit.

I. Place pictures on the bulletin board and have students try to find as many words as possible to describe the pictures. If students are old enough to use a thesaurus, allow them to do so. Place the words under the pictures and discuss them regularly.

J. Brainstorm other words for common words used most often, for example, *said*. With the assistance of the students, prepare charts with lists of synonyms for the overused words. These charts may be hung in the classroom where they can be easily seen by students. Then, when students write creative stories, encourage the students to use alternatives to the overused words. Similarly, model the use of these words when speaking to the students and encourage the students to use them in their conversations.

K. Encourage students to raise their hands whenever someone uses an unfamiliar word. Praise students for asking what a word means and indicate that such students usually have large vocabularies.

L. Develop word awareness by showing students how they often skip words for which they do not know the meaning. Promote awareness of new words by getting students to look for new words that they or other students may not know the meaning of. Write the new word on the chalkboard along with the name of the student who found it.

Vinay's new word—idealism
Darcetta's new word—afterthought

Discuss these words daily until most students know them. Keep adding new words to the bottom of the list and erase the ones from the top after they have been discussed several times.

M. Encourage students to use vocabulary cards. As students read assignments or any other reading material, have them search for new words. When a new word is found, the student writes it on a vocabulary card. Then she copies the sentence in which it was used and underlines the word. (Encourage the use of context to derive meaning.) After the student completes her reading, she locates the new word in the dictionary and writes its meaning on the card. File the new vocabulary cards in a shoebox and review them periodically.

N. Help students become aware of new words by having contests: who can find the most words that other students do not understand? Limit the contest to a particular book and one day.

O. Discuss the use of figurative language and have students look for idiomatic expressions such as "Our teacher was a bear today," "She was as quiet as a mouse," or "He lost his cool."

P. Provide a wide background of experiences for students. This can be done, to a certain extent, by taking students on field trips; showing videotapes, films, and filmstrips; and discussing a wide range of topics in the classroom. After returning from field trips, using audio-visual or computer-based materials, or engaging in class discussion, identify and discuss any new words and concepts. Also, encourage students to write down any unfamiliar words as they listen to the narration of a videotape, film, or CD-ROM or computer-based program. After viewing, list the students' words on the chalkboard or overhead projector and discuss them. In presenting each word, discuss its meaning with the class and use it in a sentence. Then have several members of the class use the word in sentences they make up. Follow this procedure with all unknown words. Finally, have students write a summary of the field trip, videotape, film, CD-ROM or computer-based program, or class discussion, and use all of the new words that were presented.

Q. Encourage students to use the dictionary to derive a word's meaning. Although only a small percentage of one's total meaning vocabulary comes from the use of the dictionary, all students should learn how to use the dictionary to derive word meaning, as well as the accompanying skills such as understanding a word's first, second, and third meaning.

R. Encourage students to use books marketed for the purpose of building vocabularies. These are constantly being updated, and new ones appear on the market each year. To find them, look under the subject of *vocabulary development* at a local bookstore. These materials present many words, and most teachers can learn much about the teaching of vocabulary by using them.

S. Teach students to use affixes as clues to word meanings. Although research indicates that the study of prefixes and suffixes is somewhat questionable, a knowledge of affixes is highly useful in understanding words in subject areas such as science, where a student might encounter such prefixes as *bio-, sub-,* and the like.

T. Teach students how to use a thesaurus and constantly encourage them to use it in their writing.

U. Use commercial materials including software programs, that have been designed for vocabulary development.

GAMES AND EXERCISES

Matching Words and Definitions

Purpose: To enrich vocabulary

Materials: Envelopes that contain slips of paper with numbered words printed on them. The envelopes should also contain a larger second set of slips with a definition of each word, numbered on the back to match the first set.

Procedure:

Have students each take an envelope and empty it on their desks. They should then place the word slips in a column in numerical order; for example:

1. candid
2. slipshod

Students try to match the definition slips with the words. Students can check the accuracy of their work when they have finished by checking to see if the numbers match. Number each envelope and give students a number sheet corresponding to each envelope. Have them check off each number as they complete the words in each envelope. Thus, each student will be sure to do each envelope.

Homonym Concentration

Purpose: To enlarge vocabulary

Materials: A set of word cards (about 8–10) with a corresponding set of homonym cards (total of 16–20)

Procedure:

Play the game the same as Concentration. Shuffle the cards and place them face down in rows on a table or on a Concentration board with squares on it. Two students play. One begins by turning over a card. Then she tries to find its homonym by turning over another card. If the words are not homonyms, she turns both cards face down, and the next student takes her turn. Whenever a student turns over a pair of homonyms, she gets to keep the cards. The student with the most cards at the end of the game is the winner. (This same exercise may be done with antonyms and synonyms.)

Phrase It Another Way

Purpose: To enrich vocabulary

Materials: Phrase cards or phrases written on the chalkboard

Procedure:

On the chalkboard each day, place a new phrase that the students or you commonly use in daily conversation and activities. Opposite the phrase, write another way of saying the commonly used phrase. Each day you and the students concentrate on using the phrase in a new way. You may wish to place the phrases on chart paper and display them as the number grows.

Old phrase	Phrasing it another way
is done	is completed
runs fast	is a rapid runner
couldn't get it	was deprived of it

Variation in Procedure:

Decide on a new *word* that can be substituted for one that is commonly used each day (see the example that follows). Place the old and new word in a chart holder. During the day both you and the students should use the new word instead of the old word. Discuss how doing this type of activity will enlarge vocabularies and make students' speech sound more mature.

Old word	New word
talk	discuss
hate	dislike
do better	improve

Drawing New Words

Purpose: To build vocabulary and improve dictionary skills

Materials: A number of 3″ × 5″ cards with new vocabulary words written in a sentence (underline the new word)
Dictionary

Procedure:

The cards are shuffled and placed face down on the table. Students then take turns picking up a card, reading the sentence, and defining the underlined word. Another student looks up the word in the dictionary to see if the definition was correct.

ENDNOTES

1. Eeds, M., & Cockrun, W. A. (1985). Teaching word meanings by expanding schemata vs. dictionary work vs. reading in context. *Journal of Reading, 28,* 492–497.
2. Bean, T. W. (1981). Comprehension strategies: What makes them tick? In E. K. Dishner, T. W. Bean, & J. E. Readence (Eds.), *Reading in the content areas: Improving classroom instruction* (pp. 188–191). Dubuque, IA: Kendall-Hunt.
3. Cunningham, J. W., Cunningham, P. M., & Arthur, V. (1981). *Middle and secondary school reading.* New York: Longman.

CHAPTER 21

Comprehension Inadequate

RECOGNIZED BY

The student cannot answer questions about subject matter he has read or cannot retell what he has read.

DISCUSSION

Definitions

The term *reading comprehension* has several different definitions. While most experts agree that reading comprehension is the meaning gained from what is written on the page, they often disagree about the source of the meaning. Currently the three most common models are the *bottom-up, top-down,* and *interactive* models. The bottom-up model emphasizes the material being read and is often described as text driven. Proponents of this model believe that the material being read is more important to the process of reading than the person who reads the material. The top-down model emphasizes the reader and is often described as concept driven. Proponents of this model suggest that the reader is more important to the process of reading than the material being read. This is because readers usually have some prior knowledge (or *schema*) about the topic. Using prior knowledge, the reader makes predictions about the meaning of the material. In other words, the reader's prior knowledge can be a powerful influence on his comprehension of the text.

The **interactive model of reading** was developed to describe the reading process as both concept and text driven, a process in which the reader relates information stored in his head with new information in the text. Most experts subscribe to the interactive model, believing that comprehension is a process of constructing meaning by interacting with the text. Many of the suggestions presented in the "Recommendations" section stress interactive strategies as the most effective way to correct and teach comprehension.

Factors That Affect Comprehension

Several factors about the reader affect his comprehension of the reading material. Other factors that affect a student's comprehension are related to the material he reads. Some factors that affect comprehension in terms of the reader are:

1. *The knowledge the reader brings to the subject.* This means that what a student knows about a particular subject is directly related to how

much he will understand about that subject when he reads. This is, of course, a major tenet of the interactive model.

2. *The reader's interest in the subject.* A student will understand more of what he reads if he is particularly interested in the subject. This interest is often a reflection of the student's prior knowledge of the subject.

3. *The reader's purpose for reading.* A student who has a purpose for reading is more likely to understand more of what he reads than a student reading the same material who has no purpose for reading. For example, if a student wishes to learn how to operate a computer to play a particular game, he will be more likely to understand more of what is read than a student of equal ability who has no desire to operate the computer or to play a particular game on that computer.

4. *The reader's ability to decode words rapidly.* If the student must stop to puzzle over new words, he cannot be expected to comprehend well. The whole process of reading, when many of the words are not easily decoded, becomes mind-boggling. The student must give so much attention to the decoding of new words that attending to comprehension to any degree is difficult, if not impossible. Teachers often experience a similar problem when they are reading a book out loud to a group of students. The demands of oral reading, watching the students in the group, showing the pictures, and so on may cause the teacher to have little or no comprehension of the story being read.

Some factors that affect comprehension in terms of the material being read are:

1. *The number of unfamiliar words.* Unfamiliar words are usually considered to be those that are not on a particular word list according to a readability formula. This means that the more words on a higher grade level, the more difficult the material is likely to be to comprehend.

2. *The length of the sentences.* Research has consistently shown that longer and more complex sentences within a passage are more difficult for most readers to comprehend than shorter, simpler sentences.

3. *The syntax.* Syntax is the way words are put together. Some writers use syntax in ways that make material more difficult to comprehend.

Comprehension Subskills

Studies on the nature of comprehension have shown that although teachers of reading often refer to comprehension subskills, they cannot really prove that these subskills exist. Reading researchers definitely know that comprehension involves both a word or vocabulary factor and a group of skills that might be referred to as "other comprehension skills." Even though they cannot prove that these other comprehension skills exist, many teachers find them useful for teaching purposes. These skills include the ability to:

1. Develop mental images
2. Recognize main ideas
3. Recognize important details
4. Follow directions
5. Predict outcomes
6. Recognize the author's organization
7. Do critical reading

Specific procedures for teaching each of these skills will be presented in the order given beginning on page 157.

Assessing Comprehension Ability

Teachers can often tell if students are having difficulty comprehending by observing their written work, their ability to answer questions, and their participation in discussions about material read. If you suspect that a student has comprehension difficulties that are not related to decoding problems, you might have the student read a passage silently, then retell the contents of the passage to you. Often it is best to have such a student read both narrative and expository selections to see if he is able to comprehend both types of material. You may use a section from a library book, literature, or reading textbook for the narrative material and a section from a science or social studies book for the expository passage. If the student is unable to retell the contents of the selection with adequate comprehension, you may assume that the student will benefit from the recommendations in this chapter.

Several methods are commonly used for more systematic assessments of students' ability to comprehend. One of the most widely used methods is the standardized test. Many standardized tests in the field of reading are divided into 2 main sections: reading vocabulary and reading comprehension. Perhaps this is a misnomer, since an adequate reading vocabulary is essential for reading comprehension. Thus, reading vocabulary is actually one of the subskills of reading comprehension. Because vocabulary is such an important subskill of comprehension, procedures for dealing with vocabulary were presented in Chapter 20.

When using standardized tests to assess reading ability, you should note whether an individual's score is higher than he could have achieved by simply guessing. Some standardized tests have no provision for enabling teachers to measure the performance of students with extremely limited reading ability; that is, by guessing, a student may be able to achieve a score that is one to three levels above that at which he is actually reading. Also remember that standardized reading tests are designed, for the most part, to measure the performance of a large group of students rather than that of an individual.

Another method of assessing reading comprehension ability is to have students read passages from their basal reader or from other material at their grade level. After reading, the students should be asked questions that test their ability to remember facts, make inferences, get main ideas, and understand the vocabulary. The major drawback with this approach is that it is difficult for the teacher to construct meaningful questions. Some questions that may appear relatively easy are seldom understood when they are used with a number of different students. At the same time and for no apparent reason, some questions are almost always answered correctly. When using this method to check comprehension, consider the student to be comprehending on a level equivalent to that at which the material is written if the student can answer at least 75% of the questions correctly.

A third approach to measuring comprehension is the use of commercial reading inventories. Although some studies have shown that the questions on some of these are sometimes irrelevant or could be answered without reading the passages over which they were constructed, in most cases the teacher can be assured that the questions are appropriate.

Another approach that is sometimes used to determine how well a student comprehends, as well as how his reading ability matches the level of the material he is reading, is the **cloze procedure.** A detailed description of how to use the cloze procedure is presented in Appendix B-11.

Methods for Teaching Comprehension

Teaching students how to comprehend what they read can be a challenging task. Certain reading methods have contributed to the problem. Comprehension is often tested but seldom taught. In fact, the only instruction some students receive in comprehension skills is in the form of questions over a paragraph or story. While this questioning may help some students to develop a strategy for comprehending on their own, it does not teach those students who most need to learn how to comprehend.

You are encouraged to have students work in pairs or groups of 3 to complete many of the recommendations that are presented in this chapter. For example, in the section titled "Ability to Recognize Important Details," the teacher asks students to write down all the details from a selection, then classify them as (1) important; (2) helpful, but not essential; or (3) unnecessary. If the classification task is done in pairs or groups of three, the resulting discussion may well include some disagreement. However, comprehension flourishes in the presence of interaction! Therefore, such a discussion should be highly beneficial. It is recommended that you limit group size to two or three students because larger groups often result in one or more students not participating actively. The active involvement that occurs when students work with each other is often crucial to the improvement of reading comprehension.

The study of **metacognition** has added much to our understanding of what educators must do to help students learn to comprehend. Cognition is the process of thinking, and metacognition is the process of understanding *how* a person thinks or the process of monitoring one's thinking. Metacognition is sometimes called "thinking about thinking." Practical methods of using metacognition to improve reading comprehension will be emphasized in the first section under "Recommendations."

RECOMMENDATIONS

Metacognitive Strategies

A. The Semantic Mapping Technique
   Definition:
   A semantic map is a diagram of relationships and ideas within a reading selection.
   Steps:
   1. The teacher selects a key word or idea from the upcoming reading selection.
   2. During class discussion, students brainstorm to come up with as many ideas as possible that are related to the key word or concept. These ideas are recorded on a chart or board.
   3. As a class, the students categorize these words and ideas.
   4. The categories are recorded in a graphic form (map) that shows the relationship of the categories to the main idea (key word) at the core of the map.
   5. The class reads the selection.
   6. New terms and ideas are added to the map after the reading selection has been read and discussed by the class. Previous categories may be changed or eliminated as the class decides. See Figure 21.1.

   Summary:
   Semantic mapping has been encouraged for three primary reasons. They are:
   1. development of critical thinking
   2. increased reasoning ability
   3. improvement of memory

B. The K-W-L Technique[1]
   Definition:
   The **K-W-L technique** is a logical, 3-step procedure named for the three basic cognitive steps required: what I *K*now (K), what I *W*ant to

FIGURE 21.1

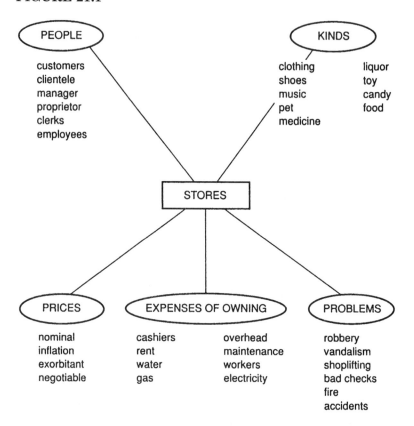

know (W), what I *Learned* (L). This reading comprehension strategy was developed by Donna Ogle.[2]

Steps:

1. The teacher selects a key concept from the upcoming reading selection.
2. The class brainstorms and lists ideas they already know (step K) about this key concept. These ideas are recorded on a chart or board.
3. As a class, the students categorize these ideas.
4. The teacher encourages students to think of questions they wish to know from the reading selection (step W). This may begin as early as step 2. The questions are recorded.
5. The class reads the selection.
6. After reading, the class discusses and records ideas they learned (step L). This may be done in the third column of the K-W-L chart, shown in Figure 21.2.

FIGURE 21.2

K	W	L
What I Know about spiders	What I Want to know about spiders	What I Learned about spiders
1. _____	1. _____	1. _____
2. _____	2. _____	2. _____
3. _____	3. _____	3. _____
4. _____		4. _____
5. _____		5. _____

Variation:
Some teachers add a fourth or even a fifth column to the chart to indicate H: *H*ow the information was obtained or S: What I *S*till want to know. (See the example in Figure 21.3.)

FIGURE 21.3

K	W	L	S
What I Know about spiders	What I Want to know about spiders	What I Learned about spiders	What I Still want to know about spiders

Summary:
With the K-W-L reading strategy, students are in charge of their learning and actively pursue knowledge. As a result, students learn to use their prior knowledge, locate key concepts in the reading, and remember to recall information.

C. Modeling Strategies for Paragraph Meaning[3]
Definition:
When **modeling strategies for paragraph meaning,** the teacher models, then directs students in the use of, a code for marking reactions to selected paragraphs. This is one of the most effective methods to teach students to monitor their thought processes when reading. The technique can be used with individuals, small groups, or an entire class. It is most effective with intermediate-age or older students, but could be modified and used with primary-grade students.

The code system will vary somewhat according to the grade level of the students involved.

Steps—Preparation:

You will need to prepare the following materials:

1. Two or more passages of 200 to 400 words, depending on the age and ability of your students. (While experts suggest that you use challenging material, we have found that the technique is successful with passages that are not too difficult.) Choose interesting passages; selections from books on science, social studies, or health make good choices.

2. The first passage should be triple spaced with generous margins and prepared as an overhead transparency (for the teacher to use in modeling the strategy). Other passages should be prepared as hard copies (for students to read on their own) and as overhead transparencies.

3. You may wish to prepare accompanying photographs or illustrations in color on overhead transparencies also.

4. Also prepare an overhead transparency (or enough hard copies for each student) of the symbols you will be using to describe your own comprehension monitoring. Choose 7 or fewer symbols, such as the ones shown in Figure 21.4.

FIGURE 21.4

GVI	=	Got a Visual Image
RA	=	Read Again
☺	=	No Sweat!
MBI	=	Must be Important
HW	=	Hard Word
LAP	=	Look at Picture
?	=	I'm Confused!

Steps—Teaching:

The technique may be taught to the whole class as follows:

1. Present the first selection to the students on an overhead transparency or on copied pages (for them to read silently). Prior to reading, you may discuss the title briefly and ask a few questions to access prior knowledge.

2. Have the students read the passage silently.

3. Present and describe your symbols to the students.

4. Place another transparency of the same passage on the overhead projector. This transparency consists of the passage triple spaced with generous margins *and* with your strategy symbols inserted in the passage in appropriate places.

5. Model how you (the teacher) would read the selection by telling the students what you did; that is, what you were *thinking* when you wrote your symbols on the passage. Discuss with the students why you made the choices you made and talk about the passage with the students, communicating your interest and enthusiasm in the material being read. *Note:* There is not one "correct" way to place your symbols. Any logical approach you use will work just fine.

6. Introduce a second selection. You may show a photograph or illustration on the overhead projector to heighten interest and use other techniques to tap into students' prior knowledge about the topic.

7. Pass out the second selection and have the students read it, either on their own or in pairs. (It often works well to leave it up to the students to make this choice.) Urge the students to monitor their own thinking as they read and explain to them that they may use your symbols or their own symbols to mark this selection as they read it.

8. Circulate around the room while the students are working, offering lots of praise and encouragement for their efforts.

9. Go over the second selection and discuss which symbols the students used and why. Explain to the students that different people may process the same material in different ways, and that is fine. Answer questions about the selection as they arise.

10. Present a follow-up lesson a day or two later. Have the students read another selection and repeat steps 6 through 9. Also, find future opportunities to inquire about students' use of comprehension-monitoring strategies when you are working with them individually or in small groups. Similarly, find additional occasions to model your own strategies with other kinds of material.

Variation:
This strategy may also be used with narrative material.

When modeling the strategy with, say, a junior novel, you may want to emphasize imagery (focus on as many of the senses as possible, not just visual), involving oneself in the selection (How would you feel if . . . ? This reminds me of when. . . .), author's purpose (Why do you think the author chose those words? focused on the setting? and so on, and prediction (What do you think will happen next?).

Another Variation:

To use this procedure with actual books, you may use a paper cutter to cut a number of strips of paper about 1″ wide and 11″ long from sheets of 8½″ × 11″ paper. Ask students to align the bottom of the strip of paper with the bottom of the page of the material they are to read. Then ask students to use these codes to mark each paragraph you have assigned.

Summary:

Although the procedure may appear complicated, students catch on quickly and are highly motivated to participate in this activity. It will help all students to think about (monitor) their reading comprehension and to learn successful reading comprehension strategies from the teacher. It will also enable less able readers to learn strategies from their peers who are more able readers.

D. Research suggests that an important metacognitive skill for students to develop is that of rereading something that does not seem to make sense when read the first time. In the beginning stages, ask students to read one sentence at a time and then ask themselves, "Do I know what the author is saying?" If the answer to this is *yes,* instruct students to keep on reading. On the other hand, if the answer is *no,* instruct students to reread that sentence. Continue to practice this skill until the students have developed the ability to monitor their thought processes while reading.

E. Young students should be counseled on the importance of getting meaning from reading. Young readers, low achievers, and disabled readers all seem to share the belief that fast, fluent oral reading is their ultimate goal. Do not take it for granted that some students know that comprehension of the material read is the most important purpose for reading. For younger students, it will also be helpful to discuss the vocabulary of reading: what is a *sound,* a *paragraph,* or a *sentence?* Studies have shown that many students, as late as first grade, do not know the difference between a letter, a word, and a sentence.

F. Stress the necessity for the student to be able to recognize words for which he does not know the meaning while he reads. Instruct the student to attempt to determine the meaning of unknown words from their context. If the student is unable to derive the meaning of the word from context, then urge the student to ask for help or use the dictionary. Most people become somewhat "expert" at omitting or ignoring words for which they do not know the meaning. Simply being aware of this habit will be most helpful in breaking it. Think back to a time when you looked up a word in the dictionary. You then may have noticed that same word several times in the very near future. Chances are that you had encountered the same word many times in the past but had simply ignored it. Once you knew the meaning of the word, you became much more aware of how often it appeared in materials that you were reading.

G. Stress the need for students to change their reading speeds depending upon the kind of materials they read. Many students read everything at the same rate. You could show students that a story problem in a math book would not be read at the same rate as a newspaper story about a familiar subject. (See Chapter 23 for additional suggestions for helping students adjust their rate of reading.)

H. Teach students to predict what may lie ahead as they read. In instructing students to do this, you may wish to have them read up to a certain point in a story or passage. Then discuss what they think the author will write next, based on what they have already read.

I. Instruct students to anticipate what questions the author or teacher might ask about a story or passage after it has been read. To do this, have students read a paragraph and then discuss what they think the author or you might ask them about the material. Practice this until students are proficient in this skill. Show students the difference between main ideas or overall comprehension of a passage and the comprehension or learning of only minor facts or details.

J. Use some type of marker for words that you think students will find difficult to understand. For example, you might put an asterisk before words that you feel will be difficult for students or an *X* before words that you believe they will not know. This will help them to be more aware of new words.

K. Talk to students about how stories progress from page to page to show a sequence of events; make students aware of the headings in social studies, science, and health books. Discuss the reason authors use headings and how they may be used to improve the students' understanding of the material they read.

L. Place all of the sentences of a paragraph on the board or on an overhead projector and discuss their importance to the overall understanding of the paragraph. You may wish to have students place the sentences in order according to their importance in the paragraph, for example, putting the most important sentence first, the next most important sentence second, and so on.

M. Teach students to learn to distinguish when text does or does not make sense to them. You may wish to provide practice in this skill by rewriting a passage and adding sentences within the text that contribute nothing to its meaning. Then have students read the material and attempt to locate those sentences that do not contribute to the overall comprehension of the material. This will help students monitor their comprehension in the future.

N. Tell students to think about the material they read, so when they complete the assignment, they will be able to explain the material to other students. This too will help students monitor their comprehension as they read.

O. Ask students to pretend they are the teacher while they read. Have them attempt to think of as many questions as they can about each paragraph.

P. Linda B. Gambrell urges teachers to make use of "think-time" in questioning.[4] She suggests that teachers allow students 5 seconds to think about a question both before and after they answer it to improve the quality of the answers they give. Teachers often observe that the same few students seem to want to answer any question the teacher asks, often before the asking has been completed. Teachers who are patient and allow think-time will get more responses from students who otherwise might not participate.

Q. Students' ability to monitor their comprehension as they read may be enhanced by using **story frames** such as those suggested by Gerald F. Fowler.[5] Fowler suggests that story frames be introduced shortly after students have read a selection. Five types of story frames are presented in Figure 21.5. Note that not all five types may be appropriate for all types of stories; however, you will find that several can often be used in many stories. It is suggested that you first introduce students to one of the simpler types of story frames, such as the one labeled "1" in Figure 21.5, after students have completed reading a story. Answers to the questions posed by the story frames may then be solicited from the entire class. After students become more adept at using each type of story frame, the frames may then be given to students prior to reading a story as an advance organizer to help them monitor their comprehension as they read.

You may have to modify these story frames to fit the story you are working on. For example, you may start with "This story begins when" and then add "and then." Following this you may add words that appropriately follow the sequence of events for the story such as, "next," "following that," and "the problem is solved when."

Procedures for Improving Overall Comprehension

A. Teach students to find material that is not too difficult for them by counting out about 100 words of the material they are about to read. Tell them that when they read these 100 words, they should not find more than one or two words they do not know. This refers to material the students would be reading without having any type of review of the words and content before they begin reading. Research in this area shows that students cannot be expected to comprehend well

FIGURE 21.5

1
Story summary with one character included

Our story is about _____ _____. _____ is an important character in our story. ____ tried to _____ The story ends when _____ _____.

2
Important idea or plot

In this story the problems starts when _____. After that, _____.

Next, _____ _____. Then, _____ _____. The problem is finally solved when _____ _____. The story ends_____ _____.

3
Setting

This story takes place _____ _____. I know this because the author uses the words "_____

_____." Other clues that show when the story takes place are _____ _____.

4
Character analysis

_____ is an important character in our story. ____ is important because _____. Once, he/she _____. Another time, _____. I think that _____ is _____
(character's name)   (character trait)
because _____.

5
Character comparison

_____ and _____ are two characters in our story. _____
(character's name)
is _____ while
(trait)
_____ is _____
(other character)   (trait)
For instance, _____ tries to _____. _____ learns a lesson when _____ _____.

unless they have rapid word recognition of the material; that is, they should be able to decode at least 98% of the words without assistance.

B. Set a purpose for reading before students begin to read. Have them skim the material and make predictions about the nature of the material and what they may expect to get from it. These predictions may be made from captions under pictures, the actual pictures, or from any headings that may appear in the story or article.

C. Have students combine sentences. This effective writing technique can also improve students' overall comprehension. Use the basal reader or a literature selection to find various sentences that can be combined. (Or create your own sentences for this purpose.) In using this method, call students' attention to connecting words such as *and, but, therefore, however, neither, either, which, that,* and so on. With your students' help, create a permanent list of these words, which can be written on chart paper and placed where all students can readily refer to it.

In doing this exercise, you may also wish to indicate which sentences should be combined by placing a number after each sentence and then giving students a sheet indicating which sentences should be combined. For example, the sheet may appear as follows:

Paragraph 1: 1 & 2
Paragraph 3: 1, 2, & 3

and so on. You may also wish to have them use words from certain sentences to form a new sentence (sometimes called *embedding.*) In this case, you may wish to indicate which words are to be embedded using a coding system such as this:

Paragraph 1: 1, 2 (cute), & 3 (stubborn)
Paragraph 1: 4, 5, & 6

Example of original paragraph:
Fred had a pet coyote. It was very cute. It was also stubborn. When Fred went to school it sometimes followed him. When the coyote followed Fred he had to take it back home. Then Fred was late for school.

Example of combined paragraph:
Fred had a pet coyote that was very cute, but also stubborn. Sometimes Fred's coyote would follow him to school and then he would have to take it back home, which made Fred late for school.

D. Constantly make the point to students that reading can be a source of information to help them with hobbies and any other subjects they would like to know more about. Refer them to various source books, encyclopedias, software, and so on.

Ability to Develop Mental Images

A. Some research indicates that the principal differences between students who comprehend well and those who do not are that the good comprehenders are able to develop mental images or visualize as they read, and they reread when they do not understand. Thus, teachers should help students develop mental images. You may teach students to be aware of mental images they are forming as they read by doing the following:

1. Select a passage and demonstrate how you visualize, by describing the mental images you are forming as you read the passage out loud to the students. Such teacher modeling is highly effective, especially if the teacher demonstrates with enthusiasm.

2. Select another passage. Have the students read a sentence or two and then ask if they were able to actually see the scene or the action described in what they read.

3. If the students cannot do this, then read the same sentences and tell the students what you saw in your "mind's eye" as you read. Ask the students to read the same material again and attempt to get approximately the same mental image. In beginning to develop this skill, be sure to use reading passages that contain information with which the students are already somewhat familiar. Keep in mind that the mental images students are able to perceive will depend on their background or experience.

B. For students to visualize a certain setting or image effectively, they must have actually or vicariously experienced it. Review the setting of a story with students before they begin. You might also supplement their information with a film or videotape or have students bring pictures from books and magazines.

C. As students read a selection, you might stop them from time to time and ask them to describe images gained from the reading. Also, students might be asked questions that combine the images from the passage and their own images. Two examples of such questions are, "What color coat do you think the person is wearing?" and, "How big was the tiger?"

D. Discuss figures of speech such as *big as a bear, black as pitch,* or *as cold as a polar bear in the Yukon.* Help the students to see that figurative language can either add meaning to a story or, in some cases, be misleading. Ask the students to listen for and collect various figures of speech. For younger students, the *Amelia Bedelia* books provide excellent examples of figurative language.

E. Ask the students to draw pictures of certain settings they have read about. Compare and discuss.

Ability to Recognize Main Ideas

A. You should work with students to help them find the main idea and supporting details of a story. You may list the main idea as well as the supporting details, as shown in the following paragraph.

A little bird sang his song day after day. The old man had heard it so many times that he knew the tune by heart. Even the students who played nearby could sing it.

Main Idea: A little bird sang his song day after day.
Supporting Details: The old man had heard it many times.
                     The old man knew it by heart.
                     Even the students who played nearby could sing it.

B. Another way of bringing out the main idea of a paragraph and showing the supporting details is to draw the paragraph as a diagram, as illustrated in Figure 21.6.

FIGURE 21.6

Some paragraphs have one main idea.

A little bird sang his song day after day.

The old man had heard it many times.
The old man knew it by heart.
Even the students who played nearby could sing it.

Other paragraphs may have two main ideas.

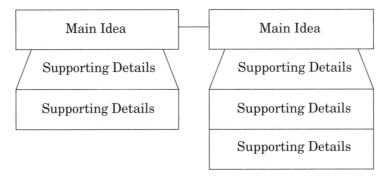

Other types of paragraphs may look like the following.

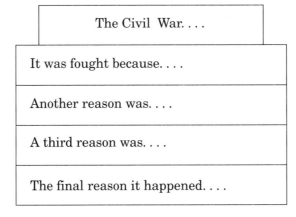

FIGURE 21.6 *(Continued)*

"X" brand of soap cleans well. . . .

"X" brand leaves no ring in the bathtub. . . .

"X" brand acts as a deodorant. . . .

therefore

You should always buy it.

Many people eat too much. . . .

Many people drink too much. . . .

Many people watch TV too much. . . .

But on the other hand there are people who. . . .

Even some of these do not. . . .

Some do not even. . . .

Sometimes there are those who. . . .

I will run for public office again if. . . .

Senator Brown must. . . .

Governor Turner should. . . .

My health. . . .

If I run I am sure. . . .

FIGURE 21.6 *(Continued)*

The first reader introduces. . . .
The second reader introduces. . . .
The third reader discusses. . . .

All of the readers in the series are deeply concerned with. . . .

Once upon a time. . . .

Therefore children, you should. . . .

When drawing paragraph diagrams with the students, do not expect to find complete agreement on how they should look. Keep in mind that the important thing is to get the students to think about paragraph structure.

C. Read the introduction or title to a story or a chapter and then encourage the students to predict what the author is going to say.

D. Select appropriate titles for paragraphs, chapters, or short selections. You might also have the students select the best title from several listed.

E. After the students read a paragraph, have them tell in their own words what the author has said.

F. Many writers use subheadings to help students organize the text. Turn these subheadings into questions and then have students read specifically to answer those questions.

G. Have the students underline the sentences in paragraphs that best represent the main idea. (Make sure there is a sentence that best represents the main idea, and also make sure the paragraph has a main idea.)

H. Find stories in the newspaper with charts or photos and remove the original captions from each of them. Give these to students and have them read each story and then write their own captions. Compare the students' captions with those of the original stories. Discuss reasons for differences and whether captions written by the students are appropriate.

I. Have each student write a paragraph and place an identifying number at the top of the paper. Then pass the paragraph to another student who reads it and writes the main idea or a caption for it on the back of the paper. Then read the various paragraphs and discuss the appropriateness of each caption or main-idea sentence.

J. Have students write paragraphs, with one sentence being the main idea of that paragraph. Pass these paragraphs around and have other students try to identify the sentence that the writer of the paragraph thought best represented the main idea.

Ability to Recognize Important Details

A. Discuss with the students the important details in several paragraphs. Students often focus on minor ideas and details that are not really important. Perhaps the kind of testing often used encourages this type of reading.

B. Help the students to find the main idea, then ask them to find significant details that describe or elaborate on the idea.

C. Ask the students to write down all the details from a selection. Have them classify the details from their list as (1) important; (2) helpful, but not essential; or (3) unnecessary.

D. Have the students answer questions or complete sentences that require a knowledge of the important details.

E. Have the students draw a series of pictures to illustrate details, for example, in the description of a scene.

F. Write three or four paragraphs about a picture; then have students read each of the paragraphs to see which one best describes the picture. The picture may be placed at the top of an 8½″ × 11″ piece of paper with each of the paragraphs arranged below it. Encourage students to select a picture and write the paragraphs, which you will duplicate, for other students to complete.

G. Have students read stories in newspapers and magazine articles and then have them attempt to answer the following: Who? What? When? Where? and Why?

Ability to Follow Directions

A. Make students aware of key words that indicate a series of instructions, such as *first, second, then,* and *finally.* Discuss the fact that, in this case, there are actually four steps, although the writer used only the terms *first* and *second.* As students read directions, have them reinforce this knowledge by having them make lists of words that were used to indicate steps.

B. Write directions for paper folding or other activities that the students can do at their seats. Have the students read and perform these directions step by step.

C. Write directions for recess activities on the chalkboard. Try to get the students in the habit of following these directions without oral explanation.

D. Ask the students to write directions for playing a game. Have them read their directions and analyze whether they could learn to play the game from a certain student's written directions.

E. Encourage the students to read written directions such as those in workbooks and certain arithmetic problems without your help.

F. Write directions for certain designs to be drawn on a certain size of paper. For example, the following directions may be given.

1. Make an X on your paper halfway between the top and bottom edges and 1″ from the left-hand side.
2. Make a Y on the same horizontal plane as the X, but 1″ from the right-hand side of the paper.
3. Make a Z directly below the Y, 1″ from the bottom edge of the paper.
4. Draw a line to connect the X and Y.
5. Draw another line to connect the Y and the Z.

After these are completed, have students examine their pictures in relation to one drawn correctly and shown on the overhead projector or on the chalkboard. Discuss reasons for some common mistakes.

Ability to Predict Outcomes

A. Show a series of pictures from a story and ask the students to tell, either in writing or orally, what they think the story will be about.

B. Read to a certain point in a story and then ask the students to tell or write their own versions of the ending.

C. Ask the students to read the chapter titles of a book and predict what the story will be about. Read the story and compare versions.

D. Encourage the students to make logical predictions and be ready to revise their preconceived ideas in light of new information.

Ability to Recognize the Author's Organization

A. Discuss the fact that all authors have some form or organization in mind when writing. Look over chapter titles and discuss other possibilities for organization. Do the same with shorter selections, including paragraphs.

B. Discuss the author's use of pictures, graphs, charts, and diagrams to clarify certain concepts.

C. Discuss the use of introductory material, headings, study questions, and summaries.

D. Explain the value of "signal" words and phrases in showing organizational patterns. Examples of signal words and phrases are: *to begin with, next, not long after, then, finally, several factors were responsible for, these led to, which further complicated it by.*

E. Write down, out of order, a sequence of events from a story the students have read and ask them to number the events in the order in which they happened. Explain before they read the story what they will be expected to do.

F. Write each of the sentences from a paragraph on a small, separate piece of paper in mixed-up order. Ask the students to arrange these sentences in a logical sequence to form a paragraph that makes sense.

G. Cut up comic strips or pictures of sequential events and have the students assemble them in the correct order.

Ability to Do Critical Reading (a higher-level reading skill)

A. Discuss the use of "loaded" words and have students search through editorials or transcripts of speeches of political candidates for these words. Some examples of these words are: *left-wing, reactionary, rightist, warlord, playboy,* and *extremist.*

B. Examine advertisements for cigarettes or alcohol to see how they are designed to appeal to various age groups. Note statements that are made about such products and examine whether these statements have merit.

C. Examine advertisements for various products in "men's" and "women's" magazines to see how they are designed to appeal to different audiences.

D. Find accounts of a political event as reported by two or more newspapers or magazines. Note ways in which the information differs.

E. Examine political cartoons and discuss whether they are designed to show an individual in a positive or negative way.

F. Examine various advertisements to see how they attempt to get the buyer to infer information about the product, which, in reality, may be quite meaningless. For example, a claim for X brand of aspirin may say, "Nine out of 10 doctors surveyed recommended the ingredients in X brand." What this may mean is that 9 out of 10 doctors recommend that people take aspirin at some time!

G. Analyze editorials to determine whether the writer of the editorial used biased statements or whether the writer wished the reader to make certain inferences. Also discuss why a certain writer may be biased in certain areas.

GAMES AND EXERCISES

Story Division

Purpose: To provide practice in comprehension and oral reading skills for students who lack self-confidence

Materials: A basal reader or other story selection for each student
Procedure:

You first divide a story, such as the following, into parts.

1. Toddle was Pam's pet turtle.
   He liked to crawl.
   He got out of his pan of water and crawled all around the house.
2. Toddle bumped into things.
   Bang! Bang! Down they went.
   Mother did not like this.
3. She said, "Please, Pam, put Toddle back into the water, and do make him stay there."

Each student studies one part of the story and reads it orally. After a whole story is read, the students are given a comprehension check. This type of procedure gives the students confidence because they know the part they will be required to read and they can practice reading it silently before reading it orally.

A Matching Board

Purpose: To provide practice on the various components of comprehension

Materials: A piece of ½″ plywood the same size as a sheet of paper
            Shoestrings
Procedure:

Drill 2 columns of holes 1″ apart down the center of the piece of plywood, as shown in Figure 21.7. Make holes the entire length of the board, spacing them the same vertical distance as four linespaces on a typewriter. The holes should be just large enough to let the shoestrings pass through them quite easily. Attach shoestrings through the holes in the left column. Tie a knot on the back side, so they will not be pulled through. Make sure each string in the left column is long enough to thread through any hole in the right column.

Prepare various exercises such as sentence completion, missing words from the context of a sentence, word opposites, sentence opposites, and so on. Space each set of opposites four vertical typewriter linespaces apart, so they will

FIGURE 21.7

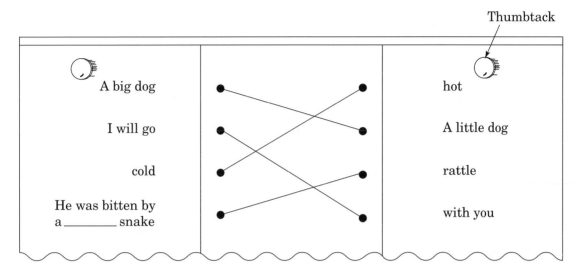

correspond with the holes on the board. Use a tack or clear tape at the top and bottom of each column of questions and answers to hold the dittoed material in place. Use these boards with individual students to provide practice in areas in which they need help.

Main Ideas

Purpose: To improve students' ability to concentrate and locate the main idea in a selection

Materials: Basal readers, library books, science or social studies textbooks
Procedure:

Before giving the students a reading assignment, show them a list of true-false questions concerning the material on the reading assignment. Construct the questions so that they test for the main ideas of paragraphs from the reading material. This test will give the students an idea of what they are expected to gather from the assignment, and it will improve their ability to recognize main ideas in future reading. Make sure students understand that the questions test for main ideas and not for details.

Directions: Some of the statements below are true and some are false. Write *T* after the true statements and *F* after those that are not true.

1. Carlos did not really want to race his car.
2. The weather was just right for racing.
3. Someone had been fooling around with Carlos's car.
4. Most of Carlos's friends felt that he could win the race if he wanted to.

Picture Puzzle

Purpose: To help students recognize, evaluate, and describe various situations

Materials: Pictures clipped from magazines or old discarded readers mounted
               on tagboard
            Word cards
            Flannel board

Procedure:

Display a picture on the flannel board. Allow the students to select from a large number of word cards the ones they feel best describe the given picture. Place these word cards on the flannel board with the picture and discuss their appropriateness to the situation.

Variation in Procedure:

Use the same procedure, except substitute sentence strips for the individual word cards or make sentences from the individual cards.

Riddles

Purpose: To provide practice in the comprehension of descriptive details

Materials: Tagboard

Procedure:

Write a series of short stories describing a particular object or animal. Have the students read the story and decide what the object or animal is. In the bottom corner, under a flap of paper, place the correct answer. The students may check their answers after they have made their decisions. See Figure 21.8.

FIGURE 21.8

My home is in the country.
I live on a farm.
The farmer's children take care of me.
They give me grain and water.
I give them eggs.
I am a good friend of yours.
What animal am I?

Answer
is here

What Do You See?

Purpose: To develop picture-word description relationships

Materials: Pictures cut from magazines
             Tagboard
             Flannel board

Procedure:

Place pictures of objects on the flannel board. On tagboard write some questions about the pictures and some questions that will act as distracters. Have the students answer the questions about the pictures posted.

Do you see a frog?
Do you see a hopping rabbit?
Do you see a fat pig?
Do you see a door?
Do you see an open window?
Do you see a red ball?

FIGURE 21.9

The Wizard

Purpose: To provide practice in reading for specific questions

Materials: A basal reader or literature selection for each student
Procedure:

One student is chosen as the Wizard. The student asks a question relating to the reading lesson and calls on a classmate to answer. If that student answers correctly, he is the Wizard, and he makes up the next question. Those students who do not answer a question correctly have another chance to be the Wizard with further play.

Classification Game

Purpose: To develop the ability to classify related words

Materials: Pocket chart
Word cards
Envelopes

Procedure:

Divide the pocket chart into four columns. In the first three columns in each row, place three related word cards. Leave the fourth column blank and have the students select a word card from their envelopes that belongs in the same class as the other three words in that row.

car	boat	airplane	_____
ball	top	doll	_____
Susan	Bill	Lassie	_____
walk	gallop	skip	_____
red	blue	green	_____

Variation in Procedure:

Instead of filling in the missing word, use four words in which one word does not fit the category represented by the other three words. Have students find and remove the "misfit."

As I See It

Purpose: To provide students with an opportunity to express the visual images they gain from reading or hearing a story

Materials: A story (preferably one with vividly described scenes)
Drawing paper and paints or colors

Procedure:

After the students have heard or read a story, have them illustrate various scenes as they perceived them. After drawing the scenes, mix the illustrations up in a box and have one student stand in front of the room and pull out pictures. After he has chosen a picture, he will try to reconstruct the story on a bulletin board from the many pictures that are in the box. Discuss various differences in drawings and discuss why some students interpreted things differently. At times you will want to reread parts of the story to see if material was interpreted incorrectly.

Furnish the Empty Room

Purpose: To develop the ability to recognize appropriate visual images

Materials: Flannel board
Pictures of specific objects cut from magazines or old books

Procedure:

At the top of the flannel board, place printed subject headings, such as "kitchen" or "playroom." Have the students select object pictures that are appropriate to the given headings. See Figure 21.10.

FIGURE 21.10

My Image

Purpose: To encourage the building of sensory images

Materials: Various materials to create sounds that are very familiar, somewhat familiar, and less familiar to students

Procedure:

Have the students close their eyes and listen as you or another student makes a noise. Have the students open their eyes and write words or phrases that describe the noise. Then have them draw pictures to represent the noise. Encourage them to use a varied vocabulary in their descriptions.

That Makes Sense

Purpose: To develop the ability to associate objects with their sources and to
develop the ability to logically complete a given idea

Materials: Pocket chart
Word cards
Envelopes

Procedure:

A series of incomplete statements is placed on the pocket chart. Word cards containing the appropriate missing words or phrases are provided for the

FIGURE 21.11

A dress is made from	in the ground
Fish usually	flour
Cocoa is made from	fly
Oil can come from	seeds
Cabbage grows	beans
Parrots can	on the ground
Strawberries have	swim in water
Cakes are made from	whales
Potatoes grow	wool

students. From these they will select the correct answer and place it in the pocket chart next to the incomplete idea. See Figure 21.11.

Ordered Phrases

Purpose: To provide practice in skimming and in determining sequence (comprehension)

Materials: Cards with phrases copied from a story, book, or basal reader
Procedure:

Have the students read the passage and place the phrases on the cards in columns in the order that the phrases occurred on the page. You should also write the number order on the back of the cards. Such numbering will enable a student to correct his own work.

Sentence Puzzles

Purpose: To help students see a sequence of ideas

Materials: Envelopes
            Paragraphs or short stories that are written in a logical order
Procedure:

Cut up the stories or paragraphs into sentences and paste each sentence on a small rectangular piece of paper. Place one story or paragraph in each envelope. Pass these envelopes out to the students and have them assemble the stories in a logical order. Number the envelopes and have the students keep a record of the stories or paragraphs (by envelope number) they have assembled. The students continue to exchange these envelopes until all have had a turn at each envelope. In some cases you may want to have stories or paragraphs graded according to the reading level of a particular group. In such a case, reading group B will do only those envelopes marked 1-B, 2-B, and so forth.

It Does—It Doesn't

Purpose: To help students classify words according to descriptive specifications

Materials: Pocket chart
Envelopes
Word cards

Procedure:

Divide the pocket chart into two columns. Place a statement and its opposite next to each other at the top of the chart. Provide each student with an envelope of word cards containing current vocabulary words. Have the students classify the words found in their envelopes according to the given statements. Use a great variety of statements and word cards that will require careful thought. Vocabulary and classification sentences will vary with grade levels.

What Did It Say?

Purpose: To develop phrase recognition and the ability to follow directions

Materials: Flash cards
Procedure:

Write specific directions on individual flash cards. As the cards are flashed before the class, call on certain students to respond. Examples of directions are:

Close the door.
Give a pencil to a brown-eyed boy.
Stand up. Turn three circles. Touch the desk behind yours.
Draw a circle inside of a triangle on the chalkboard.

Story Pantomime

Purpose: To provide practice in reading for information and following directions

Materials: Cards on which are printed directions for acting out certain activities

FIGURE 21.12

It can walk	It cannot walk

Word Cards

boy	top	boat
cup	rabbit	cow
dog	girl	pan
car	bucket	plane
coat	horse	duck

Procedure:

The cards are passed out to all the students in the class. One student is selected to act out each set. The other students watch critically for the complete acting of every detail in the directions. Example:

Pretend you are washing dishes. Stop up the sink, open the doors under the sink, and get the soap. Put the soap in the sink, turn the faucet on, test the water, put the dishes in the water, and then wash and rinse three dishes. Put the dishes in the dish rack to dry.

A story pantomime might also include such things as:

drawing water from a well
making the bed
rocking the baby

picking flowers for a bouquet
singing a hymn
winding the clock
watering the flowers
ironing
picking and eating apples
playing baseball

Good Words—Bad Words

Purpose: To provide practice in critical reading, especially concerning the purpose the author had in mind when the material was written

Materials: Various written or tape-recorded advertisements
Procedure:

Have the students locate and circle or make a list of words they can classify as either "good" words or "bad" words. Good words might include such words as *freedom, well-being, number-one rating,* and *delicious.* Bad words might include words such as *disease, cracks, peels,* and *odor.* Discuss how the use of these words influences our thinking about a certain product. Carry this exercise into the study of characters in books about whom the author wishes to convey a good or bad impression.

ENDNOTES

1. Appreciation is extended to Cathy Langmoreland for the description of the semantic mapping and K-W-L techniques.
2. Ogle, D. M. (1986). K-W-L: A teaching model that develops active reading of expository text. *Reading Teacher, 39,* 564–570.
3. This technique is adapted from Smith, R. J., and Dauer, V. L. (1984). A comprehension-monitoring strategy for reading content-area materials. *Journal of Reading, 28,* 292–300.
4. Gambrell, L. B. (1980). Think-time: Implications for reading instruction. *Reading Teacher, 34,* 143–146.
5. Reprinted with permission of Gerald L. Fowler and the International Reading Association from Fowler, G. L. (1982). Developing comprehension skills in primary students through the use of story frames. *Reading Teacher, 36,* 176–179.

STUDY SKILLS ABILITIES

CHAPTER 22

Low Rate of Speed

RECOGNIZED BY

The student is unable to read as many words per minute as would be normal for a student of her age on a certain kind of reading material. Low rate of speed usually applies to silent, rather than oral, reading.

DISCUSSION

You can determine whether certain students are slow readers by giving a timed reading exercise to an entire class. The various reading speeds listed in words per minute can be graphed or charted to determine which students are considerably below average on a particular kind of material for their class. When giving timed exercises, choose several pages that are normal reading material in story reading. You should not use pages containing questions, lists, and the like. Timed exercises from 2 to 5 minutes should be sufficient. You seldom need to worry about achieving a very rapid reading rate in the elementary grades. Therefore, the suggestions listed under "Recommendations" in items A, B, and C are more appropriate for junior- or senior-high-level students. Activities to increase speed of reading should be used only with students who have strong decoding skills and who comprehend adequately when reading slowly. In all cases, students should be expected to read with accuracy before attempts are made to increase their reading speed.

RECOMMENDATIONS

A. Have the students pace their reading with their hands. They should attempt to move across the page slightly faster than their comfortable reading speed normally allows. It should, however, be emphasized that the hand paces the eyes and the reading speed, not the opposite.

B. Focus on speed by using material that can be read fast. Give timed reading exercises followed by comprehension questions. Let the student keep her own chart on speed and comprehension. See Appendix C-8 for sample charts.

C. For older students, assign or let them pick short paperback novels that are meant to be read rapidly. Use these in conjunction with hand pacing to practice for speed.

EXERCISE

Timed Stories

Purpose: To encourage rapid reading while still focusing on improving comprehension

Materials: A number of envelopes with short stories in them, along with sets of questions about each story

Procedure:

Before doing this, you should have given speed reading tests to your class and grouped them accordingly, for example, one group that reads from 75–100 words per minute, one group that reads from 100–125 words per minute, and so on. Cut out a number of short stories from old basal readers or another source. Put one of these stories, along with approximately 10 comprehension questions, in an envelope. Develop norms for each story; for example, a certain story for the 100–125 wpm group may be labeled an 8-minute story. Label the envelopes under headings such as "Dog Stories," "Family Life Stories," and "Science Stories." Let the students choose the stories they want to read. From the labeling, the students will know that they should read the story in a certain number of minutes. This technique is a change from the timed test in which each student is reading the same subject matter. It also avoids having the faster readers wait for the slower readers; when they finish a story, students can get an envelope and begin another one. Have the students keep a record of the stories they have read and their percent of comprehension on each story.

CHAPTER 23

Inability to Adjust Reading Rate

RECOGNIZED BY

The student reads at the same rate regardless of the type of material he is reading. This applies to silent, rather than oral, reading.

DISCUSSION

Many people are in the habit of reading all kinds of material at one speed. They read a newspaper or novel as though it were a science book or a set of directions. This is a habit that can be overcome easily if the student is shown how varying his reading rate can save time and improve comprehension. To determine whether a student is reading all kinds of material at the same speed, give him a speed test on several kinds of material. The first material should be of the type found in novels or in a newspaper. Then give another speed test on material that would require more careful reading, such as the expository writing in a science book. If the student reads all of the material at approximately the same rate, he is having problems adjusting his reading rate to the difficulty of the material.

To determine reading rate, find the total number of words in the passage and the length of time, in seconds, that the student takes to read that passage. Divide the number of words by the number of seconds. Multiply the resulting figure by 60. The result will be words per minute (wpm).

RECOMMENDATIONS

A. Discuss various types of reading material and show the students how rates should vary on these materials. You may wish to construct a chart like the one shown in Figure 23.1 to explain this idea.

B. Time an entire class on a reading passage from a novel, and then time the class on a reading passage from a mathematics or science book, preferably one that explains a process. Compare the average amount of time taken to read each passage or the number of words read in a certain amount of time. Emphasize that comprehension is necessary in both cases.

C. Check the students' comprehension on easy and difficult material when each is read fast and when each is read slowly. Determine proper reading speeds for adequate comprehension of each type of material.

FIGURE 23.1

HOW WE READ DIFFERENT KINDS OF MATERIALS

Skim

1. Telephone book
2. Newspaper (when looking for one thing)

Fast

1. Novels
2. Newspaper (when reading normally)

Medium

1. Our history assignments
2. A magazine article of high interest

Slow

1. Procedures for experiments in science
2. Our mathematics book
3. A computer manual

D. Much of the material in science and social studies is presented with a number of boldfaced headings within the chapters. The student should study this material in the following manner:

1. Turn the first boldfaced heading into a question; for example, the heading may be "The New World." The student might then make a question of this by asking himself, "Where was the New World?"
2. The student then reads to answer that question.
3. When the student has read down to the next boldfaced heading, he should stop and try to answer the question he has just posed. If he cannot answer it, he should read the material again. If he can answer it, he should proceed to the next boldfaced heading and do the same with it.

E. Discuss when it may not be necessary to read every word, such as in a descriptive passage of scenery in a novel or details in newspaper articles. Have students underline only those parts that would be necessary for adequate comprehension. Then have students exchange articles or pages of a novel and read only the parts that other students have underlined. Discuss information derived by various students by reading only the underlined material. Ask the students who underlined the material to comment on the adequacy of the second reader's comprehension.

F. If the reader's rate is much too slow, then discuss when it is desirable to skim. If the reader cannot do this, then see the suggestions in Chapter 25, "Inability to Skim or Scan."

CHAPTER 24

High Rate of Reading at the Expense of Accuracy

RECOGNIZED BY

The student reads quickly but with poor recall. Often such a student completes reading assignments before the rest of the class, yet lacks comprehension of what she has read.

DISCUSSION

Reading at a high rate of speed is desirable at times. However, certain types of reading material should be read more carefully than others. For example, mathematics, science, and other content reading materials often require slow, careful reading. Many students are not able to adjust their reading rate downward as the reading material becomes difficult. This situation is especially true of the student who constantly reads novels or the newspaper and then must read material in school that requires considerable concentration.

You occasionally may find a student in the lower elementary grades who reads at a rate that impairs her accuracy. The problem is more prevalent, however, with older students who have become accustomed to reading material that requires little concentration.

RECOMMENDATIONS

A. Demonstrate and then discuss the various reading speeds that are desirable for certain types of material. You may show students how you read different types of material by preparing overhead transparencies of selections that are triple spaced. Use a pointer to indicate the speed at which your eyes move over the material and stop to explain to students why you are reading at the chosen speed and what thinking is going on in your mind as you are reading. Take time to thoroughly discuss this and to answer students' questions. Do not be concerned about telling students the *best* way to read different materials. Explain to students that they may think about other things while they are reading and that is fine. What is important is that you model the process of strategic reading. Once students see that their teacher actively thinks while reading, they will begin to do the same thing.

B. Have the students react to each paragraph using a code similar to that suggested on ideas for using metacognition, shown in Chapter 21 under "Strategic/Metacognitive Procedures," item C.

C. Ask the students to use techniques in which they are required to react to each boldfaced heading. (See Chapter 23 under "Recommendations," item D.)

D. From material found in a reading passage, ask oral and written questions that require accurate answers. Let the students know ahead of time that they will be required to answer questions about the reading passage.

E. Give students worksheets that contain reading passages and questions about subject matter in the reading passages. Ask them to underline the answers to questions as they read them.

F. Give the students study guide questions about material they are to read. Many books contain questions about a unit or chapter at the end of that unit or chapter. Encourage the students to read these questions before they begin reading the material in the chapter or unit.

CHAPTER 25

Inability to Skim or Scan

RECOGNIZED BY

The student is unable to get a general understanding of reading material through rapid, superficial reading (skimming) or to find specific information or answer specific questions about material that is read quickly (scanning).

DISCUSSION

Skimming and scanning are reading strategies to accomplish specific objectives. *Skimming* requires more comprehension than scanning but less than normal reading. It can be an effective way for students to preview reading material that they may later read more carefully. One of the causes of the inability to skim is that the students have not felt a need for this skill. People who actually need to learn to skim, and who are shown how to do so, soon become adept at this skill. To determine whether a student is able to skim, select material you wish the student to read and skim it yourself. Note how long it takes you to get the gist of the material and add some additional time for the student to do this, depending on the age and reading ability of the student and the difficulty of the material. Next, tell the student that you would like him to look at a reading selection quickly, then tell you what it is about. The best way to judge a student's ability at this task is to compare his performance to that of other students when skimming the same material.

To *scan* effectively, the student must know what he is looking for and how to use key words to find specific material or answers to specific questions. Scanning is usually more rapid than skimming and requires less comprehension. To assess students' scanning ability, list 5 to 10 facts, dates, sentences, or the like that appear in a lesson and then ask students to find the material within a reasonable time limit. Watch for those students who have completed only a little when the faster ones have finished.

RECOMMENDATIONS

For Skimming:

A. Hold a class discussion on how skimming can be beneficial. Ask students to tell when it might be appropriate to skim. Their list might be similar to the following:
   1. Wanting an idea of what an article or book is about
   2. Previewing a chapter in a textbook prior to studying it more carefully

3. Looking quickly at a controversial article or editorial to get an idea of the author's opinion

4. Looking quickly through material to see if it contains the information you are looking for; for example, skimming an article about a medical condition to see if it applies to you

B. Demonstrate to students how to skim by preparing overhead transparencies of selections that are triple spaced. Use your finger or a pointer to indicate the speed at which your eyes move over the material. Stop to explain to students what you are reading or glancing at and what thinking is going on in your mind as you are skimming. Take time to thoroughly discuss this and to answer students' questions. Do not be concerned about telling students the *best* way to skim reading materials. What is important is that you model a process of skimming. Once students see that their teacher does this, they will begin to do the same thing when instructed to do so.

C. Give students copies of newspapers, magazine articles, or other short reading selections and ask them to skim the material, without additional directions, to get a general overall impression of the contents. Use a timer and stop the students after the prescribed amount of time has elapsed. Then have the students discuss or summarize in writing what they think the material is about.

D. Using a textbook, have students skim the title, headings, introduction, the first sentence of each paragraph, and the summary to get a general overall impression of the contents. Use a timer and stop the students after the prescribed amount of time has elapsed. Then have the students discuss or summarize in writing what they think the material is about.

E. List three or four broad questions or issues on the chalkboard. Using a textbook or other reading selection, have the students skim to find out if these questions will be answered or if the issues will be discussed in this reading selection.

For Scanning:

F. Hold a class discussion on how scanning can be beneficial. Ask students to tell when it might be appropriate to scan. Their list might be similar to the following:

1. Looking for a name in a telephone book
2. Looking for a date in a history book
3. Looking for a certain number of factors to solve a problem
4. Reading the newspaper and searching for a certain article
5. Looking for a word in a dictionary

G. Demonstrate to students how to scan using the same procedure described in item B.

H. Show the students how to move their hands down a page in a telephone directory to find a certain name. After they have practiced and have become proficient with their hands, they can usually do as well without using their hands.

I. Give the students copies of newspapers and have them scan them to find things such as the article about the president, or about a certain baseball pitcher. Another good exercise with a newspaper is to have the students find a phrase on a certain page that describes something or tells a certain fact. After the students have found the phrase, ask them to paraphrase the author's meaning.

J. Give study questions on a reading assignment that can be answered by scanning the material. Keep in mind that this is not always the type of reading one wants to encourage.

K. Have the students scan to find a certain word in the dictionary.

L. Have the students scan to find a certain word (for example, the name of a city) or date in a history book.

M. Tell what a certain paragraph is about and then have the students scan to find the topic sentence of that paragraph. (Make sure there is one!)

N. Show the students that it is possible to get the meaning of some material when many words are missing. Make paragraphs in which some words unnecessary for comprehension are missing. Make sure students understand that they are not to try to supply the missing words. Another variation of this exercise is to give the students paragraphs and have them underline only the words that are really necessary for comprehension. See the example.

> The <u>superintendent</u> of <u>schools</u> in <u>Huntsville</u> spoke to a large audience. She <u>discussed reasons</u> for the <u>new building program.</u> To some extent, she <u>covered methods</u> by which <u>new revenue</u> might be made <u>available.</u> Everyone thought her <u>speech was excellent.</u>

After students have seen how this process works, have them create similar paragraphs for each other.

GAMES AND EXERCISES

Skim and Sort

Purpose: To provide practice in skimming

Materials: Old textbooks with stories in them that are somewhat varied
             Envelope

Procedure:

Cut three stories from a book and then cut each story into either paragraphs or fairly short passages. Make sure each paragraph or passage contains some subject matter that gives a clue to which story it came from. Mix all of the paragraphs or passages together and place them in an envelope. Write the names of the three stories on the outside of the envelope. Give the student this envelope and have him sort through them rapidly, putting each paragraph or passage in one of three piles to match the story title. Number each paragraph or passage. When a student has finished sorting these, give him the number key to check his work. (For example, numbers 1, 3, 5, 7, 9, 13, 15, and 16 may belong in the first story; numbers 2, 6, 8, 14, 17, and 18 may belong in the second story; and numbers 4, 10, 11, 12, 19, and 20 may belong in the third story.)

Finish It

Purpose: To provide practice in scanning

Materials: A book of which all students in the game have a copy
Procedure:

Give students the number of a page from which you are going to read. You then begin reading somewhere on that page. After reading a few words you stop, and those who have found the place continue to read to the end of the sentence.

Scanning Race

Purpose: To provide practice in scanning

Materials: Any book that is available to every student in the game
Procedure:

Divide the students into two groups. Either you or alternating captains ask a question and tell the students in both groups the page where the answer can be found. The first student to find the answer stands by his seat. The first person standing is called on to read the answer. A correct answer scores one point for that side. The object is to see who can get the most points in a specified amount of time or in a specified number of questions. If a student stands and then gives a wrong answer, take away one point from his side.

Rapid Search

Purpose: To provide students with practice in both skimming and scanning

Materials: Several copies of the same articles in magazines, basal readers, or
                newspapers
Procedure:

One student finds a part of the story that represents some action. He then pantomimes this action, and the rest of the students skim rapidly to try to find the appropriate part of the story, then scan to find the sentence in the story that describes the actions of the student doing the pantomiming.

Inability to Locate Information

RECOGNIZED BY

The student is unable to locate information in encyclopedias, the *Reader's Guide to Periodical Literature,* the card catalog or computer files of the library, the *World Almanac,* atlases, and other sources.

The student is unable to use cross-references and parts of books such as the table of contents, index, and appendix.

DISCUSSION

It is almost a necessity for students in the intermediate grades and up to be able to use some of the sources of information listed here. However, students often lack the skills needed to locate information. Even at the high school level, many students are unfamiliar with the use of the index and table of contents in their own textbooks.

Teachers can locate the types of difficulties students are encountering by giving an informal test similar to the following:

1. Name the part of your textbook that tells the beginning page number of the chapter on atoms.

2. Where would you look in your textbook to locate the meaning of the word *negotiate?*

3. Where in your textbook would you find some reference to the subject of atomic reactors?

4. Find the name of the magazine that published the following article: " _____ ."

5. Explain how you would locate the following book in the library: _____ .

6. How would you locate something on the subject of whales in the following set of encyclopedias: _____ .

7. What city in the United States has the largest population?

8. What is the purpose of the appendix of a book?

RECOMMENDATIONS

A. Discuss with the students the types of information found in encyclopedias. Also give exercises in which the students are required to locate certain volumes and then certain pieces of information using the letter and/or word guides provided.

B. Teach the use of cross-references. Ask the students to find information on certain subjects that are covered under several headings.

C. Explain the use of the library card catalog (or computerized catalog).

D. Teach the students how to locate information in the *Reader's Guide to Periodical Literature*. Assign reports that require its use for finding a number of references on a certain subject.

E. Explain the use of the *World Almanac*. Give exercises in its use. For example, ask specific questions such as the following: (1) What city has the largest population in the world? (2) What city covers the most square miles? To increase students' interest in this type of activity, use the *Guinness Book of World Records* in addition to the *World Almanac*.

F. Explain the use of the table of contents, index, and appendix. Do not take it for granted that older students know how to use these. Ask specific questions about their use. For example: (1) What chapter explains the use of maps? (2) What page contains an explanation of photosynthesis? (3) Where would you find tables showing the relationships between weights and measures in the English and metric systems?

GAMES AND EXERCISES

Reference Hunt

Purpose: To provide practice in using various reference materials

Materials: Encyclopedias
Dictionaries
Thesauruses
World Almanac
Card catalog
Other reference materials (including computer-based resources)
One prepared set of 10 questions for the first reference hunt

Procedure:

The reference hunt should be conducted after you have taught your students how to use the various reference materials. Group your students into 10 teams

FIGURE 26.1

REFERENCE HUNT

1. How did John W. Booth earn a living? _____
   Source _____ Page _____

2. What is the meaning of the word *vitiate?* _____
   Source _____ Page _____

3. What is the world record for the mile run? _____
   Source _____ Page _____

4. What is the first sentence of Lincoln's Emancipation
   Proclamation? _____
   Source _____ Page _____

5. Which country leads in the production of cotton? _____
   Source _____ Page _____

6. What is the average summer temperature of Juneau,
   Alaska? _____
   Source _____ Page _____

7. What are two other words that are synonyms for the word *lumber*
   (when used as a verb)? _____
   Source _____ Page _____

8. For how many years are United States senators
   elected? _____
   Source _____ Page _____

9. What is the Dewey Decimal classification of the book
   Blue Barns? _____
   Source _____ Page _____

10. What is another name for the gum tree? _____
    Source _____ Page _____

of 3 to 4 students each. Identify each team by a different number from 1 to 10. Give each team a copy of the prepared set of 10 questions for the first reference hunt. The questions require the students to answer each question and state the source and page number from which the answer came. (See Figure 26.1.) The first group to answer all 10 questions correctly, with the proper page indicated from an acceptable source, is the winner. (The answers to some questions may be found in more than one source.) Reward the students in the winning group by providing them with special class time so that they may prepare the next reference hunt. When the next reference hunt takes place, these students can serve as judges. (*Caution:* Look over the reference hunt questions to be sure that the students' questions are not too difficult for their classmates.)

Student Travel Bureau

Purpose: To provide practice in research and map study skills

Materials: Globes
Road maps
Travel folders and brochures
Various encyclopedias

Procedure:

When the students are studying a unit on maps, or at any other time you desire, arrange the room as a travel bureau. Advertise the class's service much the same as a travel bureau would. If students bring in information about future trips their family will be taking, student travel agents can:

1. Present the traveler with a well-marked road map after studying maps from several companies and after corresponding with state highway departments.
2. List places they may wish to visit along the way.
3. Provide a history of landmarks along the way.
4. Provide other specific information as it is needed.

Thesaurus Puzzles

Purpose: To help students increase their vocabularies through the use of synonyms and antonyms and to use a thesaurus

Materials: Pocket chart
Word cards
Envelopes

Procedure:

Divide the pocket chart into two columns, as shown in Figure 26.2. In the left-hand column, place a list of words that have synonyms or antonyms. Each student is given an envelope of word cards containing synonyms and antonyms of the word list. Each student then selects a word, which is either the synonym or antonym of one of the given words from her envelope, and places her word card in the appropriate slot on the right-hand side of the chart. A more advanced arrangement of this game can be made by using a thesaurus. Given a word in column 1, the students can use the thesaurus to make their own word cards for column 2.

FIGURE 26.2

play white eager rare easy pleasant healthy cleanse guess clear dwarf	

List Completion (for upper grades or junior high school only)

Purpose: To provide practice in the use of the thesaurus

Materials: A thesaurus
Word lists as shown

Procedure:

Provide lists of words for the student to complete as shown.

Directions:

Complete the lists with words that mean almost the same thing.

1. decide	1. erratic	1. charge
2.	2.	2.
3.	3.	3.

1. deck	1. cage	1. charm
2.	2.	2.
3.	3.	3.

Detective

Purpose: To provide practice in locating information and skimming

Materials: Copies of paragraphs from the basal reader, social studies book, or science book the students are using. (From one copy you can make multiple copies of a certain paragraph if you desire.)

Procedure:

Copy a certain paragraph from a book that the student has in her desk. Make sure the paragraph gives enough information to let the reader know from what kind of book it is taken; for example, a paragraph about clouds would be from a science book. Use paragraphs that give a clue that can be found in the table of contents or in the index of the book. Tables and graphs are appropriate if the book has a list of them. Put one of each of these paragraphs, graphs, or tables in an envelope along with a blank sheet of paper. Each student is given an envelope and the assignment to find where the paragraph came from by using the table of contents, index, list of tables and graphs, or appendix. When the student finds the answer (the same paragraph in her textbook), she writes the information on the blank piece of paper and hands it back to you. Number the envelopes and have the student keep records of which envelopes she has completed.

OTHER ABILITIES

CHAPTER 27

Undeveloped Dictionary Skills

RECOGNIZED BY

The student is unable to locate words in a dictionary, use diacritical markings in determining the correct punctuation of words, or find the proper meaning for a word as used in a particular context.

DISCUSSION

In addition to remediating the most common errors listed in the preceding section, the student needs to become proficient in a number of other dictionary skills in order to make the dictionary a useful tool. Following is a list of other skills students should learn.

1. The use of guide words
2. The use of accents
3. The use of syllabication
4. Interpreting phonetic respellings
5. Using cross-references
6. Determining plurals
7. Determining parts of speech
8. Determining verb tense

The dictionary can be a useful tool for independent word analysis. Some students become quite adept at using a dictionary in the second grade; however, most students learn in the third grade, and the skill must be learned no later than the fourth grade.

RECOMMENDATIONS

A. Follow the steps listed for teaching students to locate a word in the dictionary according to alphabetical order. Make sure the students are adept at each skill before beginning the next one.

1. Make sure the student knows the sequence of the letters in the alphabet.
2. Give several letters to be arranged alphabetically: for example, *a, g, d, b, h,* and *m.*
3. Give several words that have different first letters to be arranged alphabetically: for example, *bat, game, calf, dog,* and *man.*

4. Give several words that have the same beginning letters but different second letters to be arranged alphabetically: for example, *pie, pliers, poker,* and *pack.*

5. Give several words that have the same beginning and second letters but different third letters: for example, *pig, pie, pile,* and *picnic.*

B. Explain the purpose of the guide words at the top of the pages in a dictionary. Have the students write the beginning and ending guide words on pages that contain the words they are looking for.

C. Give students two guide words printed at the top of a piece of paper. Then list a number of words and give students a short amount of time to tell whether the words listed would be found on the same page as the two guide words (5 to 7 seconds). Time them and have them place a plus (+) after each word that would come on the same page as *key* and *kick* and a minus (−) after each word that would not come on the same page. This assignment will enable students to learn to use guide words rapidly.

key	**kick**
keyway	+
kill	−
khan	+
kibe	+
kidney	−

D. Teach the use of diacritical markings. Almost all dictionaries contain a pronunciation key at the bottom of each page that serves as a guide for teaching this skill.

E. Give students lists of words that they are not likely to be able to pronounce. Have them look up their phonetic respellings and write them beside each word. Have students then take turns reading the pronunciation of each word and let other students agree or disagree with each pronunciation.

F. Give students lists of words that have their accent in 2 places depending upon the part of speech in which they are used (such as *record* and *research*). Let students look the words up in their dictionaries and inductively decide where like words are usually accented as nouns and where they are usually accented as verbs. Other examples are *combat* and *contract.*

G. Have the students use the dictionary to find the proper meanings for the way in which certain words are used in sentences. Use words that are clearly defined by the context of the sentences. Have them write the definitions and then use the words with the same meanings in other sentences.

GAMES AND EXERCISES

Today's Words

Purpose: To provide practice in the use of the dictionary and to increase vocabulary

Materials: A dictionary for each student
Procedure:

Each morning place three or four new words on the chalkboard. Use words that the students have not previously studied. Later in the day, ask the students questions using the new words. For example, "Michael, does *pollution* affect our city?"

Synonym Race

Purpose: To provide practice in using the dictionary to find synonyms. This assignment will increase the student's vocabulary and improve his comprehension in silent reading.

Materials: A basal reader or other reading material
A dictionary for each student
Procedure:

You select sentences from the current reading lesson that include words you wish the students to study. Write these sentences on the board, underlining the words for which the class is to look up synonyms. The students race to see who can supply the most synonyms from their dictionaries.

The starfish does not *please* him.

1. satisfy   3. attract
2. amuse   4. gratify

Water ran in a puddle all over his *clean* house.

1. pure   3. unsoiled
2. spotless   4. immaculate

Written Directions

Purpose: To provide practice in following directions and in the use of the dictionary

Materials: A dictionary for each student in the game
A set of cards or pieces of paper with directions written on them

Procedure:

Give each student a piece of paper on which there is a set of directions. Be sure that the directions are simple, but also include at least one new word that the student will need to find in the dictionary before he can follow the directions. As the students find the meanings of words they have looked up in the dictionary, they can then take turns pantomiming the action described by the directions. The other students try to guess what they are doing and try to guess the word or a synonym for it. If they guess a synonym for a new word, then both the word and the synonym may be written by each student. This practice will help the whole class to remember the meanings of new words. Some examples of directions for the game are:

1. Pretend you are a vagabond.
2. Pretend you are wicked.
3. Pretend you have a halo.

Categories

Purpose: To provide practice on word meaning

Materials: Manila envelopes
Cards with words on them that the students do not know well
8½″ × 11″ paper or tagboard

Procedure:

At the top of a number of sheets of tagboard write three categories in which words may fall (see Figure 27.1). Place each sheet of tagboard in a manila envelope along with approximately 30 words that will fit one of the categories listed. Pass the envelopes out to the students and have them use their dictionaries to group the words on the small word cards under the proper

FIGURE 27.1

What animals do	Things that grow	Things that are not alive
fight	trees	rocks
run	cats	books
play	people	paper
jump	weeds	chalk
eat	frogs	chairs
sleep	elephants	pencils
walk	flowers	magnets

FIGURE 27.2

goodness	stoop	helpfulness	waning	amiability
kind	philanthropy	senile	cambered	knobby
bias	hooked	charitable	inelegant	arch
vulgar	elder	unsmooth	look	rough
aged	rippling	bowlike	chunky	curved
elderly	choppy	geriatrics	turn	

BENT	COARSE	BENEVOLENCE	OLD

categories. Number the envelopes and have the students keep a list of the envelopes that they have completed.

Matching Word Meanings

Purpose: To increase vocabulary through the use of the dictionary or thesaurus

Materials: A word sheet similar to the one shown in Figure 27.2
A dictionary or thesaurus for each student

Procedure:

Have the students place words from the word list under the capitalized word that would be the best category for them. (You may wish to have students work in pairs. This affords them the opportunity to learn from each other.)

CHAPTER 28

Written Recall Limited by Spelling Ability

RECOGNIZED BY

The student is unable to spell enough words correctly when engaging in purposeful writing.

DISCUSSION

It is important to distinguish spelling from reading. Reading ability is far more important and may be enhanced through the teaching of generalizations that are not necessarily helpful in spelling. Reading proceeds from symbols to sound (the student sees the symbols and must translate them into meaningful sound), while spelling proceeds from sound to symbols (the student knows the sound of the word she wants to spell and must think of and produce the appropriate symbols that represent that word in writing). Unfortunately, many spelling series confuse these language processes and ask students to apply phonics generalizations to spelling. Such generalizations are not always helpful. The English words most frequently misspelled by nearly all students are those words that are exceptions to the rules of phonics. Therefore, it is usually most helpful to teach students to spell correctly those words that appear most frequently in writing. Although the English language consists of several hundred thousand different words, the following eight words represent 18% of all the words used in writing: *the, of, and, a, to, in, is,* and *you.* The 100 highest-frequency words account for 60%, and 1,000 words make up nearly 90% of the words used in daily writing. Yet spelling programs may present students with more than 10,000 words.[1]

Discovering that a student makes a great number of mistakes in spelling is not difficult for the teacher. There is a reasonably high correlation between reading and spelling ability. Most good readers are good spellers and most poor readers are poor spellers. However, it is estimated that about 2% of the population are good readers but poor spellers. It appears that students who are good spellers but poor readers are rare.

A student who is not able to spell correctly as many words as would be normal for her age/grade level should be taught a mastery list of the most commonly used words. If the student must cut down on the total number of words learned, then the words sacrificed should be those of less utility. Be sure that in all subject matter you emphasize spelling. This strategy will help in motivating the students to improve their spelling and will give them the feeling that it is important to spell correctly all the time and not just during the spelling period. Indeed, spelling should not be viewed as a subject, but rather as a skill that will enable students to be more effective writers. Research on the effectiveness of various techniques for teaching spelling suggests that:

1. It is not helpful to group and teach words based on phonic generalizations or structural analysis.
2. It is not helpful to teach students to spell words that are introduced as new vocabulary words in reading or content area subjects.
3. It is not helpful to teach too many spelling rules.
4. It is not helpful to color-code parts of words.
5. It is not helpful for students to spell words through an oral presentation, such as a spelling bee.
6. It is helpful if the words taught are words that the students already know the meaning of and that appear on high-frequency lists.
7. It is better to have the student focus on learning the whole word rather than learning to spell the word by focusing on syllables or other parts.
8. It is helpful when students write the word frequently in the context of sentences or stories, rather than writing the word over and over in isolation.
9. It is best to teach only those spelling rules that apply to a great number of words and have few exceptions. It is usually most helpful to teach these rules inductively.
10. It is best to have students use many modalities (such as auditory, visual, and kinesthetic) when learning to spell words.

RECOMMENDATIONS

A. Use the following procedure to teach spelling words:
1. Be sure the student is looking at you.
2. Pronounce the word clearly, then have the student pronounce it.
3. Use the word in a sentence and have the student use it in a different sentence.
4. Write the word on the chalkboard (in manuscript or printing, not cursive); or, when working with a single student, write it on a piece of paper. Have the student write the word on a card.
5. Have the student spell the word on her card by pointing to each letter with her pencil, marker, or finger while she says it.
6. The student can use the card for further study. These cards should be kept in a file such as a shoebox.

B. Keep increasing the spelling vocabulary by adding previously missed words to new lists as well as some words with which students are more familiar. Most students can learn more words than those normally assigned to them in a spelling book.

C. Teaching the following spelling rules will be helpful to some students; however, keep in mind that there will be numerous exceptions to rules in the English language. Whenever possible, teach spelling rules inductively. An example of teaching rules inductively would be to list a number of words that exemplify a particular generalization and then let students develop the rule for themselves. This will take time, but students are more likely to remember the rules. Also, it is better to show students certain exceptions to a rule when they learn it than to let them discover exceptions for themselves. At least make clear that there will be exceptions to nearly all of the rules:

1. Write *ie* when the sound is /ee/, except after *c*, or when sounded as /a/ as in *neighbor* and *weigh*. Examples: *chief, relief;* and the exception *receive.*

2. When the prefixes *il-, im-, in-, un-, dis-, mis-,* and *over-* are added to a word, the spelling of the original word remains the same. Examples: *il-* + *literate* = *illiterate; un-* + *forgettable* = *unforgettable; over-* + *active* = *overactive.*

3. When the suffixes *-ness* and *-ly* are added to a word, the spelling of the original word remains the same. Examples: *mean* + *-ness* = *meanness; final* + *-ly* = *finally.*

4. When a word ends in a consonant + *y,* change the *y* to *i* before adding all suffixes except those beginning with *i.* Examples: *plenty* + *-ful* = *plentiful; happy* + *-ness* = *happiness; study* + *-ing* = *studying.*

5. Drop the final *e* before a suffix beginning with a vowel. Examples: *care* + *-ing* = *caring, write* + *-ing* = *writing.* (Exceptions: *noticeable, courageous, dyeing. Dyeing* is spelled as it is to prevent confusion with *dying.*)

6. Keep the final *e* in a suffix beginning with a consonant. Examples: *care* + *-ful* = *careful; care* + *-less* = *careless.* (An exception is *argue* + *-ment* = *argument.*)

7. In one-syllable words that end in a single consonant + a single vowel, and in two-syllable words that are accented on the last syllable and end in a single consonant + a single vowel, the final consonant should be doubled when adding a suffix beginning with a vowel. Examples: *fanning, beginning.*

Note: Some of the rules noted here are very difficult for even good spellers to comprehend. Keep in mind that not all students learn effectively by the use of rules.

D. Make lists of common prefixes and suffixes, as well as families of sounds. (See Appendices C-2 and C-5.)

E. Teach students how to use the dictionary to locate unfamiliar words. Practice this usage on difficult words that can be found by the sounds of the first few letters. Discuss possible spellings for certain words and sounds. Also explain the use of the diacritical markings in the dictionary.

F. Insist that your students proofread their written work. Also, encourage students to exchange papers and proofread each others' written work. The habit of proofreading is very important for nearly all forms of writing and future student assignments.

G. Allow students to correct their own papers after taking a spelling test. Some students are much more adept at correcting their own work than other students are. You will need to make periodic checks to determine whether the students are having difficulty finding and correcting their own errors.

ENDNOTE

1. Sitton, R. (1990). A turning point: Three critical connections in the spelling curriculum for the nineties. *California Reader, 23,* 11–14.

INFORMATIONAL APPENDICES

APPENDIX A-1

Scope and Sequence
of Reading Skills

PURPOSE

The purpose of the reading scope and sequence chart is to help teachers of reading recognize the points at which typical basal reader programs have historically presented certain reading skills. Use this chart with caution. Not all students learn to read by acquiring the same set of reading skills in the same order. Some students learn to read quite well with the mastery of only a few of the various skills listed.

FORMAT

Figure A-1.2 lists the various reading skills by the grade levels at which they were presented by the authors of six popular basal reading series. This information may be helpful for teachers in determining what skills generally should have been mastered by most students at each grade level, as well as what skills students should master during any particular year. For each skill, the diagonally striped box on the chart indicates the point at which the skill should have been mastered by students who are making good progress in decoding. The total number of shaded boxes on the chart indicates the range of grade levels at which the skill was taught in the various basal readers. (In some cases, as the chart will show, certain skills are taught in some basals *after* mastery of the same skill is expected in the majority of basals. This is discussed under "Rules and Notations".)

DESIGNATION OF LEVELS

Levels are designated in the scope and sequence chart as follows: below 1.3 equals readiness or kindergarten; 1.3 equals preprimer; 1.6 equals primer; 1.9 equals first reader (or end of first grade); 2.5 equals mid-second grade; 2.9 equals end of second grade; 3.5 equals mid-third grade; 3.9 equals end of third grade; 4.9 equals end of fourth grade; 5.9 equals end of fifth grade; and 6.9 equals end of sixth grade. Note that past the third grade, levels are not split, but are listed only as 4.9, 5.9, and 6.9. Most basal reader companies provide only one book per grade level past the third grade.

DEVELOPMENT

The scope and sequence chart was developed by determining the point at which six major publishers of basal readers presented each of the skills listed. The publishers were: Macmillan; Houghton Mifflin; Economy; Ginn; Harcourt Brace Jovanovich; and Scott, Foresman. (The basals used were not necessarily the most recent basals published by each company. This is because some of the more recent basals purposely made an effort *not* to present the reading skills in a systematic way.) For each skill used in the basals, a matrix was developed as follows:

FIGURE A-1.1

Skill	Economy	Ginn	Harcourt Brace Jovanovich	Houghton Mifflin	Macmillan	Scott, Foresman	Consensus
fl blend	1.3	1.6	1.6	1.3	1.3	1.3	1.6
soft *c*	1.3	1.9	1.3	1.3	1.3	1.3	1.3

Note that four of the six series examined taught the *fl* blend at the preprimer (1.3) level. However, since two did not teach it until the primer (1.6) level, the designation of 1.6 was used. On the other hand, with the soft *c* sound, five of the six series taught it by the end of the preprimer (1.3) level. Since only one company was in disagreement, the 1.3 designation was used.

RULES AND NOTATIONS

In developing the scope and sequence chart, the following rules and notations were generally observed:

1. When only one company was in disagreement with the others, the designation of that company was ignored.
2. When two companies taught the skill after the others, the later designation of these two companies appears.
3. The total number of shaded boxes on the chart indicates the *range* of grade levels at which the skill was taught in the various basal readers. For example, following the *sc* sound is a range of 1.3 to 2.5. This means that one or more series taught the skill as early as preprimer (1.3), while one or more did not teach it until the 2.5 level.
4. Following some ranges the word *varies* appears, such as with the *sn* blend. This means that the series were in considerable disagreement about the level at which the skill was taught.

5. Following other ranges just as great as for the *sn* blend, the word *varies* does not appear. In this case it means that, although the range varied a great deal, most of the series were in general agreement even though the overall range was great. In such cases, it was usually a case of one series varying considerably from the others.

6. A skill was generally not listed if it appeared in only one series.

7. If a skill was listed in only two series, then the words *2 only* appear following the shaded boxes that represent the range for that skill.

8. Where the range is limited to only one grade level, it means that all six series, or all series in which that skill appeared, were in agreement as to when it was taught.

9. The designations *K* (for kindergarten) and *R* (for readiness) were both treated as prior to 1.3.

10. Some graphemes, such as *oo,* stand for two phonemes (for example, the /oo/ in *book* and the /oo/ in *moon*). Where this was the case, a word representing each phoneme appears beside that grapheme. Note the word *book* beside one *oo* and the word *moon* beside the other.

11. Only a range is given for recognition of suffixes and prefixes. This is because the six series varied so widely that no one meaningful point could be designated.

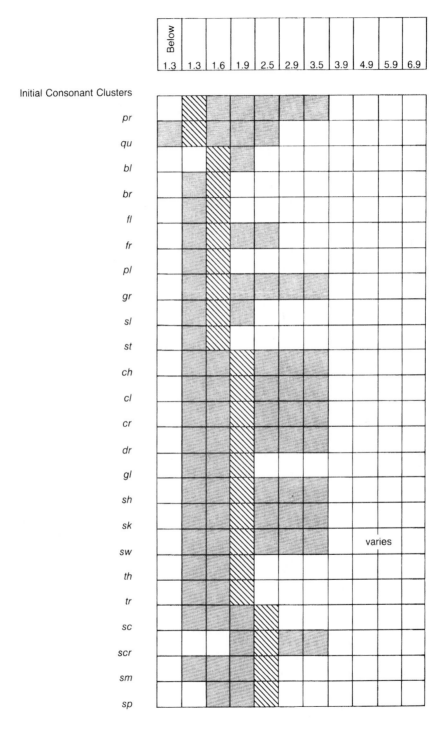

	Below 1.3	1.3	1.6	1.9	2.5	2.9	3.5	3.9	4.9	5.9	6.9

Initial Consonant Clusters

pr
qu
bl
br
fl
fr
pl
gr
sl
st
ch
cl
cr
dr
gl
sh
sk
sw
th
tr
sc
scr
sm
sp

varies

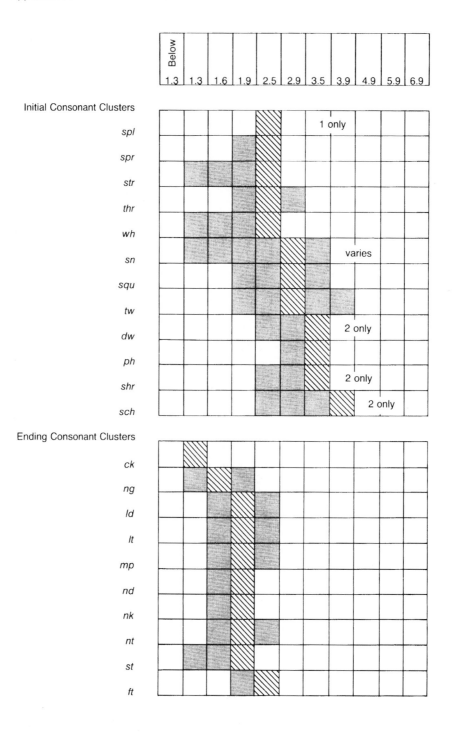

Initial Consonant Clusters

spl

spr

str

thr

wh

sn

squ

tw

dw

ph

shr

sch

Ending Consonant Clusters

ck

ng

ld

lt

mp

nd

nk

nt

st

ft

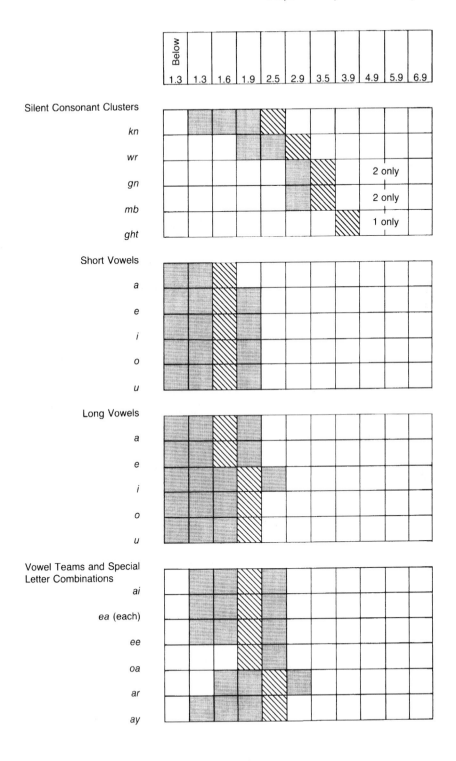

Vowel Teams and Special
Letter Combinations

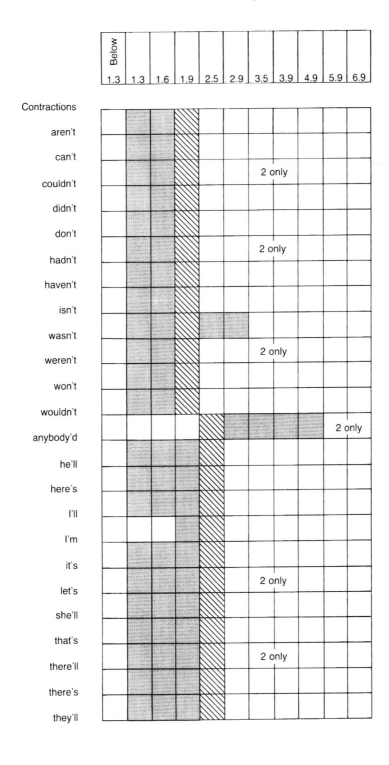

	Below 1.3	1.3	1.6	1.9	2.5	2.9	3.5	3.9	4.9	5.9	6.9

Contractions

aren't

can't
        2 only

couldn't

didn't

don't
        2 only

hadn't

haven't

isn't

wasn't
        2 only

weren't

won't

wouldn't
        2 only

anybody'd

he'll

here's

I'll

I'm

it's
        2 only

let's

she'll

that's
        2 only

there'll

there's

they'll

Prefixes (Recognition Only)

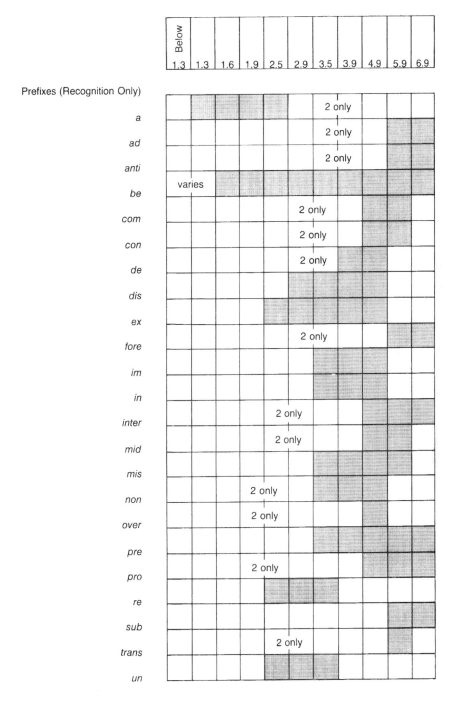

	Below 1.3	1.3	1.6	1.9	2.5	2.9	3.5	3.9	4.9	5.9	6.9
a		▓	▓	▓	▓		2 only				
ad							2 only			▓	▓
anti							2 only			▓	▓
be	varies	▓	▓	▓	▓	▓	▓	▓	▓	▓	
com						2 only			▓	▓	
con						2 only			▓		
de						2 only		▓	▓		
dis					▓	▓	▓				
ex					▓	▓					
fore						2 only				▓	▓
im							▓	▓	▓		
in							▓	▓	▓		
inter					2 only				▓	▓	
mid					2 only				▓		
mis							▓	▓	▓		
non					2 only		▓	▓			
over					2 only			▓			
pre							▓	▓	▓	▓	▓
pro					2 only				▓	▓	▓
re					▓	▓	▓				
sub										▓	▓
trans					2 only				▓		
un					▓	▓	▓				

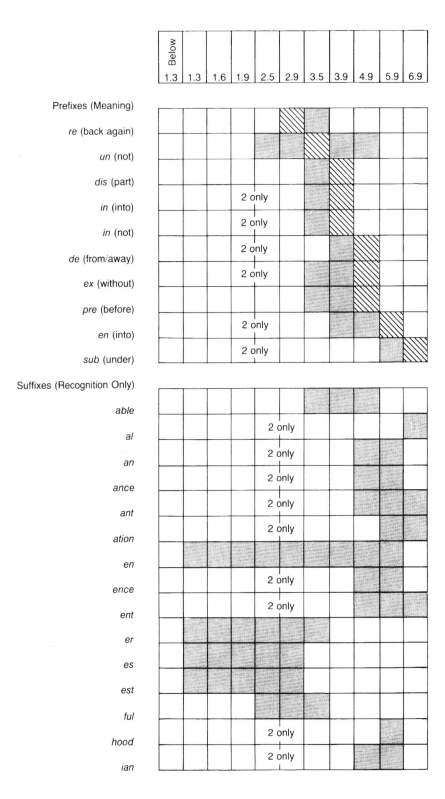

Suffixes (Recognition Only)

	Below 1.3	1.3	1.6	1.9	2.5	2.9	3.5	3.9	4.9	5.9	6.9
ible									■	■	■
ic									■	■	■
ion							■	■	■	■	
ish							■	■	■		
ist						2 only					■
ity											■
ive											■
less					■	■	■				
ly			■	■	■	■					
ment							■	■	■		
ness								■	■	■	
or						■	■	■	■	■	
ous							■	■			
ship						2 only				■	
some						2 only					■
th				2 only		■	■	■			
tion					■	■	■	■	■		
ty			2 only		■	■	■	■	■		
ure				2 only						■	■
ward				2 only						■	■
y						■	■				

	Below 1.3	1.3	1.6	1.9	2.5	2.9	3.5	3.9	4.9	5.9	6.9

Rules for *y*

1. *y* at the end of a multisyllable word
2. *y* at the end of a single-syllable word

Vowel Rules

1. A single vowel in a closed syllable is usually short.

2. A single vowel at the end of a word is usually long.

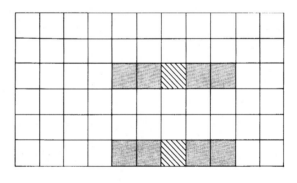

Syllable Principles

1. When two like consonants stand between two vowels, the word is usually divided between the two consonants.

2. When two unlike consonants stand between two vowels, the word is usually divided between the consonants.

Syllable Principles

3. Prefixes and suffixes are usually separate syllables.

4. When a word ends in a consonant and *le*, the consonant usually begins the last syllable.

5. Divide between compound words.

6. Do not divide between letters in a consonant digraph or consonant blend.

Accent Generalizations

1. In two-syllable words, the first syllable is usually accented.

2. In inflected or derived forms, the primary accent usually falls on the root word.

3. If two vowels are together in the last syllable of a word, it is a clue to an accented final syllable.

Accent Generalizations

4. If there are two unlike consonants within a word, the syllable before the double consonant is usually accented.

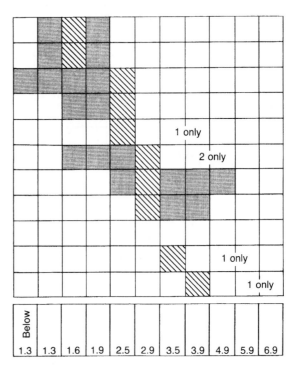

Dictionary Skills

1. Learning the alphabet in order
2. Alphabetizing letters
3. Alphabetizing words
4. Alphabetizing words to second letter
5. Selecting word meaning from context
6. Alphabetizing words to third letter
7. Using guide words
8. Interpreting syllables
9. Estimating location of a word in the dictionary
10. Interpreting accent or stress

Dictionary Skills

11. Interpreting pronunciation key
12. Using first and second spellings
13. Learning about parts of speech
14. Using cross-reference
15. Learning about word origin

A Phonics Primer

SINGLE CONSONANTS

b	bear	*l*	lake	*t*	turtle
d	dog	*m*	money	*v*	vase
f	face	*n*	nose	*w*	wagon
h	hen	*p*	pear	*y*	yellow
j	jug	*q*	queen	*z*	zebra
k	king	*r*	rat		

The following consonants have two or more sounds:

c	cat	*g*	goat	*s*	six	*x*	xylophone
c	city	*g*	germ	*s*	is	*x*	exist
				s	sure	*x*	box

When *g* is followed by *e, i,* or *y,* it often takes the soft sound of *j,* as in *gentle* and *giant.* If it is not followed by these letters, it usually takes the hard sound, as illustrated in such words as *got* and *game.*

When *c* is followed by *e, i,* or *y,* it usually takes the soft sound heard in *cent.* If it is not followed by these letters, it usually takes the hard sound heard in *come.*

Qu usually has the sound of *kw;* however, in some words such as *bouquet,* it has the sound of *k.*

CONSONANT BLENDS

Beginning

bl	blue	*pr*	pretty	*tw*	twin
br	brown	*sc*	score	*wr*	wrench
cl	clown	*sk*	skill	*sch*	school
cr	crown	*sl*	slow	*scr*	screen
dr	dress	*sm*	small	*shr*	shrink
dw	dwell	*sn*	snail	*spl*	splash
fl	flower	*sp*	spin	*spr*	spring
fr	from	*st*	story	*squ*	squash
gl	glue	*sw*	swan	*str*	string
gr	grape	*tr*	tree	*thr*	throw
pl	plate				

Ending

ld	wild
mp	lamp
nd	wind
nt	went
rk	work
sk	risk

CONSONANT DIGRAPHS

ch	chute	*sh*	ship
ch	choral	*th*	three
ch	church	*th*	that
gh	cough	*wh*	which
ph	graph	*wh*	who

VOWEL SOUNDS

Short Sounds   Long Sounds

a	bat	*a*	rake
e	bed	*e*	jeep
i	pig	*i*	kite
o	lock	*o*	rope
u	duck	*u*	mule

W is sometimes used as a vowel, as in the *aw, ew* and *ow* diphthongs (see the following list). *W* is usually used as a vowel on word endings and as a consonant at the beginning of words.

Y is usually a consonant when it appears at the beginning of a word and a vowel in any other position.

Three consonants usually affect or control the sounds of some, or all, of the vowels when they follow these vowels within a syllable. They are *r, w,* and *l* (sometimes known as <u>R</u>eally <u>W</u>eird <u>L</u>etters).

r	w	l
car	law	all
her	few	bell
dirt	now	
word		
fur		

VOWEL DIGRAPHS (Most common phonemes only)

<u>ai</u> pain
<u>ay</u> hay
<u>ea</u> each or weather   (Other phonemes are common for *ea*.)
<u>ee</u> meet
ei weight or either   (Other phonemes are common for *ei*.)
ie piece   (Other phonemes are common for *ie*.)
<u>oa</u> oats
oo book or moon
ou tough (digraph) or house (diphthong)
ow low (digraph) or cow (diphthong)

Of the various consonant digraphs, those that are most regular in their pronunciation are underlined here and are represented by the phrase: M*ai*ds m*ay* *ea*t *oa*k tr*ee*s. (Unfortunately, *ea* does have many exceptions!)

DIPHTHONGS (Pronounced: dif' thongs.)

au	haul*	*oi*	soil
au	hawk*	*ou*	trout
ew	few	*ow*	cow
ey	they*	*oy*	boy

*In a diphthong, both of the vowel letters are heard and they make a gliding sound, which is heard most easily in words like *cow* and *boy*. Some speakers may hear the examples of *au, aw,* and *ey* given here as digraphs (one sound) rather than diphthongs.

Suggestions for Interviewing Parents of Disabled Readers

Interviewing the parent or parents of a student with reading difficulties is important for several reasons. In the interview you often will be able to discover certain things that parents may hesitate to put in writing. For example, in an interview parents often will give information concerning *their* perception of their child's capabilities. If the parents have other children, they will be able to give important information on their feelings concerning the child's ability to learn compared with their other children. This will provide you with important information, not only about the child but also about the parents' feelings toward the child's capabilities. It is important that parents believe that their child has the ability to learn and that they are willing to do their part in carrying out a program of remediation.

Parents can also provide accurate information on when they first noticed the reading problem. For example, if the child has had problems from the very beginning of school, it would indicate that the reading difficulties may be severe and may take longer to remediate. However, if the child suddenly started having reading problems at a later grade level, then it might indicate that the child has developed some emotional problem because of a divorce, a death in the family, or some other traumatic event. The development of a reading problem might also indicate the onset of a physical problem such as a need for eyeglasses, a hearing difficulty, or a side effect to a prescribed medication.

The initial interview should also reveal, to some extent, whether counseling is needed. The parents may need guidance to help them make the child feel confident in his ability to learn. The parents, perhaps unintentionally, may have given their child the impression that he does not have the ability to learn. The parent interview can also provide important information on whether the parents have been consistent in dealing with the child. For example, do the parents tell the child to do something and then not carry through with requiring it to be done, or is the child allowed to find excuses for not performing certain tasks?

In the initial parent interview, it is also important that you get a verbal commitment from the parents that they are willing to do such things as the following:

1. Be prompt and responsible in providing transportation to tutoring sessions, if required.

2. Follow up in scheduling appointments for physical examinations, including vision and hearing examinations, if necessary.

3. Set aside a specific time each day when the student is required to do homework assignments or recreational reading.

4. Provide a reading environment in which the student sees his parents reading.

5. Provide a quiet place where the student can concentrate on homework or recreational reading without being interrupted by brothers or sisters or without interference from a television or telephone.

6. Check to see that homework is done.

7. Take the student to the library and learn techniques for selecting books to be read for pleasure.

APPENDICES FOR LOCATING
READING DIFFICULTIES

APPENDIX B-1

Code for Marking in Oral Diagnosis

This section, as explained in the section "How to Use This Book," is designed to teach you a shorthand method of marking oral reading errors. You should find it helpful to read the following information, which should then enable you to use this code effectively.

It is recommended that you tape-record the student's oral reading. In most cases students do not mind being recorded while reading orally. If you record the reading, you may replay it a number of times, if necessary. This will ensure that your original coding was correct or will give you a chance to make any needed changes from the original reading. Also, if you save the recording, you can compare it to a student's later reading of the same material. This is often an excellent way to document a student's progress. By listening to both the earlier and later reading of the same passages, the student, the student's parents, and you can hear noticeable growth in the student's reading ability over time.

PREPARATION FOR USING THE CODE
FOR MARKING IN ORAL DIAGNOSIS

Familiarize yourself with the shorthand method of marking students' oral reading errors before attempting to use it. There are only eight items or eight notations that are to be made to indicate errors or characteristics that readers are likely to make in oral reading. Of these eight items, only the first six are actually used to determine whether the student read a selected passage at the independent, instructional, or frustration level. Each of these notations, of course, denotes a particular kind of error or characteristic of the reader. Once they have been coded and studied, you will find that they will become a blueprint for instruction.

Study each of the eight notations, so you understand what is meant by such things as an omission, a reversal, a repetition, and the like. If you were to analyze the coded passage that follows using the code for marking in oral diagnosis, you would find the following types of errors made by the students who read this demonstration passage:

> **Tom drove his automobile to the county fair. He saw no place to park. He drove up and down between the rows of cars. Finally he decided to go home.**

1. Circle all omissions.
2. Insert with a caret (^) all insertions.

3. Draw a line through words for which substitutions or mispronunciations were made and write the substitution or mispronunciation over the word. It really doesn't matter whether the words missed were substitutions, mispronunciations, or reversals. If the student reads too fast to write in all mispronunciations, draw a line through the word and write a *P* over the word for partial mispronunciation or a *G* over the word for gross mispronunciation.

4. Use parentheses ( ) to enclose the words for which the student needed help; that is, words that you pronounced for the student if he was unable to figure it out on his own after about 5 seconds.

5. Use a wavy line to indicate repetitions.

6. Make a check (✔) over the words that were self-corrected.

7. Use an arched line to connect words in which the student disregarded punctuation. (See line connecting *fair* and *he* in Figure B-1.1.)

8. Draw two vertical lines (❘ ❘) to indicate a pause before words.

FIGURE B-1.1

Line 1: The student inserted *new* between the words *his* and *automobile*.

Line 1: The student omitted the word *county* between *the* and *fair*.

Line 1: The student did not stop or pause for the period at the end of the sentence ending with the word *fair* and the next sentence beginning with the word *He*.

Line 1: The student called the word *saw* as *was*. This could be called a substitution; however, in this case some examiners would refer to it as a reversal or inversion, since *was* is *saw* spelled backwards. For purposes of diagnosis, what you choose to call the error is inconsequential.

Line 1: The student made no attempt or did not say the word *place* after a period of time (usually 5 seconds) and was, therefore, told or given aid with the word *place*.

Line 1: The student read the word *park* as *pack* and then corrected it without help from the teacher. Since the student self-corrected the original mistake, this would not be scored as an error in analyzing the student's reading of the passage.

Line 2: The student repeated the word *He* at the beginning of the sentence. Repetitions *are* counted as errors.

Line 2: The student paused before the word *drove* for a longer period of time than the scorer believed was normal; however, the period of time was less than 5 seconds, or *drove* would have had parentheses ( ) around it to indicate that the student had been told the word. Pauses of less than 5 seconds, while marked, are not scored as errors.

Line 2: The student repeated the phrase *up and down.* All three of the repeated words count as only one total error.

Line 2: The student substituted the word *among* for the word *between.*

Line 2: The student grossly mispronounced the word *Finally.* In some cases, the teacher might note the improper pronunciation since this might be helpful in analyzing the student's problem with decoding. However, when the student reads too rapidly to write in the improper pronunciation, the teacher usually writes a *G* over the word, indicating that it was grossly mispronounced. This means that the pronunciation was so far off that it did not even sound like the original word. If you have recorded the reading, you can indicate the improper pronunciation when you listen to the tape later.

Line 2: The student partially mispronounced the word *decided.* If possible, it is best to write the incorrect mispronunciation of the word over the correct word. This will be helpful in analyzing what the student seems to be doing wrong in attacking new words. However, when the student reads too rapidly for the coder to keep up with the coding, then a *P* over the word means that it was only partially, rather than grossly, mispronounced. In this case, the student might have pronounced the word with a hard *c* or *k* sound. This could also have been quickly indicated by crossing out the *c* and putting a *k* over it.

PRACTICE IN USING THE CODE FOR MARKING IN ORAL DIAGNOSIS

In using the code for marking in oral diagnosis, you will need to duplicate something that the student will be reading orally, so you have a copy that reads the same as the one read by the student. It will be helpful if the copy on which you will be coding is double- or triple-spaced, so you can more easily

FIGURE B-1.2

write in notations on various oral reading errors made by the student. You should then seat the student so you can easily hear him as he reads the passage. Many examiners find that it is best to seat the student kitty-corner to the opposite side of your handedness. In other words, if you are right-handed, you would seat the student diagonally to your left (see Figure B-1.2).

It is a good idea to find a student at a lower grade level who is not a rapid reader when you first begin this procedure since it may become very frustrating to attempt to mark the errors of a student who reads rapidly, especially if the student makes a considerable number of errors.

INTERPRETING A CODED PASSAGE

Once the student has read the passage or has read several passages that are near his high instructional or frustration level, you can begin to interpret the meaning of the various types of errors or miscues. Chapters 2 through 11 deal directly with these kinds of errors. By studying the error pattern, you will often be able to note whether the student has difficulties with the kinds of problems listed in Chapters 12 through 19.

Preparation and Use of Materials for Testing Letter Knowledge

PREPARING FOR THE TEST

Before administering the letter recognition inventory, make multiple copies of the answer sheet on page 249, so you will have one for each student to be tested. Also remove the Letter Stimulus Sheet from page 247 and use rubber cement or tape to fasten it to a 5″ × 8″ card. You may then wish to laminate the card or place it in a plastic sleeve, so it will not become soiled from handling.

SPECIFIC DIRECTIONS FOR GIVING THE LETTER RECOGNITION INVENTORY

Before beginning this test you may first wish to have the student write all of the letters in both uppercase and lowercase. If this is done correctly, then place a plus mark (+) in the blanks by Task 1 on the answer sheet. If they are not all done correctly, you may wish to note exceptions.

A. Give the student the Letter Stimulus Sheet and ask her to read each of the letters in row 1, then row 2, row 3, and so on. Mark them as plus (+) if they are answered correctly, or you may simply wish to place a plus mark (+) in the blanks by Task 2 on the answer sheet to indicate that they were all given correctly. If they are not answered correctly, then write the answer given by the student in each blank. If the student can do this task, stop the test. If she cannot name all of the letters, continue with the following tasks.

B. Show the student the Letter Stimulus Sheet and ask her to point to letters as you name them. Name them in random order from the lowercase letters and then name them in random order from the uppercase letters. Be sure to name all of them, or enough of them so that you are certain the student can identify all letters when they are named. If the student can do this, then place a plus mark (+) in the appropriate blanks by Task 3 on the answer sheet and discontinue the testing. If the student cannot do this task, then note that on Task 3 and continue with the following tasks.

C. Show the student the Letter Stimulus Sheet and ask her to match uppercase letters with lowercase letters; for example, point to the *n* in the lowercase letters and ask the student to point to the *N* from the letters in the uppercase group. You may wish to alternate by first pointing to a letter in the lowercase group and having the student match it with the corresponding letter from the uppercase group. Be sure to do all of the letters, or do enough of them so that you are certain the student can match all letters. If the student can do this, then place a plus mark (+) in the appropriate blank by Task 4 on the answer sheet and discontinue the testing. If the student cannot do this task, then note that on Task 4 and continue with the following task.

D. Show the student the Letter Stimulus Sheet. Point to a letter from row 11 and ask the student to point to another letter that is exactly the same as that letter. Do this with all of the letters: first *b*, then *m*, and so on, until all pairs have been matched. If the student can do this, then place a plus mark (+) in the appropriate blank by Task 5. If the student cannot do this task, then note that on Task 5.

IMPORTANT POINTS TO REMEMBER

When testing for a student's knowledge of the letters, keep in mind that certain tasks concerning letter knowledge are more difficult than others. For example, note that Task 2 is more difficult than Task 3; that is, naming letters in random order from a stimulus sheet is more difficult than pointing to the letters as they are named by the teacher. Likewise, pointing to the letters as they are named by the teacher (Task 3) is more difficult than being asked to identify a lowercase *g* when shown an uppercase *G* (Task 4). Therefore, in giving this test, begin with Task 1 (if you wish), asking the student to write the letters of the alphabet in both uppercase and lowercase. Then the student will do Task 2. If she can do that task, then there is no need to do Task 3. If the student cannot do Task 3, then she should be asked to do Task 4, and so on.

FIGURE B-2.1

LETTER STIMULUS SHEET

1.	e	n	i	p	c
2.	v	x	a	j	z
3.	b	o	s	u	q
4.	k	y	f	l	d
5.	g	t	m	r	h	w

6.	C	J	P	H	K
7.	O	G	N	Q	D
8.	L	R	B	Z	Y
9.	A	S	F	M	V
10.	I	W	T	X	U	E

11.   b   m   g   d   r   p   m   b   g   r   p   d   m   o

LETTER KNOWLEDGE ANSWER SHEET

STUDENT'S NAME ——————— SCHOOL ————————————

DATE ——————————————————

TESTER ——————————————

See directions.

1. e ————— n ————— i ————— p ————— c —————
2. v ————— x ————— a ————— j ————— z —————
3. b ————— o ————— s ————— u ————— q —————
4. k ————— y ————— f ————— l ————— d —————
5. g ————— t ————— m ————— r ————— h ————— w —————
6. C ————— J ————— P ————— H ————— K —————
7. O ————— G ————— N ————— Q ————— D —————
8. L ————— R ————— B ————— Z ————— Y —————
9. A ————— S ————— F ————— M ————— V —————
10. I ————— W ————— T ————— X ————— U ————— E —————

TASK 1: ——— Student can write all lowercase letters correctly

——— Student can write all uppercase letters correctly

Exceptions noted: ————————————————————————

————————————————————————————————————

TASK 2: ——— Student can name all lowercase letters correctly

——— Student can name all uppercase letters correctly

TASK 3: ——— Student can identify all lowercase letters when named

——— Student can identify all uppercase letters when named

——— Student cannot identify all lowercase letters when named

——— Student cannot identify all uppercase letters when named

Exceptions noted: ————————————————————————

————————————————————————————————————

TASK 4: ——— Student can match all upper- and lowercase letters

——— Student cannot match all upper- and lowercase letters

Exceptions noted: ————————————————————————

————————————————————————————————————

TASK 5: ——— Student can match a letter with another one that is exactly the same

——— Student cannot match letters that are exactly the same

Exceptions noted: ————————————————————————

————————————————————————————————————

APPENDIX B-3

Preparation and Use of Materials for the Quick Check for Basic Sight Words

PREPARING FOR THE TEST

Before administering the Quick Check for Basic Sight Word Knowledge, make multiple copies of page 255, which is the answer sheet to be used in quickly assessing students' knowledge of basic sight words. Also remove the stimulus sheet on page 253. This page can then be placed on a surface such as tagboard and fastened with rubber cement or transparent tape. After it is cemented in place, you may wish to laminate it or place it in a plastic sleeve, to keep it from becoming soiled from handling.

SPECIFIC DIRECTIONS FOR TESTING BASIC SIGHT WORDS

Have your answer sheet ready and place the stimulus sheet in front of the student. Ask the student to read the words in the same order as they are numbered. Tell the student to read each word carefully and skip any word that is not known, or instruct the student to say "I don't know" when an unknown word is encountered. Mark the answer sheet as suggested in the directions. If the student pauses more than approximately one second before saying a word, count it as wrong.

IMPORTANT POINTS TO REMEMBER

The Quick Check for Basic Sight Word Knowledge is a quick way to test students' knowledge of basic sight words. If there is any doubt in your mind as to whether a student should be given an entire basic sight word test, you may give students this list first. If the student does not miss any words on this test, then he may not need to take the entire basic sight word test. However, if a student misses even one word on this list, he should be given the entire basic word test.

The Quick Check for Basic Sight Word Knowledge was developed by giving Ekwall's basic sight word list to 500 students in grades 2 through 6, using a tachistoscopic presentation. One hundred students were tested at each of these five grade levels. A computer analysis then listed, in ascending order of difficulty, the words students most often missed. From this list 36 words were chosen. The first few words are the easier ones. However, following the first few easier words are the ones students tended to miss more often. The list also includes words commonly confused by many students. When giving this test, you should make sure that the student is exposed to each word briefly (approximately one second). Given more time, the student may use word-attack skills instead of his knowledge of basic sight words. A student who misses even one word in this test should be given the basic sight word tests that appear in Appendix B-4.

Quick Check for Basic Sight Word Knowledge

1.	I	13.	both	25.	every
2.	the	14.	then	26.	ran
3.	was	15.	shall	27.	another
4.	down	16.	upon	28.	leave
5.	these	17.	while	29.	should
6.	saw	18.	draw	30.	there
7.	than	19.	thing	31.	sure
8.	start	20.	run	32.	always
9.	this	21.	thank	33.	carry
10.	want	22.	once	34.	present
11.	those	23.	wish	35.	such
12.	went	24.	think	36.	hurt

Quick Check for Basic Sight Word Knowledge

Answer Sheet

Name_____   Date_____

School_____   Tester_____

Directions: As the student reads the words from the stimulus sheet, mark those words read correctly with a plus (+) and those read incorrectly with a minus (−) or write in the word substituted. If the student says he or she does not know an answer, then mark it with a question mark (?). (If a student misses any words on this test, then he or she should be given the full list of basic sight words.)

1. I _____	19. thing _____
2. the _____	20. run _____
3. was _____	21. thank _____
4. down _____	22. once _____
5. these _____	23. wish _____
6. saw _____	24. think _____
7. than _____	25. every _____
8. start _____	26. ran _____
9. this _____	27. another _____
10. want _____	28. leave _____
11. those _____	29. should _____
12. went _____	30. there _____
13. both _____	31. sure _____
14. then _____	32. always _____
15. shall _____	33. carry _____
16. upon _____	34. present _____
17. while _____	35. such _____
18. draw _____	36. hurt _____

Preparation and Use of Materials for Testing Basic Sight Words and Phrases

PREPARING FOR THE TEST

Before administering these tests, make multiple copies of pages 261 through 269, the answer sheets to be used in assessing students' knowledge of basic sight words and phrases. You will also need an audio tape recorder and tapes. You will need to prepare flash cards for each of the 220 basic sight words and 143 basic sight word phrases. Your flash cards should be arranged in the same order as the words on the answer sheets.

To do this you may purchase 3″ × 5″ or 4″ × 6″ index cards (either blank or lined) or, if you wish, purchase heavier stock cards in a similar or slightly smaller size. Most school supply stores sell cards ready-made for this purpose in various colors. Also, they often have rounded corners, which makes them last longer. You will need 363 cards, but you should purchase a few more in case you make mistakes preparing the cards.

Once you have selected your cards, look at the lists of words on the answer sheets. Carefully print one word on each flash card, using neat lowercase manuscript printing. An alternative is to use the labelmaking feature of a word-processing program; type all of the words and phrases into the word processor and either print the words and phrases directly onto labels or print the words and phrases onto blank pages and then copy these pages onto labels using a photocopier.

You should also write the list number and the word number on the back of each card. For example, on the back of the first card, *the,* write I-1. (This indicates List I, word 1.) The designation IV-16 would be written on the back of *ride* (List IV, word 16). If your cards ever become mixed up, you will find that it is easy to reassemble them in the correct order if you designate each word on the back as described. You also may wish to use different colored cards for each list.

SPECIFIC DIRECTIONS FOR TESTING BASIC SIGHT WORDS AND PHRASES

Seat the student opposite you and place the microphone near the spot on the table where the cards will be placed after the student has responded to the words on the cards as you flash them. (Make sure the tape recorder is turned on!) Present the cards in the order they appear on the answer sheet. Say to the student: "I am going to show you some words on flash cards and I want you to say them when you see them. I will be flashing the cards quickly, so, if you don't know a word, don't worry about it and go on." Lift off 20 to 30 cards from the ordered stack. At a steady rate of approximately one to two cards per second, flash the cards to the student. Do *not* separate the cards into "right" and "wrong" piles, since this may distract you, upset the student being tested, and confuse the order of the flash cards. Continue flashing the cards until the student does not respond to four or five consecutive words or otherwise indicates an inability to successfully complete the test. If the student appears to be pronouncing most of the words correctly, continue the procedure until all cards are flashed.

After you have completed flashing the cards, you may play back the tape and mark the answer sheet with (+) for correct and (–) for incorrect responses. In scoring, *only the first response counts.* Having mastered a word, the student recognizes it instantly. If the student hesitates, the flashed word is not known *by sight.*

You may test the student's knowledge of basic sight word *phrases* using the procedures described, this time using the list of basic sight word phrases, also presented in this appendix. You may allow up to 2 seconds per phrase when flashing the cards. Each sight word test takes approximately six minutes to administer and score.

IMPORTANT POINTS TO REMEMBER

By examining the prepared lists, you can determine specifically which basic sight words and phrases the student has not mastered. These can then be taught without having to misuse instructional time teaching words or phrases that are already known.

A reasonable criterion for mastery of the entire lists is 90% or better. Even students who know all the basic sight words quite well will often miscall a few words because of the speed of the test. You may wish to recheck missed words or phrases a second time to determine whether the errors resulted from the speed of the test or from the student's lack of knowledge.

You must use judgment in evaluating a student's performance on the sight word tests. Young children may have greater difficulty with a speed of one word per second, although ultimately it is essential that the words be recognized at this rate. Similarly, students with speech difficulties may need an adjustment in the rate of flashing.

The modified Dolch list that appears in this appendix includes the 220 Dolch basic sight words, reordered according to frequency of occurrence as found in a study conducted by William K. Durr.[1] The 220 individual words are divided into 11 sublists of 20 words each for ease of scoring and instruction.

The list is presented based on the assumption that not all students will master all the words. It is therefore reasonable to begin by teaching the words that appear most often.

The phrase list is compiled so that each word from the isolated words list is presented in a phrase. Only 17 new words are added to complete phrases. These are nouns that are all drawn from the preprimer level of a basal series.

A list of basic sight word *sentences* is provided in Appendix C-1. These sentences are derived from the phrase list presented in this appendix. It is not suggested that you use the sentences for testing; however, they are quite helpful in teaching the student to recognize the individual sight words and sight word phrases in context.

ENDNOTE

1. Durr, W. K. (1973). Computer study of high frequency words in popular trade juveniles. *Reading Teacher, 27,* 37–42.

Name ———————————— Date ——————— Scores: (Pretest) ———— /220

School ——————— Tester ——————— (Posttest) ———— /220

Directions: Turn on the tape recorder and place the microphone on the table. Tell the student what you are going to do. Flash the cards to the student at a rate of one to two words per second in the order in which they appear on the list. After you have completed the flashing of the cards, play back the tape and mark the answer sheet with a (+) for correct and a (−) for incorrect responses.

Individual Diagnosis of Dolch Words (Listed in Descending Order of Frequency)   pre ☐ /220   post ☐ /220

LIST I

	pre	post
1. the		
2. to		
3. and		
4. he		
5. a		
6. I		
7. you		
8. it		
9. of		
10. in		
11. was		
12. said		
13. his		
14. that		
15. she		
16. for		
17. on		
18. they		
19. but		
20. had		
*	/20	/20

LIST II

	pre	post
1. at		
2. him		
3. with		
4. up		
5. all		
6. look		
7. is		
8. her		
9. there		
10. some		
11. out		
12. as		
13. be		
14. have		
15. go		
16. we		
17. am		
18. then		
19. little		
20. down		
*	/20	/20

LIST III

	pre	post
1. do		
2. can		
3. could		
4. when		
5. did		
6. what		
7. so		
8. see		
9. not		
10. were		
11. get		
12. them		
13. like		
14. one		
15. this		
16. my		
17. would		
18. me		
19. will		
20. yes		
*	/20	/20

LIST IV

	pre	post
1. big		
2. went		
3. are		
4. come		
5. if		
6. now		
7. long		
8. no		
9. came		
10. ask		
11. very		
12. an		
13. over		
14. your		
15. its		
16. ride		
17. into		
18. just		
19. blue		
20. red		
*	/20	/20

LIST V

	pre	post
1. from		
2. good		
3. any		
4. about		
5. around		
6. want		
7. don't		
8. how		
9. know		
10. right		
11. put		
12. too		
13. got		
14. take		
15. where		
16. every		
17. pretty		
18. jump		
19. green		
20. four		
*	/20	/20

LIST VI

	pre	post
1. away		
2. old		
3. by		
4. their		
5. here		
6. saw		
7. call		
8. after		
9. well		
10. think		
11. ran		
12. let		
13. help		
14. make		
15. going		
16. sleep		
17. brown		
18. yellow		
19. five		
20. six		
*	/20	/20

* Number of words read correctly

LIST VII

	pre	post
1. walk		
2. two		
3. or		
4. before		
5. eat		
6. again		
7. play		
8. who		
9. been		
10. may		
11. stop		
12. off		
13. never		
14. seven		
15. eight		
16. cold		
17. today		
18. fly		
19. myself		
20. round		
*	/20	/20

LIST VIII

	pre	post
1. tell		
2. much		
3. keep		
4. give		
5. work		
6. first		
7. try		
8. new		
9. must		
10. start		
11. black		
12. white		
13. ten		
14. does		
15. bring		
16. goes		
17. write		
18. always		
19. drink		
20. once		
*	/20	/20

LIST IX

	pre	post
1. soon		
2. made		
3. run		
4. gave		
5. open		
6. has		
7. find		
8. only		
9. us		
10. three		
11. our		
12. better		
13. hold		
14. buy		
15. funny		
16. warm		
17. ate		
18. full		
19. those		
20. done		
*	/20	/20

LIST X

	pre	post
1. use		
2. fast		
3. say		
4. light		
5. pick		
6. hurt		
7. pull		
8. cut		
9. kind		
10. both		
11. sit		
12. which		
13. fall		
14. carry		
15. small		
16. under		
17. read		
18. why		
19. own		
20. found		
*	/20	/20

LIST XI

	pre	post
1. wash		
2. show		
3. hot		
4. because		
5. far		
6. live		
7. draw		
8. clean		
9. grow		
10. best		
11. upon		
12. these		
13. sing		
14. together		
15. please		
16. thank		
17. wish		
18. many		
19. shall		
20. laugh		
*	/20	/20

SCORE

LIST	pre	post
I		
II		
III		
IV		
V		
VI		
VII		
VIII		
IX		
X		
XI		
TOTAL		

* Number of words read correctly

Name _____ Date _____ Scores: (Pretest) _____ /143

School _____ Tester _____ (Posttest) _____ /143

Directions: Turn on the tape recorder and place the microphone on the table. Tell the student what you are going to do. Flash the cards to the student at a rate of one to two words per second in the order in which they appear on the list. After you have completed the flashing of the cards, play back the tape and mark the answer sheet with a (+) for correct and a (–) for incorrect responses.

Individual Diagnosis of Sight Word Phrases   pre [/143] post [/143]

LIST I

	pre	post
1. he had to		
2. she said that		
3. to the		
4. you and I		
5. but they said		
6. on a		
7. for his		
8. of that		
9. that was in		
10. it was		
*	/10	/10

LIST II

	pre	post
1. look at him		
2. as little		
3. at all		
4. I have a		
5. have some		
6. there is		
7. down there		
8. then we have		
9. to go		
10. to be there		
11. look up		
12. look at her		
13. we go out		
14. I am		
*	/14	/14

LIST III

	pre	post
1. look at me		
2. can you		
3. a little one		
4. you will see		
5. what is that		
6. my *cat*		
7. I will get		
8. when did he		
9. like this		
10. get them		
11. so you will see		
12. I could		
13. we were		
14. would not		
15. yes, I do		
*	/15	/15

LIST IV

	pre	post
1. a big ride		
2. went into		
3. if I ask		
4. come over with		
5. they went		
6. I am very		
7. there are blue		
8. a long *book*		
9. an *apple*		
10. your red *book*		
11. its *name*		
12. they came		
13. just now		
*	/13	/13

* Number of phrases read correctly

LIST V

	pre	post
1. I take every		
2. the four green		
3. they don't want		
4. right around		
5. a good jump		
6. a pretty *rabbit*		
7. I know how		
8. where can I		
9. the *duck* got		
10. it is about		
11. don't put any		
12. take from		
13. too little		
*	/13	/13

LIST VI

	pre	post
1. ran away		
2. let me help		
3. going to sleep		
4. five yellow *ducks*		
5. the old *turtle*		
6. by their *mother*		
7. call after *six*		
8. the brown *rabbit*		
9. I am well		
10. will think		
11. will make		
12. you saw		
13. here it is		
*	/13	/13

LIST VII

	pre	post
1. we eat		
2. two may walk		
3. on or off		
4. before seven		
5. today is cold		
6. play by myself		
7. don't stop		
8. it is round		
9. who is eight		
10. have never been		
11. can fly again		
*	/11	/11

LIST VIII

	pre	post
1. black and white		
2. start a new		
3. must try once		
4. don't keep much		
5. it does go		
6. always drink *milk*		
7. will bring ten		
8. *Lad* goes		
9. write and tell		
10. work is first		
11. can give it		
*	/11	/11

LIST IX

	pre	post
1. open and find		
2. *Jill* ate the		
3. those are done		
4. is funny		
5. buy us three		
6. this is only		
7. gave a warm		
8. soon we ate		
9. had a full		
10. run and hold		
11. made a big		
12. it is better		
13. our *duck*		
*	/13	/13

LIST X

	pre	post
1. sit with both		
2. you use it		
3. carry a small		
4. the cut hurt		
5. the fast *car*		
6. then the light		
7. which will fall		
8. pull it in		
9. had found		
10. under here		
11. be kind		
12. pick it up		
13. *Bill* can read		
14. my own *bed*		
15. why is it		
16. I can say		
*	/16	/16

* Number of phrases read correctly

LIST XI

	pre	post
1. wash in hot		
2. because it is		
3. grow best		
4. once upon		
5. sing and laugh		
6. please thank		
7. we draw these		
8. shall we show		
9. the wish is		
10. we clean		
11. they live		
12. too far		
13. all together		
14. many *turtles*		
*	/14	/14

SCORE

LIST	pre	post
I		
II		
III		
IV		
V		
VI		
VII		
VIII		
IX		
X		
XI		
TOTAL		

* Number of phrases read correctly

APPENDIX B-5

Preparation and Use of Materials for the Quick Survey Word List

PREPARATION OF THE QUICK SURVEY WORD LIST

Remove the Quick Survey Word List on page 273 and rubber-cement or tape it to a 5″ × 8″ card. You may then wish to laminate the card or place it in a plastic sleeve, so it will not become soiled from handling.

DIRECTIONS FOR ADMINISTERING THE QUICK SURVEY WORD LIST

The Quick Survey Word List is designed to enable the tester to determine quickly whether a student has the necessary decoding skills to successfully read material written at an adult level. It may be given to students at approximately the fourth-grade level or above to determine whether it is necessary to administer other decoding tests. Students who fail this test will probably need to be given Test B-6, Phonics Assessment, and/or Test B-7, Structural Analysis Assessment.

The student is simply given the word list and asked to pronounce each word. The student should be told, however, that the words that he is about to attempt to pronounce are nonsense words or words that are not real words. The student should also be told that the words are very difficult, but that you would like to know if he is able to pronounce them. If the student can pronounce each of the words correctly, it will not be necessary to administer other decoding tests, since the ultimate purpose of learning phonics and structural analysis is to enable the student to attack new words. On the other hand, if it becomes apparent after one or two words that the student is not able to pronounce the words on the Quick Survey Word List, then it should be discontinued.

The correct pronunciation of the words on the Quick Survey Word List is shown on page 275. This key shows the correct pronunciation as well as the part of each word that should be stressed. It should be remembered, however, that accent rules or generalizations pertaining to the English language are not consistent. Therefore, if the words are pronounced correctly except for the accent or stress shown on certain syllables, they should be considered correct. It is also suggested that the page with the correct pronunciation of the Quick Survey Word List be removed, rubber-cemented or taped to a 5″ × 8″ card, laminated, and placed in your diagnostic kit.

IMPORTANT POINTS TO REMEMBER ABOUT
THE QUICK SURVEY WORD LIST

The Quick Survey Word List is designed to test a student's knowledge of such word-attack skills as structural analysis and accent generalizations. Since phonics knowledge is prerequisite for successful structural analysis, phonics skills can often be inferred from this test as well. It should be stressed, however, that students who do not do well on the list should be stopped after the first two or three words. Remember, only if the student is able to pronounce all of the words correctly (except for accent) should you continue through the entire list. Having a student attempt to pronounce the words when he is not able to do so without difficulty will only discourage him. If the student does not do well on the first one or two words, then you should simply say, "Let's stop. These words are usually meant for adults, and you are not expected to be able to read them."

QUICK SURVEY WORD LIST

wratbeling	twayfrall
dawsnite	spreanplit
pramminciling	goanbate
whetsplitter	streegran
gincule	glammertickly
cringale	grantellean
slatrungle	aipcid

PRONUNCIATION OF QUICK SURVEY WORDS

răt′-bĕl-ĭng

däs′-nīt

prăm′-mĭn-cĭl-ĭng

hwĕt′-splĭt-tər

jĭn′-kyool

crĭn′-gāl

slăt′-rŭn-gəl

twā′-fräl

sprēn′-plĭt

gōn′-bāt

strē′-grăn

glăm′-mər-tĭck-ly

grăn′-tĕl-lēn

āp′-sĭd

PRONUNCIATION KEY

l — littl<u>e</u>

ə — <u>a</u>bout

ä — f<u>a</u>ther

ə — tamp<u>e</u>r

hw — <u>wh</u>at

kyoo — c<u>u</u>te

Preparation and Use of Materials for the Phonics Assessment

THE FORMAT OF THE PHONICS ASSESSMENT TESTS

The Phonics Assessment consists of nine subtests that evaluate the student's knowledge of all the critical phonics skills. These tests can be administered quickly and easily, and provide considerable information in an easy-to-read format. All of the subtests use a common format on the answer sheets, which contain the following:

☐ Down the left column—a summary of the directions for administering each subtest, including the spoken instructions you will give to the student.

☐ Down the center—places to mark the student's responses to each test item. (Space is provided for both pre- and posttest scores on the answer sheets. You may use different-colored ink to distinguish pretest responses from posttest responses on each subtest.)

☐ Down the right column—spaces to indicate the student's total score on each subtest. (You can determine the student's mastery of each skill on both pre- and posttests by comparing the student's performance to the criterion score for mastery that is provided for each subtest.)

PREPARATION OF THE PHONICS ASSESSMENT TESTS

Before administering the Phonics Assessment tests, make multiple copies of the answer sheets on pages 291 through 297, so you will have one for each student to be tested. Remove pages 283 through 289, the Phonics Assessment test sheets, and rubber-cement or tape them to 5″ × 8″ cards. You may then wish to laminate the cards or place them in plastic sleeves, so they will not become soiled from handling.

DIRECTIONS FOR ADMINISTERING AND SCORING THE SUBTESTS

Subtest 1: Application of Phonics Skills in Context

1. Place the test sheet for Subtest 1 in front of the student and say: **"Read this story aloud until I say stop."**

2. As the student reads, indicate specific reading errors on the answer sheet. (Refer to Appendix B-1, "Code for Marking in Oral Diagnosis," for instructions on how to mark the student's oral reading errors.)

3. Encourage the student to pronounce as many words as possible. Do *not* provide assistance by pronouncing words for the student, but rather encourage the student to go on and **"do the best you can."** Cease testing if the student becomes overly frustrated.

4. Only the words underlined on the answer sheet are considered in scoring. The words that are not underlined are basic sight words, which should be pronounced without phonic analysis, or repetitions of previously underlined words.

5. To score this test, compare the oral reading transcription with the response chart just below the paragraph on the answer sheet. The chart lists the 73 phonic elements that are tested, with the underlined words from the paragraph. Circle each phonic element on the response chart that the student failed to pronounce correctly. Some of the phonic elements are tested by more than one underlined word from the paragraph. In such cases, circle the phonic element if even one of the underlined words is mispronounced. Mastery of the phonic element requires that it be pronounced correctly in all cases.

6. Circle the phonic element only if the element itself is mispronounced, regardless of the total pronunciation of the underlined word. For example, to determine the student's symbol-sound association for beginning *b,* the underlined words are *barn* and *bird.* Circle the item if *either* beginning *b* is mispronounced. If, however, the student says "bank" for *barn,* the symbol-sound association for the beginning *b* is correct, so the item is not circled.

7. Determine the number of correct responses, write this number as a fraction, and compare it to the criterion for mastery. To achieve mastery, the student must correctly pronounce 65 of the 73 phonic elements, as indicated on the answer sheet.

Subtest 2: Initial Consonants

1. Place the appropriate test sheet in front of the student and say: **"Look at number 1 and point to the letter you hear at the beginning of** *water."*

2. The student must point to the *w* from among the 5 letter choices. If the student makes an incorrect choice, circle the word *water* on the answer sheet. Then pronounce the next word, *dog,* and continue marking the answer sheet in the same way. Continue to pronounce words and circle incorrect responses until the 10 items are completed. (Of course, you may stop sooner if the student's performance reflects a total inability to succeed at this task.)

3. Determine the number of correct responses, write this number as a fraction, and compare it to the criterion for mastery.

Subtests 3–6: Initial Blends and Digraphs, Ending Sounds, Vowels, Phonograms

Subtests 3 through 6 follow the same format as Subtest 2. Subtest 3 assesses initial blends and digraphs, Subtest 4 assesses ending sounds, Subtest 5 assesses short and long vowel sounds, and Subtest 6 assesses common ending phonograms or word elements.

Subtest 7: Blending

1. Place the appropriate test sheet in front of the student, then check to see that the student can recognize and pronounce the two phonograms *at* and *in.* If the student does not know these, they should be taught to the student, which should be easy to do in a short period of time.

2. Complete the sample item for the student, demonstrating how the initial consonant *t* is pronounced /t/, then blended with the phonogram /in/, to arrive at /tin/.

3. Ask the student to do the same with the 10 items provided, while you circle the incorrect responses.

4. On this subtest and on Subtests 8 and 9, you should not only circle the incorrect responses, but also write phonetic transcriptions of the mispronounced words. This will aid in later analysis. Space is provided on the answer sheet for this.

5. Determine the number of correct responses, write this number as a fraction, and compare it to the criterion for mastery.

Subtest 8: Substitution

1. Place the appropriate test sheet in front of the student and say: "**Read these words. I will tell you the first one in each column in case you don't know it. Some of these are real words, some are not.**"

2. The student then reads the 25 words in the 5 columns, while you follow the same scoring procedure as indicated for Subtest 7.

Subtest 9: Vowel Pronunciation

1. Place the appropriate test sheet in front of the student and say: "**Read as many of these words as you can.**"

2. Follow the same scoring procedure as for Subtests 7 and 8.

INTERPRETING THE PHONICS ASSESSMENT TESTS

Subtest 1: Application of Phonics Skills in Context

Subtest 1 evaluates the student's ability to apply phonics skills in a carefully constructed passage. Phonics skills are of most benefit to a student when utilized in conjunction with context clues. For some students, context ability is sufficiently developed for them to decode successfully with only minimal phonics ability.

On Subtest 1, the student is asked to read aloud a short passage. Upon completion, you will be able to evaluate the student's application of 73 phonics elements in context. **If the student performs at mastery level on this subtest, then you may skip the other phonics tests and go on to the Structural Analysis Assessment tests, which are found in Appendix B-7.**

The passage consists of 105 one-syllable words, based on the assumption that only one-syllable words should be utilized in evaluating phonics abilities. (Words of more than one syllable usually require structural analysis, which is a separate decoding skill.) Only 44 of the words in the passage (those that are underlined) are used to evaluate phonics skills. The 61 words that are not underlined include 19 basic sight words that should be recognized instantly without phonic analysis. (Some of these words are also phonetically irregular.) These 19 words appear a total of 52 times in the passage. In addition, 4 of the underlined words are repeated a total of 9 times, and these 9 repetitions are not counted in the analysis. A few of the words that are counted do appear on lists of basic sight words. However, they tend to appear with less frequency than most basic sight words and are phonetically regular.

The 44 underlined words allow for evaluation of 16 beginning single consonant sounds, 13 ending single consonant sounds, 7 beginning consonant blends, 8 ending consonant blends, 4 beginning consonant digraphs, 1 ending consonant digraph, 5 short vowels, 5 long vowels, 5 *r*-controlled vowels, and 9 vowel digraphs, diphthongs, and other vowel combinations for a total of 73 phonic elements.

Depending on the student's reading ability, some or all of the words on this subtest may be in the student's sight vocabulary. However, for those students reading at or below a second-grade level, this subtest provides an opportunity to evaluate the student's ability to use phonic analysis in the act of reading. In addition, if a careful transcription is made, you will be able to observe the student's use of context clues and fluency skills. You should not attempt to evaluate the student's comprehension on this test.

Subtests 2–6: Initial Consonants, Initial Blends and Digraphs, Ending Sounds, Vowels, Phonograms

Subtest 2 evaluates the student's ability to identify the single consonant letter (from a choice of five) that represents the beginning sound in a word pronounced by the examiner. Subtests 3 through 6 provide for similar evaluation of initial blends and digraphs, ending sounds, short and long vowels, and common phonograms, respectively.

Subtests 2 through 6 each consist of 10 items. The mastery level for each subtest is 9 correct out of 10, excepting Subtest 4 (ending sounds), where 8 out of 10 is considered mastery. This is because ending sounds are both more difficult and less important factors in the student's phonics instruction program.

The items and the choices in Subtests 2 through 6 were carefully selected to reflect a sampling of the most critical phonic elements and to require maximum discrimination (minimal guess factor) by the student. Although guessing alone should account for 2 correct answers on the 10 items of each subtest, the mastery level requires sufficient knowledge on the student's part. You will observe that students who have mastered the items tested will work quickly and easily.

It is important to remember that these are *low-level* phonics tests. Failure on these tests does indicate that the student lacks sufficient phonics skills, but mastery does *not* prove that the student possesses adequate phonics ability *in the act of reading.*

Subtest 7: Blending

Subtest 7 evaluates the student's ability to blend a beginning sound with one of two common phonograms. High-level phonics skills are required to pronounce the beginning sound, and blending skills are required to complete the item. Two factors in this subtest may be disconcerting to the student and should be considered when analyzing the results.

First, the appearance of the test items may confuse some students. This is unfortunate, but unavoidable, since it is necessary to separate the word parts. Second, some students may balk at pronouncing nonsense words, especially older students. The use of nonsense words (which also appear in Subtest 8) is necessary to ensure that the student is not relying solely on sight recognition to pronounce the words. The subtest is designed with three nonsense words and a fourth word, *din,* which is not likely to be in the student's meaning vocabulary. Note whether the error pattern consists of only these words.

Because Subtest 7 evaluates two different skills (high-level phonics and blending), note which skill is lacking when errors are made. If the student lacks high-level phonics ability, the beginning sounds will be mispronounced. Blending will go awry if the student lacks blending ability or is confused by the format of the test or the pronunciation of the two phonograms.

The student should be discouraged from reading the words too quickly, as this will also cause errors. Correct pronunciation for each item may occur in either of two ways. For example, for the item /m/ + /at/, the student may pronounce the /m/ and the /at/ separately, then blend them together to pronounce the word /mat/, or the student may simply pronounce the whole word, /mat/. If the student is unable to correctly pronounce the word, the item is failed, even if the separate parts were pronounced correctly. (Some students may say the letter name(s) for the beginning sound, then pronounce the phonogram, and blend the word. This is acceptable, as long as the whole word is pronounced correctly.)

Subtest 8: Substitution

Subtest 8 evaluates the student's ability to substitute a new phonic element and blend it with the rest of the word. The examiner pronounces the first word in each column. The student then reads each word below the first word as a whole word. The first column requires the student to substitute and blend seven beginning single consonants. Subsequent columns require the student to substitute and blend beginning blends and digraphs, short vowels, long vowels, and ending consonants.

Most students will find that the columns are increasingly difficult. The last column (ending consonants) may be particularly difficult if the student attempts to read the words too quickly.

Subtest 9: Vowel Pronunciation

Subtest 9 evaluates the student's ability to pronounce 15 real words that represent the more difficult vowel patterns: selected digraphs, diphthongs, and r-controlled vowels. Because of the variable pronunciation of these vowel patterns, nonsense words cannot be used. Accordingly, it is possible for students to pronounce these words by relying on sight recognition. However, most of the words are not usually in the meaning vocabularies of remedial readers. This is a difficult subtest for a student who has any difficulty in phonics.

WHEN TO STOP TESTING

If the student masters Subtest 1, stop testing at that point. If the student fails to master Subtest 1, continue administering these subtests until the student consistently fails to attain mastery on the tests or when it is clear that you are no longer obtaining useful diagnostic information. It is important not to overtest. Doing so may lead to unnecessary frustration for the student.

Subtest 1: Application of Phonics Skills in Context

A Job at the Zoo

Ron has a job. He will make the fur of the cat shine. He will use a brush. Ron can fix a cage. He can pat a wet nose. He may hug a cute cub.

Ron may perk up a sad white bird with a nice word. Then Ron will clean dirt from the ground in the owl barn. He can see a fawn rest by a tree. He may bring a toy on a chain to a girl cub. The cub will make a strange noise. Ron will smile. He likes all the things he can do to work and play at the zoo.

Subtest 2: Initial Consonants

1.	l	w	h	t	b	6.	h	b	f	k	t
2.	c	b	k	q	d	7.	t	f	a	j	k
3.	m	l	t	n	b	8.	d	b	p	r	t
4.	c	k	g	b	d	9.	k	c	f	s	r
5.	b	d	p	k	g	10.	t	h	g	i	k

Subtest 3: Initial Blends and Digraphs

1.	cr	gl	gr	tr	dr	6.	sh	cr	bl	ch	sl
2.	bl	tr	br	gl	fr	7.	dr	th	tl	fl	ch
3.	sp	sn	sm	st	sc	8.	dr	bl	cr	pr	br
4.	sh	st	ch	sl	cn	9.	sm	sp	ch	sh	cr
5.	bl	pr	gl	pl	sl	10.	tr	dr	th	ch	tw

Subtest 4: Ending Sounds

1.	q	r	t	k	d	6.	nt	nk	st	ng	rk
2.	k	b	q	d	t	7.	st	ch	ss	ck	sh
3.	b	p	t	k	d	8.	sk	st	sh	ss	ck
4.	r	u	o	l	k	9.	st	nk	ng	nt	rd
5.	d	b	k	t	p	10.	nd	rd	pt	ld	rt

Subtest 5: Vowels

1.	a	e	i	o	u	6.	a	e	i	o	u
2.	e	i	o	u	a	7.	e	i	o	u	a
3.	i	o	u	a	e	8.	i	o	u	a	e
4.	o	u	a	e	i	9.	o	u	a	e	i
5.	u	a	e	i	o	10.	u	o	a	e	i

Subtest 6: Phonograms

1.	ang	and	ime	ing	ame
2.	in	ime	ame	ind	ain
3.	ite	ipe	ike	ice	eek
4.	ick	og	uck	ock	eep
5.	up	eek	ipe	eep	ime
6.	it	ate	ight	ipe	ice
7.	ung	ine	ang	ing	ind
8.	ad	ade	age	and	ape
9.	ean	ime	ad	ang	ame
10.	elp	in	ill	all	ell

Subtest 7: Blending

at   in

t   +   in

h + at   m + at

ch + in   sh + in

tr + in   str + at

bl + at   f + in

th + at   d + in

Subtest 8: Substitution

fan	track	hat	rade	bib
ran	shack	hit	rode	bif
tan	spack	hot	ride	bid
ban	frack	het	rude	big
jan	chack	hut		bim
lan	plack			
van	stack			
can	whack			

Subtest 9: Vowel Pronunciation

boat	crown	serve
paint	trout	stir
own	hawk	born
soil	haul	word
coy	card	burn

Phonics Assessment Test

Student _____ School _____
Teacher _____ Grade _____ Age_____
Examiner _____ Test Dates _____ _____
                                                        pretest   *posttest*

Subtest 1: Application of Phonics Skills in Context. Place Subtest 1 in front of the student. Say: "Read this story aloud until I say stop." (Do not assist the student by pronouncing unknown words.)

Write the mispronunciations on the story below and note the weak skill areas.

A Job at the Zoo

Ron has a job. He will make the fur of the cat shine. He will use a brush. Ron can fix a cage. He can pat a wet nose. He may hug a cute cub.

Ron may perk up a sad white bird with a nice word. Then Ron will clean dirt from the ground in the owl barn. He can see a fawn rest by a tree. He may bring a toy on a chain to a girl cub. The cub will make a strange noise. Ron will smile. He likes all the things he can do to work and play at the zoo.

Responses—Circle the Letter(s) Representing the Sounds the Student Read Incorrectly

Beginning *Single Consonants*	*Ending* *Single Consonants*	*Beginning* *Consonant Blends*	*Ending* *Consonant Blends*
b (barn, bird)	b (cub, job)	cl (clean)	nd (ground)
hard c (cage, cat, cub, cute)	soft c (nice)	pl (play)	ng (bring)
d (dirt)	d (sad)	br (bring, brush)	rd (bird, word)
f (fawn, fix, fur)	soft g (cage, strange)	gr (ground)	rk (park, work)
hard g (girl)	hard g (hug)	tr (tree)	rl (girl)
h (hug)	k (make, perk)	sm (smile)	rn (barn)
j (job)	l (owl, smile)	str (strange)	rt (dirt)
l (likes)	n (chain, clean, fawn, Ron, shine)		st (rest)
m (make, may)			
n (nice, noise, nose)	p (up)	*Short Vowels*	*Long Vowels*
p (pat, perk)	r (fur)	a (cat, pat, sad)	a (cage, make, strange)
r (rest, Ron)	s (likes, noise, nose, things, use)	e (rest, wet)	e (tree)
s (sad)		i (fix)	i (likes, nice, shine, smile, white)
t (toy)	t (cat, cute, pat, wet, white)	o (job, Ron)	o (nose)
w (wet, word, work)		u (brush, cub, hug, up)	u (cute, use)
z (zoo)	x (fix)		

Beginning Single Digraphs	*Ending Single Digraph*	*Vowel Combinations*	
ch (chain)	sh (brush)	ar (barn)	aw (fawn)
sh (shine)		er (perk)	ea (clean)
th (things)		ir (bird, dirt, girl)	oi (noise)
wh (white)		or (word, work)	oo (zoo)
		ur (fur)	ou (ground)
		ai (chain)	ow (owl)
		ay (may, play)	oy (toy)

Pretest	Posttest
/73	/73

65 = Mastery

Subtest 2: Initial Consonants   Pretest | Posttest
(Sound-Symbol)
Place Subtest 2 in front of the student.
Say: "Look at number 1 and point to   1. water   5. book   9. sit
the letter you hear at the beginning of   2. dog   6. kite   10. hide
water . . ., dog . . ." Continue for each   3. nice   7. fat
word listed.   4. goat   8. put   /10   /10

                                                    9 = Mastery

Subtest 3: Initial Blends & Digraphs
(Sound-Symbol)
Place Subtest 3 in front of the student.   1. great   5. plum   9. spell
Say: "Look at number 1 and point to   2. blue   6. church   10. those
the letters you hear at the beginning of   3. small   7. thumb
great . . ., blue . . ."   4. short   8. bring
Continue for each word listed.   /10   /10

                                                    9 = Mastery

Subtest 4: Ending Sounds
(Sound-Symbol)
Place Subtest 4 in front of the student.   1. bat   5. tab   9. pant
Say: "Look at number 1 and point to the   2. bed   6. sing   10. card
letter or letters you hear at the end of   3. drop   7. bush
bat . . ., bed . . ."   4. cool   8. mask
Continue for each word listed.   /10   /10

                                                    8 = Mastery

Subtest 5: Vowels (Sound-Symbol)
Place Subtest 5 in front of the student.   1. tip   5. mope   9. cup
Say: "Look at number 1 and point to the   2. mule   6. tape   10. keep
vowel you hear in *tip . . ., mule . . ."*   3. snap   7. pet
Continue for each word listed.   4. dot   8. fine   /10   /10

                                                    9 = Mastery

Subtest 6: Phonograms (Sound-Symbol)
Place Subtest 6 in front of the student.   1. ame   5. eep   9. ang
Say: "Look at number 1 and point to the   2. ime   6. ight   10. ill
ending part you hear: *ame . . ., ime . . ."*   3. ike   7. ing
Continue for each part listed.   4. ock   8. ade   /10   /10

                                                    9 = Mastery

Subtest 7: Blending (Sound-Symbol)
Place Subtest 7 in front of the student.   1. h + at   5. th + at   9. f + in
Make sure the student can pronounce the   2. ch + in   6. m + at   10. d + in
two phonograms *at* and *in*.   3. tr + in   7. sh + in
Say: "You are going to blend letters with   4. bl + at   8. str+ at
at and *in*. The first one is *t* plus *in* or *tin*.
Now you blend the rest."   /10   /10

                                                    9 = Mastery

Subtest 8: Substitution						Pretest	Posttest
(Sound-Symbol)							
Place Subtest 8 in front of the student.	fan	track	hat	rade	bib		
Say: "Read these words. I will tell you	r	sh	i	o	f		
the first one in each column in case you	t	sp	o	i	d		
don't know it. Some of these are real	b	fr	e	u	g		
words, some are not."	j	ch	u		m		
	l	pl					
	v	st					
	c	wh				/25	/25

22 = Mastery

Subtest 9: Vowel Pronunciation				Pretest	Posttest
(Sound-Symbol)					
Place Subtest 9 in front of the student.	boat	crown	serve		
Say: "Read as many of these words as	paint	trout	stir		
you can."	own	hawk	born		
	soil	haul	word		
	coy	card	burn	/15	/15

13 = Mastery

Preparation and Use of Materials for the Structural Analysis Assessment

THE FORMAT OF THE STRUCTURAL ANALYSIS ASSESSMENT TESTS

The Structural Analysis Assessment consists of eight subtests in a format that is similar to that used in the Phonics Assessment. Subtest 1 assesses the student's ability to apply the structural analysis skills in the context of a passage. Subtest 2 evaluates the student's ability to *hear* the separate parts (syllables) of words, a skill that is a prerequisite for structural analysis. Subtest 3 assesses the student's ability to combine the various inflectional endings with root words and pronounce the resulting new words. Subtests 4 and 5 assess the student's ability to decode prefixes and suffixes, respectively. Subtest 6 assesses the student's ability to recognize the two separate units of compound words for purposes of pronunciation. Subtest 7 assesses the student's ability to pronounce two-syllable words containing one easy affix (prefix or suffix). Subtest 8 assesses the student's ability to pronounce regular three-, four-, and five-syllable words through the use of structural analysis.

PREPARATION OF THE STRUCTURAL ANALYSIS ASSESSMENT TESTS

Before administering the Structural Analysis Assessment tests, make multiple copies of the answer sheets on pages 315 through 327, so you will have one for each student to be tested. Remove pages 305 through 313, the Structural Analysis Assessment test sheets, and rubber-cement or tape them to 5″ × 8″ cards. You may then wish to laminate the cards or place them in plastic sleeves, so they will not become soiled from handling.

DIRECTIONS FOR ADMINISTERING AND SCORING THE SUBTESTS

Subtest 1: Application of Structural Analysis Skills in Context

Note: This subtest consists of two passages. The first is easier than the second. The student may read either or both, depending on the student's reading ability. When in doubt, start the student on the first passage and proceed to the second only if the student attains mastery on the first.

1. Place the appropriate test sheet (either Part A or Part B) in front of the student and say: **"Read this story aloud until I say stop."**

2. As the student reads, follow the procedure for transcribing oral reading errors as described in Appendix B-1, "Code for Marking in Oral Diagnosis." It is essential to determine whether the underlined words are pronounced correctly. All of these words require structural analysis skills for decoding. The words that are not underlined are either basic sight words or words that can be decoded using phonic analysis.

3. Encourage the student to pronounce as many words as possible. Do *not* provide assistance by pronouncing unknown words for the student. Cease testing if the student becomes overly frustrated.

4. To score this test, evaluate the student's oral reading of the underlined words. Each word that is mispronounced should be circled on the response chart on the answer sheet. The words on this chart are categorized according to the structural analysis skill required.

5. Write the number of correct responses as a fraction on the answer sheet to be compared with the criterion for mastery. If the student meets or exceeds the criterion for the first passage (Subtest 1, Part A), then administer the second passage (Subtest 1, Part B), following the same instructions.

Subtest 2: Hearing Word Parts

1. This test requires no test sheet. Hold the answer sheet so that you can read from it and say: **"How many syllables do you hear in the word *cowboy?*"** Mark the student's response on the answer sheet.

2. Continue the test with the other 4 items, circling the incorrect responses.

3. Write the number of correct responses as a fraction on the Answer Sheet to be compared with the criterion for mastery.

Subtests 3–5: Inflectional Endings, Prefixes, Suffixes

1. For each subtest, place the appropriate test sheet in front of the student and read the first word (the root word) in each column, then ask the student to pronounce the other words in the columns. (You should not read the first word in column 2 until the student has read all the words in column 1, and so on.)

2. As the student reads the words, circle each incorrect response on the Answer Sheet.

3. Write the number of correct responses as a fraction on the Answer Sheet to be compared with the criterion for mastery.

Subtest 6: Compound Words

1. Place the appropriate test sheet in front of the student and say: "**Read as many of these words as you can. Some are not real words.**"

2. As the student reads the words, circle the errors. On this test, the errors are not determined by imprecise pronunciation, but rather by the student's failure to recognize and attempt to decode the two parts of the compound word. For example, if a student says "baskethorse" for *baskethouse,* this is considered correct, since it is clear that the student identified the two pronounceable units. However, if the student attempts to pronounce *baskethouse* by sounding the *th* as a digraph in the middle of the word, this is incorrect. Such an error reflects a lack of recognition of the two obvious word parts.

3. Write the number of correct responses as a fraction on the answer sheet to be compared with the criterion for mastery.

Subtest 7: Affixes

1. Place the appropriate test sheet in front of the student and say: "**Read as many of these words as you can. Some are not real words.**"

2. As the student reads, circle the errors. The determination of errors on this subtest follows the same restrictions as described under the previous subtest.

3. Write the number of correct responses as a fraction on the answer sheet to be compared with the criterion for mastery.

Subtest 8: Syllabication

1. Place the appropriate test sheet in front of the student and say: "**Read as many of these words as you can.**"

2. As the student reads, circle the errors. Although all of the words on this test are real words, most students will not recognize them as sight words. Count as correct pronunciations where the accent is misplaced, as long as each of the syllables is pronounced correctly.

3. Write the number of correct responses as a fraction on the answer sheet to be compared with the criterion for mastery.

INTERPRETING THE STRUCTURAL ANALYSIS ASSESSMENT TESTS

Structural analysis is a decoding skill that is analogous to phonics. It is often referred to as *morphology,* which is concerned with the study of meaning-bearing units such as root words, prefixes, suffixes, possessives, plurals, accent rules, and syllables. To use structural analysis to decode a multisyllable word, the reader first identifies the separate units in the word, then pronounces the units, then blends them together. (In using phonics, the reader goes through the same process with phonemes, or individual sounds.)

Subtest 1: Application of Structural Analysis Skills in Context

This subtest evaluates the student's ability to apply the various structural analysis skills during contextual reading. The two passages contain a total of 80 words that require the application of structural analysis. Because of the disproportionate number of long words, the readability of these passages is quite high. Part A, according to the Fry readability formula, is written at approximately the low-fifth-grade level. Part B is written at approximately the mid-seventh-grade level. You should not assume, however, that students who successfully read these passages can comfortably read other materials at these levels.

The two passages that compose this subtest are the most difficult of the structural analysis assessment tests. A student who demonstrates mastery on *both* of the passages surely is not lacking in structural analysis skills. In such a case, you should skip the other structural analysis tests. If, however, the student fails to master one or both of these passages, then you should proceed to administer the remaining subtests until you determine that you no longer can obtain useful diagnostic information.

Subtest 2: Hearing Word Parts

This subtest evaluates the student's ability to hear the separate parts (syllables) of words. If the student is unable to do this, instruction should focus on this area prior to other structural analysis skills. You should not be concerned with the student's ability to identify the specific points in words where syllable division takes place. This skill, often called *end-of-line division,* is frequently tested. Unfortunately, it is not useful for decoding purposes.

Subtests 3–5: Inflectional Endings, Prefixes, Suffixes

These subtests evaluate the student's ability to combine various inflectional endings, prefixes, and suffixes with root words, and to pronounce the resulting new words. In every case, you begin by pronouncing the root word for the student, so the task is easier than that which is required in actual reading. The student, however, must pronounce the whole word correctly to receive credit for the item. If the student fails on any of these items, your task is to determine whether the failure results from the student's inability to pronounce the structural part, blend the part with the root, or both.

Subtest 3 presents the six most common inflectional endings. Subtest 4 presents 10 of the most common and easily teachable prefixes. Subtest 5 presents 10 of the most common suffixes.

Subtest 6: Compound Words

This subtest evaluates the student's ability to recognize that many long words are the combination of two shorter, whole words. The five compound words presented consist of one real word and four nonsense words. Since it is more important for the student to recognize the two separate units of the compound words, perfect pronunciation is not required, as long as the student demonstrates recognition of the compound characteristic. Nonsense words must be used to ensure that the student is not recognizing the whole words merely by sight.

Subtest 7: Affixes

This subtest evaluates the student's ability to pronounce two-syllable words containing one common affix. On this test, you do not pronounce the root word, so the task is significantly more difficult for the student than in Subtests 3 through 5. In this case, the student must go through all three steps of decoding through structural analysis: (1) separating the parts, (2) pronouncing the word parts, and (3) blending the separate parts to pronounce the whole word. As with Subtest 6, most of the items on this test are nonsense words.

Subtest 8: Syllabication

This subtest evaluates the student's ability to pronounce 10 multisyllable words. Accurate pronunciation of these words requires the student to use the structural analysis skills previously tested as well as the ability to divide words into parts when obvious affixes are not present. Since they are particularly difficult and not likely to be recognized by sight, these words are all real words.

Subtest 1: Application of Structural Analysis Skills in Context

Part A: *Winter in the Countryside*

It was a cold winter day. The trees were bare and birds could be seen in the countryside. A grasshopper hopped across the road to hide from the cold and the foxes curled up to keep warm. A brown field mouse and her babies came running out of a hole in the ground. The babies were fighting with each other. Mother mouse looked unhappy as she sat on a big overgrown stump. It was dangerous for the mice to stay above ground but the active children wanted their lunches. Mother mouse was also nervous about her children eating the poisonous plants that were in the field. The children were curious and the plants looked so attractive.

Just that morning, Mother mouse had a disagreement with Father mouse. The question was whether or not the children should run in the field in the daytime.

Part B: *The Disappearance of Flint*

What should have been a great day turned out to be a disappointing one for David King. He found out that he would be the new quarterback for Friday night's game. Unfortunately, he was going to be taking his best friend Ron's place. Ron had gotten a disqualification notice because his grades dropped at the end of the first report. Ron felt that his concentration was poor because of his older brother's recent motorcycle crash. David was sorry about Ron's dismissal from the team; but was shocked by the resentment he saw on Ron's face when he found out who his replacement would be. This was the unfriendliest that Ron had ever treated David.

David thought about the rest of his rather uneventful day as he walked home. He turned on the flashlight he carried with him, for it had grown quite dark. David stopped short when he heard a loud and frightening scream coming from the vacant mansion just up the road.

The place had been empty for three years and was in bad shape. Fixing it up had been estimated to be costlier than most families could afford. David had always felt that the mansion had a mysterious look about it. The man who had built and lived in the mansion was believed to be knowledgeable in the ways of witchcraft. His disappearance three years ago had shocked the people of the town. What made it even scarier was that it happened on a Halloween night when so many children were out on the streets. The imaginative minds of several of the neighbors had come up with many strange stories about what had happened to old Flint.

Subtest 3: Inflectional Endings

bake	pale	slow
baker	paler	slower
baked	paling	slowest
bakes	palest	slowly
		slows

Subtest 4: Prefixes

play	mote	form
replay	remote	conform
display	promote	inform
misplay	demote	deform
take	tend	pack
retake	intend	unpack
intake	contend	prepack
mistake	extend	repack
	distend	
	pretend	

Subtest 5: Suffixes

joy	invent	base	elect
joyous	inventive	basement	election
joyful	inventable	baseness	elective
joyless		baseless	

Subtest 6: Compound Words

overdone   motorplane
laterthought   clockrunner
baskethouse

Subtest 7: Affixes

uncall   treeness
proclaim   sunning
indeem   bookful
demark   raytion
prestrain   darkous

Subtest 8: Syllabication

automotive   premeditate
displacement   imperfection
conformation   unreasonable
remarkable   misplaying
impeachable   complicated

Structural Analysis Assessment Test

Student _____ School _____
Teacher _____ Grade _____ Age _____
Examiner _____ Test Dates _____ _____
                                                    pretest   *posttest*

Subtest 1: Application of Structural Analysis Skills in Context (Part A). Place Part A in front of the student. Say: "Read as many of these words as you can."
The first story is easier than the second.

Stop if the story becomes too difficult. In both stories the words requiring the structural analysis are underlined.
Write the mispronunciations on the story below and note the weak skill areas.

Part A: *Winter in the Countryside*

It was a cold winter day. The <u>trees</u> were bare and <u>birds</u> could be seen in the <u>countryside</u>. A <u>grasshopper</u> <u>hopped</u> across the road to hide from the cold and the <u>foxes</u> <u>curled</u> up to keep warm. A brown field mouse and her <u>babies</u> came <u>running</u> out of a hole in the ground. The babies were <u>fighting</u> with each other. Mother mouse looked <u>unhappy</u> as she sat on a big <u>overgrown</u> stump. It was <u>dangerous</u> for the mice to stay above ground but the <u>active</u> children <u>wanted</u> their <u>lunches</u>. Mother mouse was also <u>nervous</u> about her children <u>eating</u> the <u>poisonous</u> <u>plants</u> that were in the fields. The children were <u>curious</u> and the plants <u>looked</u> so <u>attractive</u>.

Just that <u>morning</u> Mother mouse had a <u>disagree-ment</u> with Father mouse. The <u>question</u> was whether or not the children should run in the field in the <u>daytime</u>.

	Responses—Circle Incorrect Responses				Number Correct
Inflectional Endings	Compounds	Suffixes	Syllabication		Part A
trees	fighting	countryside	active	dangerous	
birds	wanted	grasshopper	nervous	poisonous	
hopped	lunches	overgrown	question	curious	
foxes	eating	daytime		attractive	
curled	plants			disagreement	
babies	looked	Prefix			
running	morning	unhappy			/27 /27
					24 = Mastery

Part B: *The Disappearance of Flint*

What should have been a great day <u>turned</u> out to be a <u>disappointing</u> one for David King. He found out that he would be the new <u>quarterback</u> for Friday <u>night's</u> game. <u>Unfortunately,</u> he was <u>going</u> to be <u>taking</u> his best friend Ron's place. Ron had <u>gotten</u> a <u>disqualification</u> <u>notice</u> because his <u>grades</u> <u>dropped</u> at the end of the first <u>report.</u> Ron felt that his <u>concentration</u> was poor because of his <u>older</u> <u>brother's</u> <u>recent</u> <u>motorcycle</u> <u>crash.</u> David was sorry about Ron's <u>dismissal</u> from the team, but was <u>shocked</u> by the <u>resentment</u> he saw on Ron's face when he found out who his <u>replacement</u> would be. This was the <u>unfriendliest</u> that Ron had ever <u>treated</u> David.

David thought about the rest of his rather <u>uneventful</u> day as he <u>walked</u> home. He turned on the <u>flashlight</u> he <u>carried</u> with him, for it had grown quite dark. David <u>stopped</u> short when he heard a loud and <u>frightening</u> scream <u>coming</u> from the vacant <u>mansion</u> just up the road.

The place had been empty for <u>years</u> and was in bad shape. <u>Fixing</u> it up had been <u>estimated</u> to be <u>costlier</u> than most <u>families</u> could afford. David had always felt that the mansion had a <u>mysterious</u> look about it. The man who had built and <u>lived</u> in the mansion was <u>believed</u> to be <u>knowledgeable</u> in the ways of <u>witchcraft</u>. His <u>disappearance</u> three years ago had shocked the people of the town. What made it even <u>scarier</u> was that it <u>happened</u> on a <u>Halloween</u> night when so many children were out on the <u>streets</u>. The <u>imaginative</u> <u>minds</u> of <u>several</u> of the <u>neighbors</u> had come up with many strange <u>stories</u> about what had happened to old Flint.

Responses—Circle Incorrect Responses					Number Correct
Inflectional Endings		*Compounds*	*Syllabication*		*Part B*
turned	carried	quarterback	disappointing	estimated	
night's	stopped	motorcycle	Unfortunately	costlier	
going	coming	flashlight	disqualification	mysterious	
taking	years	witchcraft	concentration	believed	
Ron's	Fixing		dismissal	knowledgeable	/53 /53
gotten	families	*Prefixes*	resentment	disappearance	48 = Mastery
grades	lived	report	replacement	Halloween	
dropped	scarier	recent	unfriendliest	imaginative	Total Score
older	happened		uneventful	several	
brother's	streets	*Suffixes*	frightening	neighbors	
shocked	minds	notice			
treated	stories	mansion			
walked					/80 /80
					72 = Mastery

	Directions	Responses—Circle Incorrect Responses	Number Correct
			Pretest Posttest
Subtest 2: Hearing Word Parts			
Say: "How many syllables do you hear		1. cowboy (2) 4. disagreement (4)	
in the word *cowboy* . . . , *intention* . . . ,		2. intention (3) 5. randomly (3)	
steam . . . , *disagreement* . . . , *randomly*?"		3. steam (1)	/5 /5
			4 = Mastery

Subtest 3: Inflectional Endings

Place Subtest 3 in front of the student. Say: "Read these words. I will read the first one in each column."

	bake	pale	slow	Pretest	Posttest
	er	er	er		
	ed	ing	est		
	s	est	ly		
			s	/10	/10

9 = Mastery

Subtest 4: Prefixes

Place Subtest 4 in front of the student. Say: "Read these words. I will read the first one in each column."

play	mote	form	take	tend	pack	Pretest	Posttest
re	re	con	re	in	un		
dis	pro	in	in	con	pre		
mis	de	de	mis	ex	re		
				dis			
				pre		/20	/20

18 = Mastery

Subtest 5: Suffixes

Place Subtest 5 in front of the student. Say: "Read these words. I will read the first one in each column."

joy	invent	base	elect	Pretest	Posttest
ous	ive	ment	ion		
ful	able	ness	ive		
less		less		/10	/10

9 = Mastery

Subtest 6: Compound Words

Place Subtest 6 in front of the student. Say: "Read as many of these words as you can. Some are not real words." (It is more important for the student to recognize the separate units of the words than to pronounce them perfectly.)

overdone	motorplane	Pretest	Posttest
laterthought	clockrunner		
baskethouse			
		/5	/5

4 = Mastery

Subtest 7: Affixes			Pretest	Posttest
Place Subtest 7 in front of the student.	uncall	treeness		
Say: "Read as many of these words as you can.	proclaim	sunning		
Some are not real words."	indeem	bookful		
(It is more important for the student to recognize	demark	raytion		
the separate units of the words than to	prestrain	darkous		
pronounce them perfectly.)			/10	/10
			9 = Mastery	

Subtest 8: Syllabication				
Place Subtest 8 in front of the student.	automotive	premeditate		
Say: "Read as many of these words as	displacement	imperfection		
you can."	conformation	unreasonable		
	remarkable	misplaying		
	impeachable	complicated	/10	/10
			9 = Mastery	

Preparation and Use of Materials for Testing Knowledge of Contractions

PREPARING FOR THE TEST

Before administering the test, remove page 333 and duplicate it so that you will have multiple copies to use as answer sheets for testing each student. Also remove page 331 and use rubber cement or tape to fasten it to a 5″ × 8″ card. You may then wish to laminate the card or place it in a plastic sleeve, so it will not become soiled from handling.

SPECIFIC DIRECTIONS FOR TESTING FOR KNOWLEDGE OF CONTRACTIONS

Have your answer sheet ready (p. 333) and give the student the stimulus sheet (p. 331). Then read the directions on the answer sheet.

IMPORTANT POINTS TO REMEMBER

A rather high percentage of students have occasional problems with the pronunciation of contractions; however, you are likely to find a greater percentage who do not know what two words each contraction stands for. Keep in mind that pronunciation is important for reading purposes, but students will not use a contraction in their writing until they know the two words for which it stands.

Knowledge of Contractions

1.	aren't	25.	there's
2.	can't	26.	we'll
3.	don't	27.	there'll
4.	weren't	28.	what's
5.	couldn't	29.	you'll
6.	didn't	30.	doesn't
7.	wasn't	31.	hasn't
8.	hadn't	32.	you'd
9.	won't	33.	he'd
10.	haven't	34.	you're
11.	isn't	35.	he's
12.	wouldn't	36.	I'd
13.	anybody'd	37.	we've
14.	he'll	38.	I've
15.	it's	39.	they've
16.	here's	40.	she'd
17.	I'll	41.	who'd
18.	let's	42.	she's
19.	she'll	43.	they'd
20.	that's	44.	we'd
21.	where's	45.	they're
22.	they'll	46.	we're
23.	I'm	47.	you've
24.	who'll		

Knowledge of Contractions
Answer Sheet

Name _____ Date _____

School _____ Tester _____

Directions: Say, "Here is a list of contractions. I want you to begin with number one and say the contraction and then tell what two words it stands for." Following each contraction are two lines. If the student is able to pronounce the contraction correctly, put a plus (+) in the first blank. If he or she can then tell you what two words it stands for, put a plus (+) in the second blank. Mark wrong answers with a minus (−). The grade-level designation following each blank stands for the point at which the contraction should be known.

1.	aren't	___	___	1.9	25.	there's	___	___	2.5
2.	can't	___	___	1.9	26.	we'll	___	___	2.5
3.	don't	___	___	1.9	27.	there'll	___	___	2.5
4.	weren't	___	___	1.9	28.	what's	___	___	2.5
5.	couldn't	___	___	1.9	29.	you'll	___	___	2.5
6.	didn't	___	___	1.9	30.	doesn't	___	___	2.9
7.	wasn't	___	___	1.9	31.	hasn't	___	___	2.9
8.	hadn't	___	___	1.9	32.	you'd	___	___	2.9
9.	won't	___	___	1.9	33.	he'd	___	___	2.9
10.	haven't	___	___	1.9	34.	you're	___	___	2.9
11.	isn't	___	___	1.9	35.	he's	___	___	2.9
12.	wouldn't	___	___	1.9	36.	I'd	___	___	2.9
13.	anybody'd	___	___	2.5	37.	we've	___	___	2.9
14.	he'll	___	___	2.5	38.	I've	___	___	2.9
15.	it's	___	___	2.5	39.	they've	___	___	2.9
16.	here's	___	___	2.5	40.	she'd	___	___	2.9
17.	I'll	___	___	2.5	41.	who'd	___	___	2.9
18.	let's	___	___	2.5	42.	she's	___	___	2.9
19.	she'll	___	___	2.5	43.	they'd	___	___	2.9
20.	that's	___	___	2.5	44.	we'd	___	___	2.9
21.	where's	___	___	2.5	45.	they're	___	___	2.9
22.	they'll	___	___	2.5	46.	we're	___	___	2.9
23.	I'm	___	___	2.5	47.	you've	___	___	2.9
24.	who'll	___	___	2.5					

Preparation and Use of Materials for Testing Ability to Use Context Clues

PREPARING FOR THE TEST

Pages 339 through 349 contain materials that you may use to test students' ability to use context clues. Each page contains materials for testing context clues at a level from grade 1 to grade 6. To prepare the materials for testing, remove these pages from this appendix. Cut each page in half along the dotted lines and use rubber cement or magic tape to fasten each half of the page to separate sides of a 5″ × 8″ card. You may then wish to laminate the card or place it in a plastic sleeve to keep it from becoming soiled with use. In fastening the materials to the 5″ × 8″ card, make sure that the material on one side of the card is in the same position as the material on the other side, so both you and a student can read the materials at the same time. (An alternative is to place each half page on separate cards, one for the student being tested and the other for you. If you do this, you may wish to use different colored cards to distinguish the student's cards from the examiner's cards. This method has the advantage of allowing the student to hold his card so that it will be easier for him to read.)

When all cards are completed, you should place them in grade-level order, so that the front of the first card contains the material to be read by a student reading at first-grade level, the second card contains the materials to be read by a student reading at second-grade level, and so on. The other side of the cards (to be read by the tester) will then contain the same passages as those to be read by the student, except that the words omitted on the student's passage will be underlined on the side seen by the tester. This side of the card also shows the grade level at which the material is written.

SPECIFIC DIRECTIONS FOR ADMINISTERING THE TEST

Begin the test at a level at which you are sure the student can function at his low instructional or independent reading level. Hold the card so the student can read the material on his side. Read the directions printed at the top of the card and then let the student proceed to read orally the passage printed on the other side. It should not be necessary to record the student's errors; however, as the student reads, if you believe you have chosen too difficult a passage to begin with, or too easy a passage to begin with, then move to the next passage that is either easier or more difficult. If the student uses a word that is a logical substitute for the one that is omitted, then count it as correct. No norms have been developed for how well students should do in using context clues. However, in these passages it is suggested that you use the following criteria in determining student performance:

No errors	Excellent
One error	Good
Two errors	Fair
Three or more errors	Poor

IMPORTANT POINTS TO REMEMBER

It is often taken for granted that students will automatically attempt to use context clues even though they have not been taught how to do so. This is simply not true. Many readers require a considerable amount of instruction and a great deal of practice in using this skill.

The pages that follow contain materials for testing students' ability to use context clues. It should be stressed that most students will be unable to use context clues effectively unless they are reading at a level that is rather easy for them (their independent or easy instructional level). Therefore, in using the materials, be sure to use only passages that the student would be able to read fairly easily if no words were omitted. If you wish to develop materials for testing students' ability to use context clues, other than those presented on the following pages, the section that follows will be helpful.

DEVELOPING YOUR OWN MATERIALS FOR TESTING STUDENTS' KNOWLEDGE OF CONTEXT CLUES

In constructing materials for testing context clues, you should first keep in mind that students must be aware of context in their oral language. Depending upon the age/grade level of the students with whom you are working, the following sequence is suggested:

1. Make a tape recording of a passage in which certain words are omitted. Replace words that are omitted with the sound of a bell or tone of some type. When the bell or tone sounds, ask the student to give orally the word that he feels should have appeared in place of the tone. In making either a tape recording or a written exercise for testing context clues, make sure the words that are omitted are ones that can be gotten from the context of the sentence, as in the following example:

   Lori was going to (beep) a party.

   It was going to (beep) on Saturday.

   She invited some of (beep) friends to come.

   She was (beep) happy.

2. Progress to written materials in which the word omitted is replaced with a __ for each letter omitted as follows:

Lori was going to __ __ __ __ a party.

It was going to __ __ on Saturday.

She invited some of __ __ __ friends to come.

She was __ __ __ __ happy.

3. Progress to written materials in which the word omitted is replaced with the first letter of the word omitted, and the rest of the letters are replaced with a blank line as follows:

Lori was going to h _____ a party.

It was going to b __ on Saturday.

She invited some of h _____ friends to come.

She was v _____ happy.

4. Finally, progress to written materials in which the word omitted is replaced with a line. At this point, be sure to make all lines equal length.

Lori was going to _____ a party.

It was going to _____ on Saturday.

She invited some of _____ friends to come.

She was _____ happy.

Teacher reads these directions: Here is a story with some words left out. Each time a word is left out, it has been replaced with a line. When you come to a line, try to figure out what word should be in that blank. Ready—begin.

Jan has a cat.

The cat's <u>name</u> is Tab.

Tab does not <u>like</u> dogs.

One day <u>a</u> dog ran after Tab.

<u>Tab</u> ran up a tree.

The dog could not go <u>up</u> the tree.

Then <u>the</u> dog went away.

Grade one reading level

Jan has a cat.

The cat's _____ is Tab.

Tab does not _____ dogs.

One day _____ dog ran after Tab.

_____ ran up a tree.

The dog could not go _____ the tree.

Then _____ dog went away.

Teacher reads these directions: Here is a story with some words left out. Each time a word is left out, it has been replaced with a line. When you come to a line, try to figure out what word should be in that blank. Ready—begin.

One day Sam was going to school.
He was riding with his father in their car.
He looked out of the window and saw an elephant.
He said, "Look, father, there goes an elephant."
Sam's father did not even look because they were
   in a large city.
That day Sam's father heard that
   an elephant had escaped from a circus.
That evening Sam's father said, "I'm sorry, Sam,
   you did see an elephant this morning."

Grade two reading level

One day Sam was going to school.
He was riding with _____ father in their car.
He looked out of the window and _____ an elephant.
He said, "Look, father, _____ goes an elephant."
Sam's _____ did not even look because they were
   in a large city.
That day _____ father heard that
   an elephant had escaped from a circus.
That evening Sam's father said, "I'm sorry, Sam,
   you did _____ an elephant this morning."

341

Teacher reads these directions: Here is a story with some words left out. Each time a word is left out, it has been replaced with a line. When you come to a line, try to figure out what word should be in that blank. Ready—begin.

Ann and her brother Mike like to play basketball in a park that is far from their home. When they want to play, they usually take a bus to get to the park. There are other boys and girls that play there, too. Sometimes when they go to the park, their father and mother go with them. Their father and mother like to take some food and have a picnic while they are at the park.

Grade three reading level

- - - - - - - - - - - -

Ann and her brother Mike like to play basketball in a park that is far from their home. When they _____ to play, they usually take a bus to get _____ the park. There are other boys and girls _____ play there, too. Sometimes when they _____ to the park, their father and _____ go with them. Their father and mother like to take some food and _____ a picnic while they are at the park.

343

Teacher reads these directions: Here is a story with some words left out. Each time a word is left out, it has been replaced with a line. When you come to a line, try to figure out what word should be in that blank. Ready—begin.

Most kinds of dogs make excellent pets. They can learn fast, <u>and</u> they also <u>have</u> an excellent memory. An intelligent dog can learn <u>to</u> respond to many commands. Many dogs that have been taught <u>well</u> can learn more <u>than</u> 100 words and phrases.

Grade four reading level

Most kinds of dogs make excellent pets. They _____ learn fast, _____ they also _____ an excellent memory. An intelligent _____ can learn _____ respond to many commands. Many dogs that have been taught well can learn more _____ 100 words and phrases.

Teacher reads these directions: Here is a story with some words left out. Each time a word is left out, it has been replaced with a line. When you come to a line, try to figure out what word should be in that blank. Ready—begin.

Fire is very important to all of us today. Wherever ruins of early man have been found, there has always been evidence of fire in that civilization. It is thought that early man may have first found fire when lightning struck trees and caused them to burn. Some people think that man might have been able to start fires by getting them from active volcanoes.

Grade five reading level

Fire is very important to all of us today. Wherever ruins of early man have _____ found, there has always been evidence _____ fire in that civilization. It is thought _____ early man may _____ first found fire when lightning struck trees and caused _____ to burn. Some people think that man might have been able _____ start fires by getting them from active volcanoes.

347

Teacher reads these directions: Here is a story with some words left out. Each time a word is left out, it has been replaced with a line. When you come to a line, try to figure out what word should be in that blank. Ready—begin.

One of the most famous eagles in the entire world is not the one we see on stamps or coins. It was an eagle caught by an Indian named Blue Sky who lived in Wisconsin. Blue Sky sold the eagle to a man that sold him to a soldier in the Civil War who named him Old Abe. Before the eagle died, he had been through four years of war and had survived twenty-two battles.

Grade six reading level

One of the most famous eagles in the entire world is not the one we see on stamps or coins. It was _____ eagle caught by an Indian named Blue Sky _____ lived in Wisconsin. Blue Sky sold _____ eagle to a man that sold him to a soldier _____ the Civil War _____ had been who named him Old Abe. Before the eagle died, _____ through four years _____ war and had survived twenty-two battles.

Preparation and Use of Materials for the Reading Interest Survey

PREPARING FOR THE TEST

Before administering the test, remove page 353 and duplicate it so that you will have multiple copies to use as test/answer sheets for each student. (With this test, the one page serves as the total test.)

PURPOSE OF THE READING INTEREST SURVEY

This test is designed to assess the student's attitude toward reading and school, areas of reading interest, reading experiences, and conditions affecting reading in the home.

DESCRIPTION

This test enables you to assess quickly a student's reading attitudes and interests. The test may be given orally to young children or students unable to read the questions. Older students or more able readers may complete the form in writing.

ADMINISTRATION AND SCORING

1. You might want to give this test orally regardless of the student's reading ability. This will allow you to discuss with the student her responses to some of the questions.
2. Encourage the student to give you candid responses to these items. Reassure the student that there are no right or wrong answers; you want to know how the student honestly feels about these questions.
3. Part I consists of seven open-ended statements. Write down the student's responses as she finishes the sentences.
4. Part II assesses the student's reading interests. If necessary, explain to the student what some of the categories are.
5. Part III assesses the student's reading experiences and some of the factors that may affect the student's reading behavior at home.

Reading Interest Survey

I. Open-Ended Questions

I like school if _____

I wish _____

When I grow up _____

Reading makes me _____

Books are _____

I like to read when _____

Teachers should _____

II. Reading Interests

I like to read about:

_____ Science   _____ Dogs

_____ Biography   _____ Mysteries

_____ Sports   _____ Science Fiction

_____ People   _____ Riddles

_____ History   _____ Plays

_____ Horses   _____ Monsters

_____ Fantasy   _____ Poetry

I do *not* like to read about _____

If I had my choice, I would really like to read about _____

_____

III. Reading Experiences

The last book I read was _____

My three favorite books are _____

_____

People in my family read:

_____ Books   _____ Magazines   _____ Newspapers

I watch television or play video games about _____ hours per day.

The hours I watch television or play video games are from _____ to

_____ .

I visit the public library:

_____ Often   _____ Seldom   _____ Never

Using the Cloze Procedure

DEVELOPING, ADMINISTERING, AND SCORING CLOZE PASSAGES

In constructing cloze passages, you could omit every third, fifth, or tenth word. However, most of the research is based on the deletion of every fifth word. Blank lines of equal length replace each of the deleted words. It should also be stressed that the commonly used percentages for determining students' independent, instructional, and frustration levels are based on the deletion of every fifth word. If every eighth or tenth word were deleted, these commonly used percentages would not apply.

Passages may vary in length depending on the grade level of the students; however, for students of ages equivalent to third- or fourth-grade level or above, passages of about 250 words are often used. The entire first and last sentences are usually left intact. If passages of 250 words plus intact first and last sentences are used, and if every fifth word is omitted, there will be 50 blanks, and every blank or answer will be worth two percentage points.

Cloze passages may be administered in a group situation much as with standardized reading tests. However, in administering cloze passages, there are usually no specific time limits for completion of the work.

For passages in which every fifth word has been deleted, the percentages for the various reading levels are as follows:

Independent Level = 57% to 100%

Instructional Level = 44% to 56%

Frustration Level = 43% or below

In scoring the passages, only the exact word omitted is usually counted as correct; that is, appropriate synonyms are not counted as correct. Research has shown that the overall percentages change very little regardless of whether synonyms are counted as correct or incorrect. Furthermore, if words other than the exact word omitted were counted, scoring would be much more difficult; that is, what one teacher might consider an adequate answer, another teacher may not, and we would tend to lose interscorer reliability. In scoring cloze passages, however, students are not usually penalized for incorrect spelling as long as there is little or no doubt about which word they meant to use.

A plastic overlay such as an overhead projector transparency can be made of each cloze passage with the correct answers appearing on the plastic overlay.

When this is superimposed on the student's copy, you can readily check the number of right and wrong answers. These can, in turn, be converted to percentages. From these percentages you can then determine whether the material is at the student's independent, instructional, or frustration level.

USING THE CLOZE PROCEDURE TO PLACE STUDENTS IN GRADED MATERIALS

1. Select 6 to 12 passages from a book or material that students will possibly be using. (If the results of the test show that the book is too easy or difficult for the students, another must be selected.) Pick them randomly but equally distributed from the front to the back of the book.

2. Give the tests to 25 to 30 students in a class in which the text is commonly used.

3. Calculate the mean score on each test and then the mean of the means (see pp. 357–358).

4. Select the test that is closest to the mean of the means and throw the rest of the scores away.

5. When a test has been selected for each of the texts a teacher is likely to use, the tests can be duplicated and compiled into booklets that can be administered as group tests. When a student's score is 57% or higher, the student is reading at his independent reading level. A score from 44% to 56% is equivalent to the student's instructional reading level. A score of 43% or less is considered to be at the student's frustration level. (In a textbook, of course, one is concerned with placing the student in the textbook that is represented by the passage in which the student scored at his instructional reading level.)

USING THE CLOZE PROCEDURE TO MEET THE NEEDS OF THE STUDENTS

1. Divide the book into sections and select two or more passages from each section. The same length passages as described earlier can be used.

2. Make a random selection of the students for whom the book will be used.

3. If you are using a great number of students, you may wish to put them into a number of groups and then let each group take some of the tests. (Make sure, however, that the selection of the subgroups is done randomly.)

4. If students are able to score at their instructional level on the passages from the book, then it would be considered suitable for them. On the other hand, if most students scored at their frustration level on the passages from the book, it would be considered too difficult for them.

THE RELIABILITY OF THE CLOZE PROCEDURE

The reliability of the cloze procedure will essentially depend on the following factors:

1. If longer tests are used, the students' scores will probably be more accurate, but it will take longer to correct them.

2. If a larger number of tests is used when selecting the one to represent the material, the test selected will more accurately represent the difficulty of the material.

3. Some materials are uneven in difficulty. These materials should be avoided if possible.

4. The procedure outlined here must be followed exactly or the results will not be accurate.

PROCEDURE FOR DETERMINING THE MEAN OF THE MEANS

The example in Figure B-11.1 illustrates how to find the mean of the means. In this example there were 10 passages and 5 students. (In determining the mean of the means one would, of course, be likely to have more than 5 students.) Note that there are 10 means: 52.4, 34.6, and so on. These means were added and their total was 480.6. When this figure (480.6) was divided by the number of means (10), the mean of the means was 48.06. This figure was closest to the mean of passage number 8 (47.4). Therefore, that passage was most representative of the difficulty of the material. As a whole, passage number 8 would be kept, and the rest of the passages would be discarded.

Passage number 8 is then given to new students with whom you may wish to use the text from which number 8 was derived. If they can read passage number 8 with an accuracy of between 44% and 56%, this text would be appropriate for them at their instructional reading level. If they scored at 43% or lower, the text would be at their frustration reading level. If they scored at 57% or better, the text would be at their independent reading level.

FIGURE B-11.1

	1	2	3	4	5	6	7	8	9	10
Mary	56	42	84	12	48	34	51	47	75	49
Sam	42	41	83	10	40	30	49	50	74	42
Sally	32	36	74	18	42	41	55	51	75	45
Joe	76	26	66	26	47	31	60	38	69	39
Fred	56	28	54	41	49	33	59	51	72	54
Totals	262	173	361	107	226	169	274	237	365	229
Means	52.4	34.6	72.2	21.4	45.2	33.8	54.8	47.4	73.0	45.8

Total of the Means = 480.6

Mean of the Means = $\dfrac{480.6}{10}$ = 48.06

APPENDICES FOR CORRECTING
READING DIFFICULTIES

APPENDIX C-1

Basic Sight Word Sentences

HOW TO USE THE BASIC SIGHT WORD SENTENCES

This appendix contains a list of basic sight word sentences that may be used to provide students with practice in learning the basic sight words in context. Each of the basic sight word phrases listed in Appendix B-4 were used to create these sentences.

Students may practice these sentences alone, with other students, or with parents at home. You may also make an audio tape of the sentences as described in Appendix C-4. Since it is important for students to *master* basic sight words, it is appropriate for students to practice these sentences over and over. They may also create their own sentences using the sight word phrases or incorporate them in language-experience activities. The underlined words that appear on the list are nouns drawn from the preprimer level of a basal series.

A common approach that teachers use in teaching the basic sight words, phrases, and sentences follows these steps:

1. First, the student learns the basic sight words from one sublist at a time. (Each sublist contains 20 words.)

2. Then, the student learns the basic sight word phrases from the same sublist.

3. Then, the student learns the basic sight word sentences from the same sublist.

4. Reinforce the learnings in each previous step by having the student read as much as possible from low-level texts that incorporate many basic sight words and by having the student participate in language-experience activities.

5. After the basic sight words from one sublist are mastered, go on to the next sublist and repeat steps 1 through 4.

Basic Sight Word Sentences

List I

1. She said that it was you.
2. He and I had the <u>duck</u>.
3. They said he had to.
4. But she said it was his.
5. It was on that turtle.
6. He said that it was in it.
7. A <u>duck</u> was for you.
8. They had that for you.
9. She said that of you.
10. <u>They</u> said it was for you.

List II

1. Look at him out there.
2. There is some for her.
3. We have to go out there.
4. Then look up at him.
5. I have to go with her.
6. They had as little as he had.
7. All of it is there.
8. Go down there and look.
9. I am little.
10. Be there with him.

List III

1. I will get them a <u>cat</u>.
2. See what you can do.
3. I like this one a little.
4. Would you look at it for me.
5. My <u>turtle</u> is not little.
6. Could you get some for her?
7. When will you see him?
8. Yes, they were there.
9. He did it for them.
10. Get it so I can see it.

List IV

1. Get the big blue <u>book</u>.
2. When it's over, come to see me.
3. Its ride is very long.
4. No one came to ask her.
5. I would like an apple that is red.
6. He came in just now.
7. If you ask, they will come.
8. They went in to see him.
9. They are your books.
10. He will ride out.

List V

1. I can take it from there.
2. They don't want to do it now.
3. How did you know it was right?
4. She got her four pretty little <u>rabbits.</u>
5. Don't jump around there.
6. Where did he put the good one?
7. It was too little for me.
8. I take every red and green one.
9. It is about this long.
10. Don't put any around there.

List VI

1. They ran away from here.
2. Call after six, then come over.
3. He ran and got his yellow <u>duck.</u>
4. I think I saw the brown <u>turtle.</u>
5. He can help to make her well.
6. I like going to sleep here.
7. Five old <u>turtles</u> are there.
8. Let me ask her to come.
9. He will come by after five.
10. Their cat ran around here.

List VII

1. We can help you eat.
2. The two <u>ducks</u> may walk over there.
3. He will take off the round can.
4. Help him to come before seven.
5. It is very cold today.
6. I do not like to play by myself.
7. I don't know where to stop.
8. When can it fly again?
9. They have never been there.
10. Who had eight yellow ducks?

List VIII

1. Their cat was black and white.
2. May we start to play?
3. You must try once, then try again.
4. Always write your name before you start.
5. Tell her to give it to him.
6. You must drink all of it.
7. Do the work first, then play.
8. You may keep the ten new <u>turtles.</u>
9. How much does he bring?
10. He goes to him for help.

List IX

1. Soon they will find only three of us there.
2. He ate it before it got warm.
3. Our work gave them much help.
4. Will you buy those funny yellow ducks?
5. Hold it open for her.
6. He has made a cold drink.
7. Better start to work right now.
8. It is all done for you.
9. It is cold, so run and jump around.
10. He said he can make it fall.

List X

1. Use the right light when you read.
2. Both of you will sit here.
3. Run too fast and you may fall.
4. They found it under here.
5. Can you pick it up?
6. The cut hurt very much.
7. Say which one you want.
8. I will carry the small one myself.
9. Why pull it up there?
10. My own work is kind of good.

List XI

1. Please thank him for the cold drink.
2. I live far from here.
3. It will grow best over here.
4. I like to laugh and sing, don't you?
5. I wish these were together.
6. How many shall come here?
7. Wash, because you must keep clean.
8. Draw it, then show it to him.
9. She gave him a hot drink.
10. She will start to say, "Once upon. . . ."

Phonograms and Words for Use in Teaching Phonics

In this appendix you will first find an explanation of how the phonogram list was developed. Following that, on pages 369 through 372 you will find an explanation of how to use the phonogram list (and word lists on pages 373 through 384) to teach phonics.

HOW THE PHONOGRAM LIST WAS DEVELOPED

The phonogram list was developed by taking the phonograms from the words listed in *Basic Reading Vocabularies*. This is a vocabulary list derived through an analysis of eight sets of basal readers. In the book *Basic Reading Vocabularies,* words are listed alphabetically, by frequency, and by grade level. The phonogram list was developed using the list by grade level. The list is graded in the following order: Preprimer, primer, first reader, second reader, and so on.

The phonogram lists are not cumulative; only the new phonograms for each level are listed. Therefore, you should begin instruction with the preprimer list regardless of the student's grade placement. In developing the final list, the following rules were used:

1. Each word at preprimer, primer, first-reader level, and so on, was examined, and the phonogram(s) in those words were listed. For example, in the list shown in *Basic Reading Vocabularies,* the following 10 words first appear at the preprimer level: *a, all, am, and, are, at, be, bear, big,* and *blue.* From this list one would then have the following phonograms: *all, am, and, are, at, ear, ig,* and *ue.*

2. Because certain of the phonograms listed in item 1 begin with vowel pairs or contain a vowel controlled by the consonant following it—for example, *ea, ar,* and *al* (which are not introduced at the preprimer level)—they are not listed in the phonogram list until that particular vowel pair or vowel-controlled sound is introduced in the scope and sequence chart shown in Appendix A-1. For example, the vowel pair *ea,* as in the word *each,* is not taught until the first-reader level; therefore, it does not appear in the phonogram list until first-reader level. Likewise the *l*-controlled *a* is not taught in most basal readers until the 2-2 level; therefore, it would not appear in the phonogram list until second-grade level.

3. In some cases words contain phonograms in which the phonogram is different from the sound it takes in most common words, for example, *are*. When this was the case, it was not used at all. For example, it would be confusing to a student to first say *are* and then *bare, care, dare,* and so on.

4. Where a phonogram such as *is* appeared with only one common word such as *his*, it was not included in the list. The assumption here was that to teach such phonograms would be akin to teaching an obscure rule in phonics that pertained to only a few words. The word and phonogram *is* is also somewhat confusing in that it appears in such words as *this* with a different *s* sound. In this case, of course, the student would also probably know both *is* and *his* as sight words.

5. Certain phonograms, such as *ull*, were omitted. This was done in some cases because the words in which they appear are of rather low utility, such as *dull, gull,* and *skull*. The *ull* sound heard in *gull* also takes on a slightly different pronunciation in words such as *bull*.

6. Only one-syllable words were used in making words from phonograms.

7. Vowel pairs are introduced in the phonogram list at the level at which they appear in the scope and sequence. For example, *oo* appears with the long /o/ sound as in *moon* at the third-reader level. The *oo* then appears with the short /o/ sound as in *book* at the second-reader level. Therefore, both appear in the third-reader list of phonograms. However, when both appear they are separated by a line so that students will tend to differentiate between the two different sounds. See the following example of this:

ook—book, brook, cook, crook, hook, look, shook, took

---

oof—goof, hoof, proof, spoof, woof

8. Vowel pairs do not appear by themselves (*aa, ee, ii, oo, uu*). Only vowels or vowel pairs with consonants appear in the phonogram list.

9. There are only about four vowel pairs that are consistent in following the rule that when two vowels appear, the long sound of the first one is heard. Or as you may have been taught, "When two vowels go walking the first one does the talking." These vowels are *ai, ay, oa,* and *ee*. (These vowel pairs, or vowel digraphs, appear in the clever mnemonic, "M*ai*ds m*ay* *ea*t *oa*k trees." Unfortunately, the *ea* vowel pair has many exceptions.)

10. Vowel pairs of low utility or vowel pairs that stand for a number of different sounds have, for the most part, been omitted. However, there are several vowel pairs for which two sounds are rather common. Examples of these are *ea* (each, head); *ow* (crow, owl); and *oo* (moon, book). When these appear, they are handled as described in item 7.

USING THE PHONOGRAM LIST TO TEACH PHONICS

Research in the field of reading shows that the practice of looking for little words in big or longer words is a poor practice since the shorter word often changes in longer words. For example, in the word *government* we would find the words *go, over,* and *men;* yet of these three words only *men* retains the normal sound of the shorter or smaller word. You may wish to experiment with other words.

There is, however, another similar approach that works well for students who need help with word-attack skills. In using this approach one looks for phonograms in words. A phonogram, as defined here, is a common word family beginning with a vowel or vowel pair followed by a consonant or consonants, and sometimes ending in *e.* A high percentage of phonograms retain the same sounds in longer words that they stand for in the simple phonograms themselves. (See the section titled "How the Phonogram List Was Developed.") Helping students learn many phonograms will, in turn, help them immediately identify these same sounds in longer words. In learning phonograms, students also learn many consonant and consonant cluster sounds, as well as the sounds for long and short vowels, vowel pairs, and *r-, l-,* and *w*-controlled vowels.

Many students who have problems in learning to read also seem to have problems learning various rules for vowel and consonant sounds. These same students also have difficulty learning sounds in isolation. In using the phonogram approach, the student learns automatically and is not required to learn rules. We have found that many students can greatly expand their knowledge of phonics in a very short time using the phonogram list. Following is an example that illustrates how you can use the phonogram list to teach students vowel sounds as well as the sounds represented by various consonants and consonant clusters.

Recording and Learning Phonograms by Row

You will note that the phonogram list that follows has each of the rows numbered by grade level. The first three rows of phonograms, at the preprimer level, appear as follows:

1. ake —bake, cake, fake, lake, make, take, rake, wake
2. am —ham, dam, jam, ram, Sam, yam
3. ame—came, dame, game, fame, lame, name, same, tame

Using a tape recorder, record the following script:

"I am going to say a number and then some words. As I say the words you are to point to each word and say it right after you hear it on the tape recorder. Be sure to point to the word as you say it. Number one: *ake, bake, cake, fake, lake, make, take, rake, wake.* Number two: *am, ham, dam, jam, ram, Sam, yam.* Number three: *ame, came, dame, game, fame, lame, name, same, tame.*"

In recording the words, pause slightly after each word so that the student will have time to look at the word and say it before you say the next word on the recording. *However, it is very important to keep a rather brisk pace so the student does not become bored. It is also very important that the student be required to point to each word as she says it. The importance of this cannot be overemphasized.*

When teachers first begin to use this method, they often ask, "How many rows should I expect the student to learn at one time?" The answer to this is not a simple one, but will depend on how fast the student learns. To make this determination, begin with about 10 rows on the first recording. Have the student listen to the tape enough times so that she can do the exercise without listening to the tape recording; that is, have her point to the words and say them just as she did when listening to the tape recorder. If you find the student does not know nearly all of the phonograms already studied, or that it takes an inordinate amount of time for her to learn 10 rows, then next time do only 5 rows. Adjust the number of rows so that the student can learn all the words without a great deal of difficulty. However, this is not to say that the student should not have to listen to the tape and go over the words many times.

Another frequently asked question is, "How many times should the student have to listen to the tape recording and say the words before she learns them?" Again, the answer to this question is not a simple one. The best approach to this is probably to simply tell the student that you want her to listen to the words enough times to learn all the words on the recording. The student will then probably be the best judge of just how many times she needs to listen to the tape to learn all of the words.

If you find that approximately 10 rows is best for the student, then continue to give her about 10 rows at a time until she knows all of the phonograms and words up to her grade level. When she has mastered this task, not only will she know the phonograms found in most words, but she will also have learned nearly all of the initial consonants and consonant clusters. The student will probably also have internalized several of the most common vowel rules.

Using the Phonogram List and Word List to Teach the Most Common Vowel Rules

Following the phonogram list you will find a word list for teaching the most common vowel rules. The two vowel rules that beginning readers should learn are as follows:

1. *When a single vowel appears in a closed syllable, it usually stands for the short sound of the vowel.* (This is often referred to as the CVC rule.) A closed syllable is one that has a consonant at the end; for

example, the words *in, did, on,* and *Fred* are all closed syllables. On the other hand, the words *go, he,* and *me* are open syllables. Remember that a closed syllable is one that has a consonant at the end and an open syllable is one that has a vowel at the end.

2. *When a word has a vowel, consonant, and final* e, *the first vowel will be more likely to be long and the final* e *will be silent.* (This is often referred to as the VCE rule.) More accurately, the student should probably be taught that when she encounters a word with a VCE ending, she should try the long sound first.

In order to use the phonogram and word list to teach these 2 vowel rules, do exercises as follows:

A. Write the following words and ask the student to say each word (or help her, if necessary):

   can   cap   dam   pan

   After doing this, explain to the student that the *a* sound heard in these words stands for the short *a* sound. Have the student give you more words in which the short *a* sound is heard.

B. Write the following words and then ask the student to say each word (again, help her if necessary):

   cane   cape   dame   pane

   Following this, explain to the student that the *a* sound heard in these words stands for the long *a* sound. Have her give you some more words in which the long *a* sound is heard.

C. Now write the word *cane.* Then cross off the *e* at the end. Ask the student what word you now have. Do the same with the words *cape, dame,* and *pane.* Following this, ask the student what happens to the vowel sounds in the words when you remove the *e* from the end. She should, of course, tell you that removing the *e* changes the vowel sound of the first vowel from long to short.

D. Following this, do words the other way around. That is, take words such as *mad, fat,* and *man* and have the student pronounce them. (Help her again, if necessary.) Then put an *e* at the end of each word and ask her to pronounce the words as they now appear. Ask her what happens when you add an *e* to the end of words such as these. The student should, of course, tell you that the first vowel sound changes from short to long when an *e* is added.

In doing this it is not necessary to use real words all of the time; therefore, you may wish to use the phonogram list to supplement the word list. Students enjoy doing the same exercises with nonsense words; for example, changing *slam* to *slame,* or *bam* to *bame.*

E. After teaching the two vowel rules, dictate various words and non-sense words to students and have them write them from your dictation. *This is a very important part of learning these rules.*

F. Provide the student with practice in the act of reading. Have the student read simple sentences or stories that you have created that use the words just taught along with other easy words the student already knows. You may also have the student dictate simple stories to you in which she uses the newly learned words in context. Later, the student can copy over her simple stories for additional practice. Finally, have the student read published easy readers that provide repetitive practice on these phonic elements.

Preprimer

1. ake — bake, cake, fake, lake, make, quake, rake, sake, take, wake

2. am — cam, dam, ham, jam, lam, ram, Sam, tam, yam

3. ame — came, dame, fame, game, lame, name, same, tame

4. an — ban, can, Dan, fan, Jan, man, pan, ran, tan, van

5. and — band, hand, land, sand

6. at — bat, cat, fat, hat, mat, pat, rat, sat, tat, vat

7. ed — bed, fed, Jed, led, Ned, red, Ted, wed, Zed

8. elp — help, kelp, yelp

9. et — bet, get, jet, let, met, net, pet, set, wet, yet

10. id — bid, did, hid, kid, lid, mid, rid

11. ide — bide, hide, pride, ride, side, tide, wide

12. ig — big, dig, fig, gig, jig, pig, prig, rig, wig

13. ike — bike, dike, hike, like, Mike, pike

14. ill — bill, dill, fill, gill, hill, Jill, kill, mill, pill, sill, till, will

15. ime — dime, lime, mime, prime, rime, time

16. in — bin, din, fin, gin, kin, pin, sin, tin, win

17. ing — ding, king, ling, ring, sing, wing, zing

18. ish — dish, fish, wish

19. it — bit, fit, hit, kit, lit, pit, quit, sit, wit

20. og — bog, cog, dog, fog, hog, log, tog

21. old — bold, cold, fold, gold, hold, mold, sold, told

22. op — cop, fop, hop, lop, mop, pop, prop, sop, stop, top

23. ot — cot, dot, got, hot, jot, lot, mot, not, pot, rot, sot, tot

24. ump — bump, dump, hump, jump, lump, pump, rump, sump

25. un — bun, dun, fun, gun, nun, pun, run, sun, tun

26. up — cup, pup, sup

27. ut — but, cut, gut, hut, jut, nut, rut

Primer

1. ace   —   brace, face, grace, lace, mace, pace, place, race

2. ack   —   back, black, hack, jack, lack, pack, quack, rack, sack, slack, stack, tack

3. ad   —   bad, brad, cad, dad, fad, gad, had, lad, mad, pad, sad

4. ade   —   blade, fade, grade, jade, lade, made, wade

5. ag   —   bag, brag, flag, gag, hag, lag, nag, rag, sag, slag, stag, tag, wag, zag

6. alk   —   balk, calk, stalk, talk, walk

7. ank   —   bank, blank, dank, flank, frank, Hank, plank, rank, sank, stank, tank, yank

8. ask   —   bask, cask, flask, mask, task

9. ast   —   blast, cast, fast, last, mast, past, vast

10. ate   —   bate, date, fate, gate, grate, hate, late, mate, Nate, plate, rate, slate, state

11. aw   —   caw, flaw, haw, jaw, law, maw, paw, raw, saw, slaw, taw, yaw

12. each   —   beach, bleach, breach, leach, peach, preach, reach, teach

13. ell   —   bell, cell, dell, fell, hell, jell, Nell, quell, sell, tell, well, yell

14. em   —   gem, hem, stem

15. en   —   Ben, den, fen, hen, Ken, men, pen, ten, wen, yen, zen

16. end   —   bend, blend, fend, lend, mend, rend, send, tend, vend, wend

17. ent   —   bent, Brent, cent, dent, lent, pent, rent, sent, tent, vent, went

18. ext   —   next, text

19. ick   —   brick, Dick, flick, kick, lick, nick, pick, prick, quick, sick, slick, stick, wick

20. im   —   brim, dim, grim, him, Jim, Kim, rim, slim, Tim

21. ive   —   dive, five, hive, live, rive, wive

22. ix   —   fix, mix, nix, six
23. ob   —   blob, bob, cob, fob, gob, job, lob, mob, rob, slob, sob
24. ost —   host, most, post
25. ox   —   box, fox, lox, pox, sox
26. uch —   much, such
27. uck —   buck, duck, luck, muck, puck, pluck, stuck, suck, tuck
28. us   —   bus, flus, nus, plus, pus
29. ust —   bust, dust, gust, just, must, rust

First Reader

1. able — cable, stable, table

2. aid — braid, laid, maid, paid, raid

3. ail — bail, brail, fail, frail, hail, jail, mail, nail, pail, quail, rail, sail, tail, trail, wail

4. ain — brain, chain, drain, gain, grain, lain, main, pain, plain, rain, slain, stain, vain

5. aint — faint, paint, quaint, saint, taint

6. air — chair, fair, flair, hair, lair, pair, stair

7. ang — bang, fang, gang, hang, rang, sang, slang

8. ant — pant, plant, slant

9. ass — bass, brass, class, glass, grass, lass, mass, pass

10. aste — baste, haste, paste, taste, waste

11. ave — brave, cave, crave, Dave, gave, grave, nave, pave, rave, save, shave, slave, stave, wave

12. eal — deal, heal, meal, peal, real, seal, steal, teal, veal

13. ean — bean, clean, dean, glean, Jean, lean, mean, skean, wean

14. ear — clear, dear, fear, gear, hear, near, rear, sear, shear

15. ease — please, tease

16. eat — beat, bleat, cheat, cleat, feat, heat, meat, neat, peat, pleat, seat, treat

17. eed — bleed, breed, creed, deed, feed, freed, greed, heed, need, reed, seed, steed, teed, treed, weed

18. eel — creel, feel, keel, peel, reel, steel

19. een — green, keen, peen, queen, seen, sheen, teen

20. eep — beep, cheep, creep, deep, jeep, keep, peep, sheep, sleep, steep, sweep, weep

21. eet — beet, feet, fleet, greet, meet, sheet, sleet, sweet

22. elf — pelf, self, shelf

23. ere — here, mere, sere

24. ess   — bless, chess, cress, dress, guess, less, mess, press, tress

25. est   — best, blest, chest, crest, jest, lest, nest, pest, quest, rest, test, vest, west, zest

26. ice   — dice, lice, mice, nice, price, rice, slice, trice, vice

27. ine   — brine, dine, fine, line, mine, nine, pine, shine, swine, thine, tine, wine

28. ink   — blink, brink, chink, drink, fink, kink, link, mink, pink, rink, shrink, sink, slink, stink, think, wink

29. int   — flint, glint, hint, lint, mint, print, quint, stint, tint

30. ip   — blip, chip, clip, dip, drip, flip, grip, hip, jip, kip, lip, nip, pip, quip, rip, ship, sip, skip, slip, tip, trip, zip

31. irl   — girl, swirl

32. iss   — bliss, hiss, kiss, miss, Swiss

33. oad   — goad, load, road, toad

34. oat   — bloat, boat, coat, float, gloat, groat, moat, shoat, stoat, throat

35. ole   — bole, dole, hole, mole, pole, role, sole, stole, tole

36. ong   — gong, long, prong, song, thong, tong

37. ood   — brood, food, mood, rood

38. oom   — boom, bloom, broom, doom, gloom, groom, loom, room, zoom

39. oon   — boon, coon, croon, loon, moon, noon, soon, swoon

40. ope   — cope, dope, grope, hope, lope, mope, pope, rope, slope, trope

41. ose   — chose, close, hose, nose, pose, rose, those

42. ote   — cote, dote, mote, note, quote, rote, tote, vote

43. ove   — clove, cove, drove, grove, stove

44. unch   — brunch, bunch, crunch, hunch, lunch, munch, punch

45. ung   — bung, clung, dung, flung, hung, lung, rung, slung, stung, sung, swung

Second Reader

1. ab — blab, cab, crab, dab, drab, flab, grab, jab, nab, scab, slab, stab, tab

2. afe — chafe, safe, strafe

3. age — cage, gage, page, rage, sage, stage, wage

4. ale — bale, Dale, gale, hale, Kale, male, pale, sale, scale, shale, stale, tale, wale, whale

5. all — ball, call, fall, gall, hall, mall, pall, small, squall, stall, tall, wall

6. amb — jamb, lamb

7. amp — camp, champ, clamp, cramp, damp, lamp, ramp, scamp, stamp, tamp, tramp, vamp

8. ane — bane, cane, crane, Dane, lane, mane, pane, plane, sane, Shane, vane, wane

9. ange — change, grange, mange, range, strange

10. ap — cap, chap, clap, crap, flap, gap, hap, lap, map, nap, pap, rap, sap, scrap, slap, snap, strap, tap, trap, wrap, yap, zap

11. ape — cape, drape, grape, nape, scrape, shape, tape

12. ar — bar, car, char, far, gar, jar, mar, par, scar, spar, star, tar

13. arch — larch, march, parch, starch

14. ard — bard, card, guard, hard, lard, sward, yard

15. arge — barge, charge, large

16. ark — bark, Clark, dark, hark, lark, mark, park, quark, shark, spark, stark

17. arm — charm, farm, harm

18. arn — barn, darn, tarn, yarn

19. arp — carp, harp, sharp

20. art — cart, chart, dart, hart, mart, part, smart, start, tart

21. ase — base, case, chase, vase

22. ash — bash, brash, cash, clash, crash, dash, flash, gash, gnash, hash, lash, mash, rash, sash, slash, smash, splash, stash, thrash, trash

23. ath — bath, lath, math, path

24. ause — cause, clause, pause

25. awl — bawl, brawl, crawl, drawl, pawl, shawl, scrawl, sprawl, trawl, yawl

26. awn — brawn, dawn, drawn, fawn, lawn, pawn, prawn, spawn, yawn

27. ay — bay, bray, cray, day, Fay, flay, fray, gay, gray, hay, jay, lay, may, nay, pay, play, pray, quay, ray, say, slay, spay, splay, spray, stay, stray, sway, tray, way

28. ayed — bayed, brayed, flayed, frayed, grayed, payed, played, prayed, rayed, spayed, sprayed, stayed, swayed

29. ead — bread, dead, dread, head, lead, read, spread, thread, tread

30. ead — bead, lead, plead, read, stead

31. eam — beam, cream, dream, gleam, ream, scream, seam, steam, stream, team

32. eap — cheap, heap, leap, reap

33. earn — learn, yearn

34. ease — please, tease

35. east — beast, feast, least, yeast

36. eck — check, deck, neck, peck, speck, wreck

37. edge — hedge, ledge, sedge, wedge

38. eek — cheek, creek, Greek, leek, meek, peek, reek, seek, sleek, week

39. eem — deem, seem, teem

40. eer — beer, cheer, deer, freer, jeer, leer, peer, queer, seer, sheer, sneer, steer, veer

41. eeze — breeze, freeze, sneeze, squeeze, tweeze, wheeze

42. eft — cleft, deft, left, theft, weft

43. eg   —   beg, dreg, Greg, keg, leg, peg

44. eld   —   geld, held, meld, weld

45. ence   —   fence, hence, pence, thence, whence

46. ench   —   bench, blench, clench, drench, French, quench, stench, trench, wrench

47. ept   —   crept, kept, slept, swept, wept

48. er   —   her, per

49. esh   —   flesh, fresh, mesh, thresh

50. ew   —   blew, brew, chew, clew, crew, dew, drew, few, flew, grew, hew, Jew, knew, mew, new, pew, screw, skew, slew, spew, stew, strew, threw, yew

51. idge   —   bridge, midge, ridge

52. ife   —   fife, knife, life, rife, strife, wife

53. ift   —   drift, gift, lift, rift, shift, sift, swift, thrift

54. ile   —   bile, file, mile, Nile, pile, rile, smile, stile, tile, vile, while, wile

55. ilk   —   bilk, milk, silk

56. ince   —   mince, prince, quince, since, wince

57. ipe   —   gripe, pipe, ripe, snipe, stripe, swipe, tripe, wipe

58. ird   —   bird, gird, third

59. ire   —   dire, fire, hire, lire, mire, quire, shire, sire, spire, squire, tire, wire

60. irt   —   dirt, flirt, girt, shirt, skirt, squirt

61. ist   —   fist, grist, jist, list, mist, twist, wist, wrist

62. ite   —   bite, cite, kite, mite, quite, rite, site, smite, spite, sprite, trite, white, write

63. ize   —   prize, size

64. oach   —   broach, coach, poach, roach

65. oak   —   cloak, croak, soak

66. oal   —   coal, foal, goal, shoal

67. oar   —   boar, roar, soar

68. oast — boast, coast, roast, toast
69. ock — block, bock, chock, clock, cock, crock, dock, flock, frock, hock, knock, lock, mock, pock, rock, shock, smock, sock, stock
70. od — clod, cod, God, hod, mod, nod, plod, pod, prod, rod, scrod, shod, sod, trod
71. ode — bode, code, lode, mode, node, rode, strode
72. oft — loft, soft
73. oice — choice, voice
74. oil — boil, broil, coil, foil, moil, roil, soil, spoil, toil
75. oin — coin, groin, join, loin, quoin
76. oke — broke, choke, coke, joke, poke, smoke, spoke, stoke, stroke, woke, yoke
77. old — bold, cold, fold, gold, hold, mold, scold, sold, told
78. ond — blond, bond, fond, frond, pond
79. ong — gong, long, prong, song, strong, thong, throng, tong
80. ood — good, hood, stood, wood
81. oof — goof, poof, proof, spoof
82. ook — book, brook, cook, crook, hook, look, nook, rook, shook, took
83. ool — cool, drool, fool, pool, spool, stool, tool
84. oot — boot, coot, hoot, loot, moot, root, scoot, shoot, toot
85. ore — bore, chore, core, fore, gore, lore, more, pore, score, shore, snore, sore, spore, store, swore, tore, wore, yore
86. ork — cork, fork, pork, stork, York
87. orn — born, corn, horn, morn, scorn, shorn, sworn, thorn, torn, worn
88. ort — fort, port, short, snort, sort, sport, tort, wort
89. oss — boss, cross, floss, gloss, loss, moss, toss
90. oud — cloud, loud, proud
91. ought — bought, brought, fought, sought, thought, wrought

92. ould — could, should, would

93. ound — bound, found, ground, hound, mound, pound, round, sound, wound

94. ount — count, fount, mount

95. our — dour, flour, hour, scour, sour

96. ouse — blouse, douse, grouse, house, louse, mouse, souse, spouse

97. out — bout, clout, flout, gout, grout, lout, pout, rout, scout, shout, snout, spout, stout, trout

98. ow — brow, chow, cow, how, now, plow, pow, prow, scow, vow, wow

99. ow — blow, crow, flow, glow, grow, low, mow, row, show, slow, snow, throw, tow

100. oy — boy, cloy, coy, joy, ploy, Roy, soy, toy, troy

101. ube — cube, rube, tube

102. udge — budge, drudge, fudge, grudge, judge, nudge, sludge, smudge, trudge

103. uff — bluff, cuff, fluff, gruff, huff, muff, puff, ruff, scruff, scuff, sluff, snuff, stuff

104. ug — bug, chug, drug, dug, hug, jug, lug, mug, plug, pug, rug, slug, smug, snug, thug, tug

105. um — bum, chum, drum, glum, gum, hum, plum, rum, scum, slum, strum, sum, swum, thrum

106. umb — crumb, dumb, numb, plumb, thumb

107. une — dune, June, prune, rune, tune

108. ur — blur, bur, cur, fur, slur, spur

109. ure — cure, lure, pure, sure

110. urn — burn, churn, spurn, turn

111. urse — curse, nurse, purse

112. usk — dusk, husk, musk, rusk, tusk

113. uss — buss, cuss, fuss, muss, truss

114. uzz — buzz, fuzz

Third Reader

1. awk — hawk, squawk
2. ere — here, mere, sere
3. inch — cinch, clinch, finch, flinch, pinch, winch
4. olt — bolt, colt, dolt, jolt, molt, volt
5. oop — coop, droop, goop, hoop, loop, scoop, sloop, snoop, stoop, swoop, troop, whoop
6. oose — goose, loose, moose, noose
7. ove — clove, cove, drove, grove, stove

Words for Teaching the
CVC & CVCE Rule

A Vowels

can	cane
cap	cape
dam	dame
fad	fade
fat	fate
gap	gape
hat	hate
mad	made
mat	mate
nap	nape
pal	pale
pan	pane
Sam	same
tam	tame
tap	tape
plan	plane
scrap	scrape
shad	shade
sham	shame

E Vowels

bed	bede
pet	Pete
met	mete

I Vowels

bid	bide
bit	bite
dim	dime
din	dine
fin	fine
hid	hide
kit	kite
mil	mile
mit	mite
pin	pine
rid	ride
rip	ripe
Sid	side
sit	site
Tim	time

I Vowels (continued)

tin	tine
quit	quite
grim	grime
grip	gripe
prim	prime
shin	shine
slid	slide
slim	slime
snip	snipe
spin	spine
spit	spite
strip	stripe
trip	tripe
twin	twine

O Vowels

rob	robe
cod	code
dot	dote
hop	hope
lop	lope
mop	mope
not	note
pop	pope
rod	rode
rot	rote
ton	tone
tot	tote
glob	globe
slop	slope

U Vowels

Long *u* sound:

cub	cube
cut	cute

Long *oo* sound:

dun	dune
jut	jute
tub	tube
crud	crude
plum	plume

Words, Sentences, and Stories for Teaching Structural Analysis

The materials in this section were developed by Cheryl Milner, Director of Assessment and Staff Development in the San Mateo/Foster City (California) School District. The word lists, sentence lists, and stories contained herein have been used to teach thousands of students how to decode "big words" in both one-to-one settings and small groups in classrooms.

Unfortunately, most developmental reading programs (basal readers) provide teachers with few materials or lessons to achieve this important goal. Students who get off to a good start in reading and continue to read widely as they progress through the grades usually have little difficulty in figuring out on their own how to attack (pronounce) multisyllable words. Many students, however, have no strategy other than guessing to assist them in this aspect of decoding.

These materials provide you with two important tools to teach students to decode using structural analysis. First, a sample direct instruction lesson is provided. This lesson consists of six critical steps. The first three teach students how to strategically identify, separate, and blend parts of multisyllable words. Students then get guided assistance in pronouncing whole words (step 4), reading the words in sentence context (step 5), and finally reading the words in story context (step 6).

The scope and sequence of the program is as follows:

Lesson 1: Inflectional endings *-s, -ed, -ing*
Lesson 2: Inflectional endings *-er, -est*
Lesson 3: Inflectional endings *-es, -ies, -ied, -ier, -iest*
Lesson 4: Inflectional endings *double consonants*
Lesson 5: Inflectional endings *-ly, -en, final -e*
Inflectional endings: Review Story
Lesson 6: Compound Words
Lesson 7: Contractions
Lesson 8: Prefixes *re-, un-*
Lesson 9: Prefixes *pre-, pro-*
Lesson 10: Prefixes *com-, im-*
Lesson 11: Prefixes *con-, dis-, ex-*

Lesson 12: Prefixes *de-, in-*

Prefixes: Review Story

Lesson 13: Suffixes *-ion, -ive*

Lesson 14: Suffixes *-able, -ment*

Lesson 15: Suffixes *-ful, -less, -ness*

Lesson 16: Suffixes *-al, -ous*

Suffixes: Review Story

Lesson 17: Syllabication

For each lesson, a word list, a sentence list, and a story are provided.

The sample lesson was created for teaching the very first lesson in the program: Inflectional Endings *-s, -ed, -ing*. However, the same six steps in the sample lesson may be used along with the word lists, sentence lists, and stories to teach the full range of structural analysis skills. Students begin this program learning how to read words with simple inflectional endings, such as *sees* and *asking*. By the end of the program, you will see that you can teach these same students to decode long, difficult words, such as *paleontologist* and *uncontaminated*.

The sample lesson is presented here. Following that are the word lists, sentence lists, and stories.

Sample Lesson

Step 1: Identify Word Parts

Materials: Chalkboard, word list

1. Review roots: **clean, born, cover, dress**
2. Write on the chalkboard:

   List 1

   look   looked
   looks   looking

   List 2

   asks   worked
   works   calling
   called   asked
   asking   working
   calls

3. Direct the students' attention to List 1.
   Say: "How are these words alike?" (They all have the root **look**.)

4. Circle the root *look:*   **look   s**
                              look   ed
                              look   ing

   Say: "How are these words different?" (They have different endings.)

5. Write these headings across the chalkboard:

   <u>s</u>   <u>ed</u>   <u>ing</u>

6. Direct the students' attention to List 2.
   Say: "These words have some of the same endings you saw on the word **look**. Which column would you place the word **asks** under? (Under the **s** because it has an -**s** ending.)

7. Repeat step 6 with the words: **called, asking, calls, worked, calling, asked,** and **working.**

8. Ask the students to read the -**<u>s</u>** words, the -**<u>ed</u>** words, and the -**<u>ing</u>** words.

Step 2: Separate Word Parts (Optional)

Materials: Each student should have a magnetic board with magnetic letters, a small chalkboard, a magic slate, a white board with a marker, or a pencil and paper

1. Review roots: **turn, help**

2. Using the medium you have chosen, have the students form or write the word **turns.** Say: "Show me how you take away the **s** from **turns.** Assist the student to separate the magnetic letters (between the **n** and the **s**), or draw a line between the appropriate letters on the chalkboard, magic slate, white board, or paper.

3. Repeat Step 2 for **helping, turning, helps,** and **helped.**

Step 3: Blend Word Parts (Optional)

Materials: Same as Step 2

1. Say: "Make or write the word **turn.** Now add the ending **-ed.** Put the parts together. What is the word?" **(turned)**
"If you take away the **-ed,** what is left?" **(turn)**
"If you take away the **turn,** what is left?" **(-ed)**
"What is the whole word?" **(turned)**

2. Repeat Step 1 for: **helped**
turns
helps
helping
turning

3. Ask each student to read all the words aloud.

Step 4: Pronounce Whole Words

Materials: Word List 1

1. Select a number of words from the word list with **-s, -ed,** and **-ing** endings.

2. Have the students read these words out loud, chorally, to themselves, and with a partner.

3. Have the students read these words as often as necessary until they can be read quickly and easily.

Step 5: Read in Sentence Context

Materials: Sentence List 1

1. Read the first sentence slowly to the students. Have the students look at the words, not at you, and have the students point to each word in the sentence as you read it.

2. Repeat your reading of the sentence (slowly). This time have the students read out loud (chorally) with you, while they also point to each word in the sentence as it is read.

3. Have the students read the first sentence to a partner, then switch and listen while the partner reads the sentence.

4. Repeat the steps 1, 2, and 3 with the remaining sentences. (If the students catch on quickly and you find that you can skip some of the steps, then do so. But remember: accurate decoding is the goal, not speed of reading.)

5. Provide opportunities for the students to read the sentences over and over, to the teacher, to an aide, to another student, or into a tape recorder.

6. Encourage the students to read the sentences to parents or siblings at home.

7. If a student is able to do steps 1 through 4 successfully but has difficulty reading the words in sentences (step 5), try color-coding the variants. To draw the student's attention to the root plus the inflectional ending, underline or write the roots with one color and the inflectional endings with a different color to draw the student's attention to the two known word parts.

Step 6: Read in Story Context

Materials: Story 1—A Long Camping Trip

1. The story *should* be:
   a. copied and distributed to each student in the group.
   b. introduced to the group.
      Say: "This is a story about a boy with a problem. Some strange things happen to him that do not make sense. We are going to read to find out what they are."
   c. read silently.
   d. read chorally (all students reading out loud together) after silent reading.
   e. discussed by the group.
   f. practiced as seatwork or a free-time activity.
   g. read orally by each student to an aide, into a tape recorder, with a partner (either together or taking turns), and/or to the teacher.
   h. taken home to be read to parents or siblings *after* mastery at school.

2. The story *may* be:
   a. placed on a transparency for introduction to the group.
   b. read to the principal or another group of children for extra oral practice.
   c. placed along with other stories into a booklet.

3. If a student has successfully completed steps 1 through 5, but has difficulty reading variants in context:
   a. try color-coding the variants on one copy of the story. Underline the roots with one color and the endings with another color.

b. ask the student to read the color-coded story orally. Direct his attention to the color-coded ending and root when he has difficulty with the longer word.

c. *encourage the student to read the whole sentence and think of a word that makes sense as well as focusing on the word parts.*

d. after mastery of the color-coded story, have the student read the same story without color-coding.

e. remember that repeated readings of the same story are helpful to students who are learning to decode longer words, and students are usually highly motivated by such repeated readings. This is especially true when students discover that practice leads to success in the form of fluent reading of the story.

Words, Sentences, and Stories for Teaching Structural Analysis

CONTENTS

Word List 1:
Inflectional Endings -s, -ed, -ing

-s

acts	eyes	mothers	slams
answers	fades	naps	sleeps
apples	finds	Nells	slows
asks	flowers	news	smells
backs	friends	nuts	smiles
bangs	frowns	odds	stairs
bats	gaps	opens	starts
birds	gets	paints	steps
blows	girls	pants	stops
boys	glares	pats	streets
bumps	grows	pets	tags
burns	gusts	picks	takes
cakes	hands	plants	tells
calls	hates	plays	thinks
camps	helps	pleases	ticks
cans	hems	pops	times
casts	hints	puffs	tips
chugs	hopes	punts	tracks
clears	hops	puts	trees
clicks	hugs	reds	trips
climbs	jabs	rings	trunks
comes	jams	rolls	tugs
costs	jumps	rows	turns
cuts	kicks	runs	uses
days	kills	sands	waits
dims	kinds	says	walks
dogs	knows	schools	warms
doors	lights	scores	waters
dots	likes	scrubs	waves
dreams	loads	sees	weds
drills	longs	shakes	works
drips	looks	shines	years
dusts	logs	shorts	
eats	makes	skates	
ends	melts	skips	

Word List 1 (continued)

-ed

acted	crashed	lighted	shocked
answered	crossed	loaded	shorted
asked	dreamed	looked	slowed
backed	dressed	melted	smelled
banged	drilled	mothered	started
boxed	dusted	opened	ticked
bumped	filled	painted	tossed
burned	fixed	panted	tracked
called	flowered	picked	turned
calmed	frowned	planted	waited
camped	gusted	played	walked
casted	handed	puffed	warmed
clashed	helped	punted	watered
cleaned	hinted	reached	wished
cleared	jumped	sanded	worked
clicked	kicked	schooled	
climbed	killed	seemed	

-ing

acting	dreaming	knowing	singing
answering	dressing	lighting	sleeping
asking	drilling	loading	slowing
backing	drying	longing	smelling
banging	dusting	looking	starting
blowing	eating	melting	teaching
boxing	eyeing	morning	telling
bumping	feeling	mothering	thinking
burning	finding	opening	ticking
calling	fixing	painting	tossing
calming	flowering	panting	tracking
camping	flying	picking	treeing
casting	freeing	planting	trying
clashing	frowning	playing	turning
cleaning	frying	puffing	waiting
clearing	going	punting	walking
clicking	growing	reaching	warming
climbing	gusting	ringing	watering
cooking	handing	sanding	wishing
costing	helping	saying	working
crashing	hinting	schooling	yelling
crossing	jumping	seeing	
crying	kicking	shorting	
doing	killing	shying	

Sentence List 1:
Inflectional Endings -s, -ed, -ing

She turns and helps the girls.

She turned and helped the girl.

She is turning and helping the girl.

Mother knows when the family eats, plays, and sleeps.

The family likes being mothered.

The family will be eating, playing, and sleeping here.

He opens the doors for his friends.

He opened the door and called his friend.

He is opening the door and calling his friend.

Bob stops and looks up and down the streets.

Bob looked before he crossed the street.

Sis likes trees, walks, and dogs.

Sis watered and walked the dog.

Sis will be watering and walking my dog.

Sam waits and thinks about how many days it takes.

Sam played while he waited.

Sam is waiting and thinking about the day.

Story 1:
Inflectional Endings *-s, -ed, -ing*
A Long Camping Trip

It all started when I came home from camp. I was walking home from the bus stop. As I turned down my street I saw some friends a block away. I called hello, but they acted like they did not hear me.

I was feeling a little sad as I opened the doors to our house. I needed a snack, so I went to find Mom and get some nuts and apples. When I saw her I laughed and said, "Here I am!" Mom seemed not to hear or see me. I started yelling. I jumped up and down. It was no use. She just went on cooking. "She does not look the same as before," I thought.

I walked out the back door. First my friends, and now my mother! What had I done? Was no one glad to see me? The trees were blowing, and the birds were singing, but I felt like crying as I climbed a tall tree near the gate.

I started thinking. My dog Rags would be happy to see me! I jumped from the tree and ran to find Rags. He would be in my room sleeping. I ran up the steps. When I walked into my room I was shocked to find it filled with trunks, junk, and all kinds of odds and ends.

Just then my little sister Kate ran up the stairs. To my surprise she walked right by me too. She looked to be about five years too old to be little Kate! As I walked down stairs I saw the date in the hall—July 16, 2008. But this is only 1998!

Word List 2:
Inflectional Endings *-er, -est*

-er

asker	faster	painter	starter
backer	finder	passer	stronger
boxer	fixer	picker	swifter
brighter	frowner	planter	taller
bumper	grower	player	teacher
burner	helper	puffer	teller
caller	higher	punter	ticker
calmer	hinter	quicker	thicker
camper	jumper	quieter	thinker
clearer	kicker	reacher	tosser
clicker	killer	ringer	tracker
climber	kinder	sander	turner
colder	leader	sayer	waiter
crasher	lighter	shorter	walker
crosser	loader	sleeper	warmer
damper	longer	slower	wisher
dreamer	looker	smaller	worker
dresser	melter	smarter	younger
driller	newer	smeller	
duster	older	softer	
eater	opener	sooner	

-est

brightest	highest	shortest	swiftest
calmest	kindest	slowest	tallest
clearest	longest	smallest	thickest
coldest	newest	smartest	warmest
crossest	oldest	softest	youngest
dampest	quickest	soonest	
fastest	quietest	strongest	

Sentence List 2:
Inflectional Endings *-er, -est*

The ball player used to be a boxer.

He is slower than Roger, but he is not the slowest.

This is the longest I have seen you work.

You have been a faster worker than I have.

I am a quieter eater than you are.

Tom is the longest passer on our team.

When the baby is older she can sit in a walker.

The sky is clearest after a rain.

That moon is the brightest I have ever seen.

He is the quickest fox in the woods.

This has been the warmest day all week.

I have the oldest bike, but the newest paint job.

Story 2:
Inflectional Endings *-er, -est*
The Slowest Kid on the Block

Jack was the smartest, the strongest, the tallest, and the oldest kid on our block. The younger kids always came to him for help. He was also kinder than most older boys I knew. Bob was like a teacher or leader to us, a big brother.

I went to him for help once a few years ago.

"I am slower than all my friends," I told him. "I am also the smallest and the shortest. I would not mind being slower at SOME things. I would not mind being slower than SOME of my friends. But ALL of my friends are faster at ALL things. My friend Bob is a faster climber, a faster eater, a faster walker, and a faster worker. Bob is the fastest at all things."

I went on talking to Jack. "I thought that if I grew taller, I would get faster. So at each meal I ate longer than any of my friends. I did not get taller. I am still the shortest, thickest kid on the block. What can I do?" I asked. "I need your quickest answer."

Jack told me to wait one week and I would find an answer quicker than I thought. I thought it would be the longest week of my life.

Three days after our talk I went to Fun Park U.S.A. with some friends. We were having fun at the Killer Whale Show when I looked down and saw Bob's sister, Sue, looking over the wall of the pool. The killer whales began their fastest swim across the pool to make their highest jump to grab the smallest ring from the pole over Sue's head. When the whales came down they would hit Sue!

I made the swiftest move of my life and reached Sue sooner than Bob. I pulled her away just as the two whales shot out of the water.

Bob said, "You were by far the quickest thinker and the fastest on your feet this time, Mike. Sue may be quicker than me, but not quicker than my best friend, Mike." He took Sue's hand. "And you, little one, are the dampest girl at the park. We should go home before you get any colder."

I guess Jack knew I couldn't always be the slowest at all things.

Word List 3:
Inflectional Endings
-es, -ies, -ied, -ier, -iest

-es

boxes	clashes	fixes	teaches
branches	crashes	foxes	tosses
bushes	crosses	goes	watches
buzzes	dishes	reaches	wishes
churches	dresses	searches	

-ies

babies	cries	funnies	scurries
berries	dries	hurries	tries
carries	flies	muddies	
copies	fries		

-ied

babied	copied	fried	muddied
busied	cried	hurried	tried
carried	dried	married	scurried

-ier

busier	flier	merrier	slier
carrier	frier	muddier	sneakier
copier	funnier	prettier	speedier
crazier	furrier	rustier	tinier
crier	happier	scarier	uglier
drier	heavier	sillier	

-iest

busiest	happiest	rustiest	tiniest
craziest	heaviest	scariest	ugliest
driest	merriest	silliest	
funniest	muddiest	sneakiest	
furriest	prettiest	speediest	

Sentence List 3:
Inflectional Endings
-es, -ies, -ied, -ier, -iest

After the rain the ground was muddier than before.

He jumped in the mud and tried to be the muddiest of all his friends.

His mother cries when she tries to wash the mud out of his clothes.

These boxes are the heaviest I have ever carried.

My brother lives alone and has never married.

Tom cried when he saw that the rain had made his bike rustier.

The foxes hurried across the field.

The mother fox watches her babies.

He was the tiniest baby I had ever seen.

That tinier bee buzzes as it flies.

If I had three wishes I would wish to be the funniest, craziest clown, so that I could make people happier.

The funnies in the paper are funnier than before.

Story 3:
Inflectional Endings
-es, -ies, -ied, -ier, -iest
The Ugliest Ogre

In the very deepest part of the woods lived the ugliest ogre that had ever lived. Every ogre said that he was scarier and uglier than any other ogre. I had tried many woods before I came here to live. I came here because of the many bushes and tall trees. It was the prettiest place I had ever been. It was prettier than any picture I had ever seen. I was happier here than I had ever been. One day all of the ogres in the woods came to visit me.

They all cried at once, "We must go away from our beautiful woods, away from the trees with their beautiful branches, away from the sliest foxes, away from the sweetest berries, away from each little mouse who scurries around under our feet, and away from all of our friends. We will miss the woods."

"If you like it so much, then why must you leave?" I asked. "That is the silliest thing I have ever heard."

"Over near those bushes lives the ugliest, meanest ogre of the woods. He searches for the tiniest ogres he can find, and he fries them for his dinner!"

With that, the tiny ogres hurried and scurried away to look for a new home.

"How do you know this?" I called after them. They did not hear me.

I did not think that the ugliest ogre fried tiny ogres like me.

I went to visit him. I thought he looked funnier than any ogre I had seen before, but not scarier. I tried to say hello, but the ugly ogre just cried.

"I was much happier before I came here," he said. "My life was merrier. I am going away."

"That's the craziest thing I ever heard of," I said. "You must talk to the others and let them know that you are *not* the ugliest, scariest, sneakiest ogre, but that you are the merriest and the friendliest. They will like you if they get to know you. Why I like you already and I just met you."

I took his hand and we both felt happier.

Word List 4:
Inflectional Endings
Double Consonants

Roots

bat	gap	pet	step
beg	get	plan	stop
bet	hem	pop	swim
big	hit	put	tag
bob	hop	rob	tip
can	hot	run	trap
chug	hug	scrub	trot
dig	jab	shop	wed
dim	jam	sit	wet
dot	log	skip	zip
drip	nap	slam	
flap	pat	spot	

Sentence List 4:
Inflectional Endings
Double Consonants

The digger used a shovel to do the digging of the hole.

Some days I can hear the water dripping, dripping while I am napping.

This must be the hottest day of the year.

She petted and patted the dog.

The corn is popping in the corn popper.

The bride planned a big wedding.

The boy zipped up the zipper of his coat and skipped out to play.

When she tugged on the strap, the horse trotted down the path.

The rabbit stopped hopping.

We stepped across the brook on the stepping stones.

Story 4:
Inflectional Endings
Double Consonants
Monster from Outer Space

It was the hottest day of the year when that strange shape popped out of the sky and zipped back and forth before my eyes. I was sitting by the pool thinking about going in swimming when there it was! It stopped over the pool, and a strange dotted monster hopped out.

I jumped up to run just as the monster was hitting the water. He bobbed in and out of the pool three times, tipped his head to one side, and was still dripping as he stepped back into the ship. The door slammed, and the ship zipped off.

I never saw the strange dotted monster again. What a strange swimmer to have dropping in my pool!

Word List 5:
Inflectional Endings *-ly, -en, final e*

-ly

brightly	dimly	openly	strongly
calmly	dryly	quickly	swiftly
churchly	freely	sadly	thickly
clearly	friendly	shortly	timely
costly	greatly	shyly	warmly
crossly	lightly	slowly	
daily	motherly	softly	

-n, -en

brighten	hidden	quicken	soften
broken	known	redden	sunken
dampen	lengthen	sadden	taken
eaten	lighten	shaken	thicken
grown	olden	shorten	widen

Sentence List 5:
Inflectional Endings *-ly, -en, final e*

The friendly boy has broken the glass.

I saw his face redden when I said, "My, how quickly
you have grown."

"We must go home shortly," Mother said calmly.

It will sadden me greatly to give away my bike.

The fox will be running very swiftly.

She timed Bob running, while I was timing Jack.

The sunken ship was found under the water.

Mother will shorten my dress after baking a cake.

The book was hidden under some papers.

We were hoping to find a seat in the front.

Story 5:
Inflectional Endings *-ly, -en, final e*
The Hidden Mummies

One day as I was walking home from school, I saw a sunken door in the broken brick wall near the old Miller place. I pushed on the door. As the opening began to widen I felt my heartbeat quicken. I wanted to run swiftly away.

"Lighten up!" I thought calmly as I peered into the dimly lit room.

That is when I saw them! Four hidden mummies! The white tapes of one mummy slowly waved in the wind. They were clearly not friendly mummies.

There I was, a hater of mummies, glaring at four of them. Or were they glaring at me? One wrong move could be very costly.

I quickly turned and closed the sunken door. I must say, I was pretty shaken. How was I to have known there were mummies at the old Miller place?

Inflectional Endings: Review Story
The Land of Giants and Elves

Who could have known that there really was a land of thrilling giants and friendly elves? Joe had found this olden land one evening while trimming the hedges for his Aunt Sue. As he clipped the back of the largest hedge, he spotted a good-sized hole hidden there, covered with ivy.

He started trimming the ivy when he spied a flowered path leading to a funny-shaped building. Cutting through the ivy to get a better look, he saw newly made tracks. The only thing Joe could do was follow the tracks.

No sooner had Joe started walking than he saw a motherly-looking elf brightly dressed in the prettiest clothes Joe had ever seen. She was watering the plants. The elf clearly did not see Joe at all.

Joe crossed a bubbling stream and then sat down while his dripping boots dried. All of a sudden he heard a crashing, bumping noise. He looked up just in time to see a frowning giant swiftly rushing down the hill to the building at the end of the winding path. All around the building with its tall towers were lots of the littlest people Joe had ever seen. As the giant rushed nearer, the little elves scattered and ran away. The giant went into the building, and things were much quieter than they had been earlier. The elves did not come back.

Slowly Joe walked back to the hole in the hedge. He could hardly wait to go home and find Tom!

Word List 6:
Compound Words

aircraft	butterfly	hardwood	pineapple
airfield	classmate	headline	playground
airliner	cowboy	herself	policeman
airplane	cupcake	highlight	popcorn
airport	doghouse	himself	racecar
anywhere	downhill	homesick	railroad
babysit	draftsman	horseshoe	rainbow
backboard	dragonfly	however	raincoat
backbone	dressmaker	icebox	rattlesnake
background	drugstore	indeed	raygun
bagpipe	earache	inside	roadblock
barnyard	everyone	into	roadside
baseball	fairway	kingfish	rooftop
basketball	firebell	landslide	rowboat
bathtub	firehat	lifeboat	sailboat
because	fireman	lipstick	schoolhouse
bedside	fisherman	mailbox	seafood
bedspread	flagman	mailman	seaman
bedtime	flapjack	mainland	seaport
behind	flashlight	milkman	seesaw
beside	flatworm	motorbike	shipmate
birthday	football	myself	shipwreck
birthmark	foremost	nearby	shotgun
birthplace	forgot	newspaper	skyline
birthright	freeway	oatmeal	skyscraper
birthstone	fruitcake	onto	slipknot
blackberry	glassblower	outdoors	smallpox
blackboard	glassware	outfit	snowball
blacklist	godfather	outlaw	snowflake
blackmail	grandfather	outline	snowman
blackout	grandmother	outrage	snowmobile
blindfold	grapevine	outside	snowshoe
blowhole	groundwork	overdone	someone
bluebell	grown-up	overdose	something
bluebird	gunpowder	overnight	sometime
brainstorm	hailstorm	pancake	somewhere
brakeman	hairbrush	peanut	sourdough
briefcase	haircut	peppercorn	southeast
buckskin	halfback	peppermint	southwest
buckwheat	hallway	pigtail	spaceman

Word List 6 (continued)

spaceship	storyteller	toadstool	waistline
spotlight	strawberry	today	waterproof
staircase	streamline	toenail	watershed
stairway	sunburn	trademark	weekend
steamboat	sunshine	turnpike	wheelchair
steelhead	supermarket	underground	windmill
stepladder	tadpoles	upstairs	without
stereotype	tailbone	waistband	

Sentence List 6:
Compound Words

The airplane landed on the airfield at the airport.

The butterfly flew around the barnyard in the sunshine.

The little boy took a bath in the bathtub with his toy sailboat.

Mother sits at my bedside to read a story at bedtime.

The boys and girls ran downhill and onto the playground.

The boys are playing football nearby.

My grandmother and grandfather gave me a horseshoe game for my birthday.

The mailman left the mail in my mailbox.

The spaceman jumped into his spaceship and flew away.

The flagman stood on the freeway to flag the cars by.

Story 6:
Compound Words

Little Brother, Anyone?

My little brother Bobby just had his fifth birthday. He can be very hard to live with. He likes to make everyone think he is something he is not. Like cute! Cute indeed! If they knew him like I do, they would not think he was so cute. I sometimes think I would like to live by myself.

Today Bobby thinks he is a fireman. He even ate lunch with his raincoat and firehat on. Mom would have a fit if I came to the table with a hat on! Bobby said that he needed to be ready when the firebell rang.

Last weekend I took Bobby to the playground beside the schoolhouse. Mom will not let him go by himself, so I always have to take him. She does not seem to know that I have better things to do than babysit my little brother. First he wanted to play spaceman. He cried because his swing did not look like a spaceship. He cheered up when I let him shoot me with his raygun, however. Next, he climbed the staircase to the rooftop. He said he was an airplane and could land on the grass like a butterfly. I had to say that I would buy him a cupcake and give him my old flashlight before he would come down. Then Bobby wanted to make a snowman. There was not a snowflake to be found anywhere. We made snowballs without snow. Bobby made a snowman in a snowmobile. After it was done we had a snowball fight. Bobby used rocks for snowballs. It was like being hit by a landslide. I hid behind a nearby mailbox. It was a good thing none of my classmates saw me hiding from my little brother.

On the way home we passed the drugstore and the supermarket. Bobby wanted his cupcake.

Every day with Bobby is like that. The last time he went to stay overnight with Grandmother and Grandfather he called home at bedtime. He wanted to come home because he had forgotten his cowboy outfit. He said that cowboys never sleep without their guns. Dad had to take the freeway and bring

Bobby home. I think he was homesick. Sometimes I do not know why they put up with him.

I like to hunt tadpoles, look at motorbikes, make model racecars, and play football and baseball. Bobby wants to do all of these things too. He never lets me be alone. Mom says it is because I am such a great brother that Bobby wants to be grown-up like me.

I guess Bobby is not such a bad brother. He just may be as good a brother as I am someday.

Word List 7:
Contractions

aren't	he'll	o'clock
can't	he's	one's
couldn't	I'd	that's
didn't	I'll	they'll
doesn't	I'm	wasn't
don't	isn't	you're
haven't	it's	you've
he'd	I've	

Sentence List 7:
Contractions

He doesn't know that it's six o'clock.

We can't find the keys, so we aren't ready to go.

Tom couldn't play handball because he didn't have
anyone to play with.

I don't think he'll be home because I've been calling
all day.

I'm sure we haven't met before.

Dad said he'd be home soon, but he's not here yet.

I'd like to know what time you're having dinner.

I'll make sure the meat isn't too well done.

This one's not as big as that one is.

That's not a nice thing to say.

They'll be here before you've cleaned up.

She wasn't at school today.

Story 7:
Contractions
Jumping Seeds

Mexican jumping beans aren't beans, but they'll sure jump. The bean isn't really a bean but a seed. It's a seed with a caterpillar inside.

A moth lays an egg on the plant. After the egg hatches he'll chew his way into a seed. The seed doesn't jump, but it does fall to the ground. The larva in the seed can't do much but wiggle around. This makes the bean or seed move. Some people think he's jumping because of the heat from the ground.

Now the larva couldn't live in the seed forever. He'd run out of food. I'll tell you how he gets out. He chews a hole in the seed. Next he turns into a pupa and then into a moth. The moth climbs out the hole. He didn't go in as a moth, but that's how he comes out.

If you've ever kept a jumping bean for a long time you may have seen a moth come out. If you have some jumping beans, and you haven't seen one move for a long time, it may mean that that one's a pupa. If you wait you're sure to have a moth.

I'd better warn you! If your jumping bean stops moving, don't keep the seeds in your house, unless you don't mind sharing your home with a moth or two.

Word List 8:
Prefixes *re-*, *un-*

re-

react	refill	remorse	respond
readjust	refine	remote	response
rebate	reflect	remove	restore
rebel	reflex	renew	restrain
rebirth	reform	reorder	restrict
rebloom	refrain	repack	result
reborn	refresh	repair	retail
rebuild	refuse	repay	retain
rebury	refute	repeat	retard
rebut	regain	replace	retest
recall	regard	replay	retire
recap	regress	reply	retold
recede	regret	report	retouch
receive	rehearse	repress	retrace
recess	reject	reproach	retreat
recharge	rejoice	repulse	return
recite	relate	request	reveal
reclaim	relax	require	revenge
reclean	relay	rerun	reverse
record	release	research	revert
recount	relent	resemble	review
recover	relief	resent	revise
redeem	relieve	reserve	revolt
redo	rely	resist	revolve
redone	remain	resort	revue
redress	remind	resource	reward
reduce	remiss	respect	rewrite

un-

unable	uncertain	uncover	uneven
unafraid	unchain	uncross	unfair
unaware	unclaim	uncut	unfasten
unbalance	unclean	undo	unfit
unbecoming	unclear	undone	unfold
unbolt	unclench	undress	unfurl
unborn	unclose	undue	unglue
unbroken	uncoil	undying	unhappy
unbuckle	uncommon	unearth	unhealthy
unbutton	unconcern	uneasy	unheard
uncap	uncork	unequal	unhook

Word List 8 (continued)

_un-_ (continued)

unjust	unmask	unsaddle	untidy
unkind	unpack	unsafe	untie
unknown	unpaid	unscramble	until
unlace	unpin	unscrew	untouch
unlatch	unpleasant	unseal	untrue
unlearn	unplug	unseat	untwist
unleash	unravel	unseen	unused
unless	unread	unsnap	unveil
unlike	unready	unsnarl	unwell
unload	unreal	unsteady	unwind
unlock	unrest	unstrung	unwise
unlucky	unripe	unsung	unwrap
unmarried	unroll	unsure	unzip

Sentence List 8:
Prefixes *re-*, *un-*

The weatherman will repeat the report on our unpleasant weather at six o'clock.

My dog will refuse to unclench his teeth and release the stick after I throw it.

Unlace and remove your shoes, unzip your coat, and relax until dinner is ready.

Unless we repair the old chair it will be unsafe, and we will be unable to sit in it.

Please remind me to unload the washer after we return from the store.

Bob was feeling a little uncertain and very uneasy about trying out for the class play.

They had to unwind the ropes and release the sails as a wind came up in order to return the boat to the dock.

It would be unwise to unfasten the ribbon and unwrap the present before the party.

You must review the story and rewrite this paper before I retest.

As he began to unsaddle his horse and unpack the saddlebags, the sheriff said, "I regret having to lock you up, Sam, but I can't let you get revenge for your brother's death."

Story 8:
Prefixes *re-*, *un-*
The Mystery of Sea Creatures

Long ago, unlucky sailors would relate unpleasant stories about unknown sea creatures when they returned from the sea. These creatures had long arms and might attack the ship. They might refuse to release it until the ship sank or many men were eaten or drowned.

Today, scientists who review those stories think that some of them were untrue. The creatures may have been real, but the size may have gotten larger each time the story was retold.

A sailor who looked into the water as he tried to unfasten the ropes or unfurl the sails might become very uneasy if he saw a large animal with long arms. Today we know these were not uncommon monsters, but an octopus or a giant squid.

Other sea creatures that may have made fishermen and sailors a bit unsteady on their feet are eels, lizards, and whales. How would you feel if, as you bent to recover your fishing net, you found a seven-foot eel? The result could be another untrue story about sea monsters.

Some iguanas, or lizards, remove food from the sea bottom by prying it loose with their teeth. They can remain underwater for fifteen minutes. These uncommon creatures are found around the islands off the coast of South America.

After much research, or study, scientists think that many of the creatures thought to be monsters were whales. Grey whales have bumpy backbones, grow to be fifty feet long, and have been reported to attack boats. These attacks may have been the result of a mother whale trying to keep her baby safe.

In a storm or thick fog anything might be reported to look like a monster. Even a remote island in an unclear fog could resemble a sea monster. Maybe unknown creatures do live in the sea, but so far scientists have been unable to uncover real sea monsters, only real animals.

Word List 9:
Prefixes *pre-*, *pro-*

pre-

prearrange	prejudice	pretend
precede	prepack	pretense
precise	prepare	pretest
preclude	prescribe	prevail
precook	present	prevent
predict	preserve	preview
prefect	preside	prewash
prefix	presume	

pro-

proceed	program	proscribe
proclaim	project	protest
procure	prolong	proton
produce	promote	protrude
profane	pronoun	provide
profess	pronounce	provoke
profile	propane	
profound	propose	

Sentence List 9:
Prefixes *pre-, pro-*

We must promote the program before the preview show on March 10th by putting up posters.

I presume, or take for granted, that my pretest score will be lower than my posttest score.

At a yellow blinking light, proceed with care to prevent an accident.

Sometimes I pretend to know how to pronounce very long words when I don't.

If you provoke me again by calling me names, I will project my voice throughout this whole room in an angry protest.

If you precook the meat and prewash the produce, it is easier to prepare meals when camping.

Story 9:
Prefixes *pre-, pro-*
Gerbils

I don't profess to like gerbils, but I can't pretend that they don't make perfect pets, because they do. Most people love the furry animals. They are clean and easy to feed. These animals have a mouselike profile with tiny feet, whiskers, and long tails.

In the wild, gerbils dig tunnels in the desert sand and live underground, but you can prepare a good home for a pet gerbil almost anywhere. If you proceed as follows, I predict you will have lots of fun with your pet.

First, procure a healthy gerbil from a pet store. Provide the gerbil with a tank or wire cage, wood chips for bedding, a water bottle, and gerbil food. Prearrange the supplies so that you will be able to find them as you need them. If your gerbil acts slow or sleepy, I prevail upon you to take it to a pet doctor. Protect your pet from dogs, cats, and small children. Try not to provoke or upset your pet.

Preserve or keep a quiet place for your gerbil. Finally, I presume you will also give your gerbil lots of love.

Word List 10:
Prefixes *com-*, *im-*

com-

combat	common	complex
combine	commune	comply
comfort	commute	compose
command	compact	compound
commence	compare	compress
commend	compass	comprise
comment	compel	compute
commerce	compile	comrade
commit	complain	
commode	complete	

im-

image	impact	imply
imbed	impair	import
imbue	impale	impose
immature	impart	impound
immense	impasse	impress
immerse	impeach	imprint
immobile	impede	improper
immodest	impel	improve
immoral	impend	impulse
immortal	implant	impure
immune	implore	

Sentence List 10:
Prefixes *com-*, *im-*

It is common for mothers to complain that their children's rooms are messy.

It would impress me if you would improve your math grades.

Mr. J. P. Marsh bought the four smaller farms to combine them into one immense 15,000-acre ranch.

Everyone tries to compare me with my brother, but we are nothing alike.

If you like to sleep in comfort, try a waterbed.

You can make an imprint in the wet sand with a shell.

It is improper to clean your teeth at the dinner table.

The map was too complex for me to follow.

Story 10:
Prefixes *com-, im-*
Dinosaurs

The word *dinosaur* means "terrible lizard." Try to compare the dinosaurs that lived more than 65 million years ago to the animals of today, and you may think of lizards or snakes. Some scientists believe that common birds of today and the dinosaurs may both be related to early reptiles that crawled on the land over 200 million years ago. The history of the dinosaur is very complex and not at all complete.

Scientists learn more every day. Not all dinosaurs were immense in size. Some were as small as a chicken. Scientists have found fossils, or imprints of bones and footprints that became imbedded in the earth.

In 1964 Dr. John Ostrom found some unusual fossils in Montana. He found the remains of a four-to-five-foot dinosaur that must have run fast on its hind legs to catch its prey. Research seems to imply that

this animal may have been a warm-blooded ances-
tor of today's birds.

Some dinosaurs were very terrible and would have
been unpleasant to meet. One such dinosaur was
the Sauropod (*SOAR*-oh-pod), which weighed about
30 tons. It might impel you to run if it were not for
the fact that its size would impede your path.

Of course, humans did not live during the age of the
dinosaurs. Everything we know is just what scientists think from studying the remains they have
found. We should commend scientists like Dr. Ostrom for their hard work and study.

Word List 11:
con-, dis-, ex-

con-

concave	conform	consume
conceal	confound	contain
conceit	confront	contempt
conceive	confuse	contend
concept	congest	contest
concern	congress	context
concert	connect	continue
concise	connote	contort
conclude	conquer	contour
concord	conquest	contract
concrete	consent	contractor
concur	conserve	contrast
condemn	consider	control
condense	consist	convene
condone	console	converge
conduct	conspire	convert
confess	constant	convex
confide	constrain	convey
confine	constrict	convict
confirm	construct	convince
conflict	consult	

dis-

disaffect	discomfort	disloyal
disagree	disconnect	dismiss
disallow	discontinue	dismount
disappear	discord	disobey
disappoint	discount	disorder
disapprove	discourage	disown
disarm	discover	dispatch
disarray	discrete	dispel
disaster	discuss	dispense
disband	disfigure	disperse
disbar	disgrace	displace
disbelief	disguise	displease
disbelieve	disgust	dispose
discard	dishonest	disprove
discern	dishonor	disserve
discharge	disinfect	distend
disclaim	disjoin	distort
disclose	dislike	disturb
discolor	dislodge	

Word List 11 (continued)

ex-

exact	exhaust	explode
exam	exile	exploit
excel	exit	explore
except	expand	export
excess	expanse	expose
exchange	expect	express
excite	expel	extend
exclaim	expend	extent
exclude	expense	extinct
excrete	expert	extract
excuse	expire	extreme
exhale	explain	

Sentence List 11:
Prefixes *con-, dis-, ex-*

I must confess that I did not win the contest fairly.

Tom had to convince his father to consent to drive his friends home after the party.

The building contractor sank the beams in concrete to make the building safe.

The rock concert will conclude at 1:30 a.m.

I disagree with the way some people dispose of, or discard, their empty cans and gum wrappers.

We watched with disbelief as he made the rabbit disappear.

The little boy will discover a Santa Claus disguise when he looks into the old trunk.

Mom dislikes disorder, and she is always making me clean my room.

I could not think of a good excuse for my low score on the math exam.

She tried to explain to the clerk why she wanted to exchange the gift.

You must exhale into the balloon to make it expand.

They walked through the exit of the spaceship to explore the world beyond.

Story 11:
Prefixes *con-, dis-, ex-*
The Family of Ants

Experts consider the life of the ant to discover more about it. Few people disagree, and most would concur, or agree, that ants live like humans in many ways. Some live in towns or villages. The queen or mother ant lays the eggs and is treated with extreme care by the workers. She controls the colony or village. Some ants are builders and construct nests. They may construct a nest or shelter from their own bodies. Farmer ants grow food, and tend other insects the way people tend cattle.

Some ants excrete something they contain in their bodies to mark their nests and to make trails for other ants to follow.

Don't expect to meet an army of ants in your backyard, but army and driver ants may move by the thousands to conquer anything in their path. In constant motion, they disappear quickly and build a new nest each night. The sting of the Australian bulldog ant can cause great discomfort also.

If you were to discuss the ant with your friends, it could be hard to convince them that people live anything like the tiny ants who disturb picnics. But it is true. With a little study you would discover that the ant has been around for millions of years. Except for their looks, the ant may be like humans in many ways.

Word List 12:
Prefixes *de-*, *in-*

de-

debar	deform	deprive
debark	degrade	derail
debate	degree	derive
debrief	deice	descend
decal	delay	descent
decay	delete	describe
decide	delight	deserve
declare	deliver	design
decline	deluxe	desire
decode	demand	despise
decoy	demean	despite
decrease	demise	destroy
decry	demon	destruct
deduct	demote	detach
deface	denote	detail
default	deny	detain
defeat	depart	detect
defect	depend	detest
defend	depict	detract
defense	deplete	develop
define	deplore	device
deflate	deport	devise
deflect	deprave	devote

in-

inboard	index	infield
inborn	indirect	infirm
inbred	indoor	inflame
inbreed	induce	inflate
incense	induct	inflect
incise	indulge	inflict
incite	inept	influx
incline	inert	inform
inclose	inexact	ingest
include	infancy	inhale
income	infant	inject
increase	infect	injure
indeed	infer	injury
indent	infest	inlaid

Word List 12 (continued)

in- (continued)

inland	inspire	intent
inlay	instance	intern
inlet	instant	intrude
input	instead	invade
inquire	instep	invalid
insane	instill	invent
inscribe	instinct	invert
insect	insult	invest
insert	insure	invite
inset	intact	invoice
insist	intake	involve
inspect	intend	inward

Sentence List 12:
Prefixes *de-*, *in-*

I detest people who insult me.

I got so cold the last time I went camping that I intend to invent an indoor campground.

If you deflate the tire tube, it will decrease in size.

When you inflate the tire tube, it will increase in size.

They will develop a new device to detect planes flying overhead.

Please describe your feelings as the plane began its fast descent.

The infant had a very intent look on his face as she tried to reach the rattle.

In infancy a baby will hold its breath and not inhale when placed underwater.

I am afraid that if the store does not deliver my new bike soon, Mom and Dad may decide I really don't need it.

Story 12:
Prefixes *de-, in-*
Birds That Don't Fly

Have you ever heard anyone describe a bird that flies under water or runs faster than you can pedal your bike? Does this sound insane? Well, it isn't. The penguin uses its wings to push itself through an inlet of water so that it can rest inland on the rocks. The ostrich can run as fast as 35 miles an hour. Neither of these birds can fly. Here are a few details about other birds that do not fly.

The emu does not try to defend itself when in danger. Its instinct tells it to depart or run away as quickly as it can.

The kiwi will inhale the smell of a worm through the nostrils at the end of its beak, and then insert its long beak into the ground to get dinner.

The demise of the dodo bird came soon after it was discovered on an island in the Indian Ocean. This bird did not develop a fear of humans and soon began to decrease in number. Finally, humans did destroy all of these birds. The dodo is now extinct.

The rhea of South America is very tall. This helps the mother to spot enemies and insure the safety of her chicks.

One funny-looking bird can defend itself with a crash helmet on its head and spikes on its feet. This strange bird is the cassowary (CASS-uh-ware-ee).

The design of these birds is not for flying. Many of these birds do not have the right kind of breastbone for flying. Instead, they find food and protect themselves in other ways.

Prefixes: Review Story

The Unusual Bats

People may compare bats to "flying foxes." They sleep by day and compete for food at night. Some bats can see at night, but most use sound waves or echoes to hunt. These bats read sounds so well that even human sonar does not compare. Bats use their own sounds to guide them through the forest and to reveal insects or other prey to feed on. If humans could detect with their own ears the complex display of sounds that bats produce, they would most likely react with surprise. But the human ear cannot detect these sounds. These unusual animals produce more sounds more often than any other group of mammals.

Some types of bats include fruit bats, tomb bats, hammerhead bats, whitelined bats, and spearnosed bats. The whitelined bat weighs no more than three dimes. Its home on the side of a tree may often expose it to plain view. One colony may consist of 40 bats. The whole colony leaves to feed at night and then returns at dawn. Two males may bark at each other and shake or snap a gland under their wing in a fight for space. In this strange display the males may shake their wings many times. Scientists presume that this shaking causes the gland to disperse some scent or odor. When the females return to the roost, the males stop fighting and begin to sing. Scientists have been able to record these songs and reveal just how complex they really are.

Bats hunt and eat many things. A fishing bat may impale a small fish in an instant. Other bats have a tongue which protrudes and extends to lap nectar from plants. Bats can consume at night most kinds of food that birds hunt and eat during the day.

Only in the past 30 years have humans begun to extend their knowledge of the bat and its ways. Scientists still have much to learn about the unusual bats.

Word List 13:
Suffixes -*ion*, -*ive*

-ion

abrasion
action
addition
adhesion
admission
affliction
ambition
attention
attraction
auction
aversion
caption
caution
circulation
citation
combination
communication
concession
condition
confession
confusion
connection
construction
convention
conversation
correction
creation
deception
decision
declaration
deduction
definition
delusion
depression
description
destruction
detection
determination
dictation

direction
discrimination
discussion
distinction
diversion
division
edition
education
election
elevation
emotion
equation
erosion
evacuation
eviction
evolution
exception
excursion
exemption
expansion
expensive
explosion
expression
extension
fiction
fission
flotation
formation
fraction
function
ignition
imagination
imitation
impression
induction
information
intention
invasion
invention
inversion

invitation
junction
legislation
lesion
limitation
location
lotion
mansion
mention
mission
mutation
nation
notation
notion
nutrition
objection
obligation
occlusion
occupation
operation
option
ovation
partition
passion
pension
perception
percussion
permission
persuasion
population
position
potion
probation
production
profession
protection
punctuation
question
radiation
ration

Word List 13 (continued)

-ion (continued)

reaction	salvation	television
reception	sanction	tension
reduction	satisfaction	tradition
reflection	section	vacation
regulation	selection	variation
relation	session	version
reproduction	station	vision
revolution	suction	

-ive

abusive	excessive	positive
active	executive	productive
attractive	expansive	reactive
captive	expensive	relative
cooperative	impressive	representative
defensive	inventive	repulsive
destructive	locomotive	
elective	objective	

Sentence List 13:
Suffixes *-ion, -ive*

The new building was attractive to some and repulsive to others.

I need to make a correction to this division problem or the fraction will not be correct.

Defensive driving will help keep the traffic on our highways in much better condition.

A good education may help you to become a more productive person.

I have a relative who was very active in the election of our president.

The expression of your emotions can help get rid of tension and anger.

The construction of the bridge was very expensive.

The television version of this book of fiction was not very impressive.

Story 13:
Suffixes *-ion, -ive*
Diving in "Inner Space"

A new focus of attention has been given to the expansive reaches of "inner space" in recent years. Skin and scuba diving have become an attractive sport to active people of all ages seeking information about the seas. Men and women like Jacques Cousteau have become concerned about the protection of the ocean and its resources as humans begin their exploration of this new world.

Divers must be fit and in very good condition. They must have excessive knowledge of the ocean, and of the reaction of the human body in these strange conditions. Divers must also have training in first aid.

A diver must have the right tools for diving. Scuba gear can be purchased or rented, but either way it is expensive.

For a diving session in the cool waters off the California coast, it is necessary to wear a wet suit, a dry suit, or both to prevent excessive loss of body heat. A weight belt must be worn to offset the positive effect of the body and the wet suit that causes one to float. A diver also needs a face mask with a good seal, a snorkel, a set of boots and regulation fins, and a flotation vest. Gloves are an option. A scuba tank and a regulator are used to breathe underwater. A diver should also carry a knife and compass for direction. A float and a flag are used to caution boats and other divers. There are other tools in addition to these for taking pictures, fishing, or studying.

A good diver never dives alone, obeys all safety rules, and leaves the ocean as he or she found it so that it will remain productive and attractive for many years to come.

Word List 14:
Suffixes *-able, -ment*

-able

accountable	distractable	recoverable
admirable	durable	redeemable
adorable	employable	reliable
agreeable	enjoyable	remarkable
available	honorable	renewable
capable	knowledgeable	respectable
changeable	liveable	retrainable
cleanable	lovable	suitable
comfortable	movable	touchable
conceivable	notable	treatable
curable	payable	washable
dependable	questionable	
desirable	readable	

-ment

agreement	disappointment	judgment
amazement	disarmament	movement
amendment	discontentment	pavement
amusement	discouragement	payment
appointment	disenchantment	placement
argument	displacement	punishment
arrangement	employment	replacement
assignment	enjoyment	resentment
basement	equipment	settlement
concealment	excitement	statement
department	government	treatment
development	instrument	
disagreement	investment	

Sentence List 14:
Suffixes -*able*, -*ment*

After payment was made for tickets at the amusement park, we began our day of excitement and enjoyment.

The adorable little girl picked up the lovable puppy and kissed its nose.

The dog was quite capable of finding a comfortable spot on the pavement to sleep.

I bought a durable pair of jeans at the department store.

The doctor is very knowledgeable about the treatment of sick children.

The basement was too dark and dirty to be suitable for living.

My teacher said that the assignment was not readable.

I would be agreeable to a settlement of this argument.

To our amazement, the injured cat made an admirable attempt at movement toward its master.

Story 14:
Suffixes -*able*, -*ment*
Archery

Archery has played a notable role in human development. Early humans used their archery skills for protection, as a means of getting suitable food, and for their own amusement and enjoyment. They had to have sure judgment and quick smooth movements. The bow was also used throughout the world as an instrument of music.

Today archery is an enjoyable sport that is available to the whole family. It is also conceivable that poor posture, if caught at a young age, may be curable through regular practice of the sport on the archery range.

Archery tackle refers to the equipment used by the archer while shooting. The statement, "Athletes will be as good or poor as their equipment," applies to archery. Matched arrows and bows must be suitable to the individual using them. Equipment may be purchased from a respectable, reliable archery shop.

Equipment from a department store is a poor investment. Fiber-glass arrows may be best for beginners and are quite durable. There is disagreement about what is the best bow. A good recurve bow is probably the most dependable bow on the market. It is usually desirable for a beginner to use a lighter bow than a skilled archer. Other available tackle includes a bow sight, a finger tab, and an arm guard.

Archery has its place in history, literature, art, and religion. There is also agreement that it will have a place in the future.

Word List 15:
Suffixes *-ful, -less, -ness*

-ful

armful	doubtful	peaceful
awful	dreadful	playful
bashful	fearful	powerful
beautiful	forceful	restful
cheerful	graceful	truthful
colorful	hateful	useful
cupful	helpful	watchful
deceitful	hopeful	wishful
delightful	joyful	

-less

careless	flawless	priceless
cheerless	friendless	sightless
colorless	helpless	sleepless
doubtless	homeless	speechless
effortless	hopeless	thoughtless
fearless	noiseless	

-ness

brightness	humanness	quickness
directness	illness	sadness
emptiness	kindness	sickness
fullness	lateness	softness
gladness	loneliness	sweetness
goodness	madness	thickness
happiness	neatness	weakness

Sentence List 15:
Suffixes *-ful, -less, -ness*

The fearful child stood motionless in the noiseless room.

The graceful dancer did a joyful dance of happiness.

The delightful sweetness of the cake kept me speechless.

I am doubtful that this dreadful emptiness in my stomach will be gone after just one apple.

I love to watch the beautiful ocean because it makes me feel so restful and peaceful.

The playful puppy was homeless.

I am hopeful that you will be truthful.

He spoke in a powerful voice and flashed a watchful look toward the sky.

Story 15:
Suffixes *-ful, -less, -ness*
The Match

Bob: Hi! Ready for a restful tennis match?

Tim: Sure! Beating you is always effortless.

Bob: Effortless? You're the one with the hopeless backhand.

Tim: Ha! And you have the quickness of a turtle on the court.

Bob: Enough of this talk. Let's play tennis.

Hey, that was really a forceful serve! I'd better keep a watchful eye on you.

Tim: What an awful shot. I'm just careless. I act like I have an armful of bricks. Thoughtless!

Bob: To be truthful, I'd be grateful for a little weakness on your part. I just can't seem to get my flawless game together today.

Tim: That's wishful thinking!

Bob: I am rather graceful today, aren't I?

Tim: Dreadful is more like it. Well, that's the match. Better luck next time!

Bob: Thanks, that was fun. It was a good match. That last shot of yours was priceless. Let's get a soda.

Tim: Fine! You showed no weakness today. That was a good workout. Let's play again tomorrow.

Word List 16:
Suffixes *-al, -ous*

-al

additional	formal	political
alphabetical	functional	postal
bifocal	historical	regional
brutal	hysterical	rehearsal
central	legal	terminal
chronological	musical	tribal
coastal	numeral	typical
electrical	personal	
focal	physical	

-ous

ambitious	glorious	poisonous
courageous	gracious	previous
dangerous	humorous	prosperous
delicious	joyous	religious
enormous	mysterious	studious
envious	nervous	various
famous	numerous	

Sentence List 16:
Suffixes *-al, -ous*

That enormous slice of cake was delicious.

The mysterious story was not easy to understand.

The lovely gracious queen became famous for her numerous religious speeches.

The central coastal region has examples of the typical sea life in this state.

Some tribal customs seem brutal and involve physical pain.

I have always been nervous before my previous speeches, but today I will remain calm.

There will be a rehearsal of the historical play in the central lobby at 8:00.

This enormous list must be put in alphabetical order.

Story 16:
Suffixes *-al, -ous*
Sailing on Ice

Iceboating or hard-water sailing is a regional sport since you need cold weather to do it. Central and eastern New York get cold enough for a typical day of iceboating. The cold wind can be brutal, so the captain must be courageous.

Sailing on the ice can be dangerous and requires about the same physical strength as sailing on water. A typical iceboat glides on three metal runners. There are various boat styles, since numerous ambitious boaters build their own iceboats.

Racers wear functional safety equipment such as helmets and goggles. The boats may look a little humorous sailing along the ice, but their captains say they get a glorious, joyous feeling of personal freedom while iceboating.

Suffixes: Review Story

Another Way to Ride

Horse vaulting provides excitement and enjoyment for sports lovers all over the world. This team sport demands the gracefulness of a gymnast, the quickness in movement of a hockey player, and the courageous ambition of a high diver. The German version of this impressive sport was brought to the United States over 24 years ago. News of this remarkable sport spread with unbelievable rapidness.

There are now about forty additional U.S. teams in the competition. Reaction to the sport has been excellent. After many rehearsals, the precision riding of these teams is flawless and leaves their audiences speechless.

Beginning riders may be nervous before a national competition. After a while the riders lose their tension and provide enjoyable entertainment with their remarkable routines. Each team member must do a set of special exercises and is then able to do an original program. To be successful, the team must work together.

Word List 17:
Syllabication

abominable
additional
adjoining
allergic
alphabetical
alternately
amplifier
anthropologist
anticipation
apparatus
apparition
application
apprehensive
archaeologist
armadillo
arrogantly
artifact
artificial
association
astronaut
astronomical
atmosphere
barnacle
barometer
barometric
barracuda
bedraggled
beneficial
bibliography
bicentennial
binoculars
calamity
casserole
centimeter
charity
circulation
circumstance
collapsible
combination
commercial

compassionate
completion
composition
compressed
concentration
confidential
congregation
continent
continual
contribution
contributor
conventional
convulsively
correspondent
craftsmanship
decapitated
decaying
declaration
decompression
defiance
definition
delicatessen
delicious
demonstration
descended
description
detection
deteriorate
detestable
devouring
diameter
diminutive
dinosaur
diplomatic
disintegrate
distributor
duplicate
egotistical
electrical
electricity

elevation
emotion
emphatic
evacuation
evaporate
evolution
executive
expedition
experience
explosion
extension
extraordinary
fantastic
fertilizer
flotation
formation
frustrating
generosity
geologist
gravitational
gravity
hallucination
historian
horizontal
hurricane
ignition
ignorant
illuminated
imagination
imaginative
imitation
immaculate
immediate
immobilize
immortality
implication
impossible
inconvenience
incredible
incredulous

indignation
inducement
industrial
information
inhabitant
initiate
intelligent
intention
intervals
intimidate
intricate
invasion
investigate
investigating
irritated
isolation
jettisoned
lacerate
legislation
librarian
limitation
limitlessly
listlessly
locomotive
luminous
malignant
malingering
manuscript
meditation
melancholy
melodious
miraculously
monotonously
mysterious
neighborhood
obligation
occupation
ominous
paleontologist
parasites

Word List 17 (continued)

particles	presently	respiration	testified
pedestrian	proficient	revolution	testimony
perception	publisher	satisfaction	theoretically
permission	radial	sensibilities	tolerance
perspiration	rapidly	sensitivity	tradition
persuasion	ravenous	sincerity	tremendously
pestilential	refrigerate	sombrero	trillions
petition	regression	specifications	ultimately
phenomenon	regulate	spectacle	uncontaminated
photographic	relative	speculation	unimaginable
population	reluctant	stalagmite	universe
position	representative	statistics	unreasonable
potato	reproduction	submicroscopic	unrelenting
precision	reproductive	substantial	variation
preparation	repulsively	superficial	vicinity
prescription	residential	television	visibility
presentation			

Sentence List 17:
Syllabication

The amplifier made the music louder.

The archaeologist studied the bones of the dinosaur and the other artifacts found near the caves.

Sara is a kind, compassionate person.

The twelve contributors contributed five hundred dollars to the charity.

That delicatessen has delicious potato salad.

After the explosion there was an evacuation of the building.

The horizontal lines on the television screen make it impossible to see the picture.

The intricate puzzle is very frustrating.

The hurricane did substantial damage to our neighborhood.

The barometric pressure is falling rapidly.

Story 17:
Syllabication

A Black Hole in Space

Do black holes really exist? The answer may lie beyond our present imagination.

In our galaxy there are trillions of stars. Most of them are unnamed. At any given time, some of these stars are dying. Some consume themselves, some explode, and others contract or draw in upon themselves. When a decaying star contracts, the matter of which it is made is tremendously compressed. The star shrinks limitlessly. It theoretically shrinks past pinpoint size, to submicroscopic size, to zero volume. Its surface gravity rises. This unrelenting gravity or gravitational whirlpool sweeps luminous gases and star particles into its core. Scientists don't know what happens ultimately. Maybe a new presently unimaginable universe is formed.

If the earth were to collapse from a diameter of nearly eight thousand miles down to two thousand miles, its increased gravity would cause a 175-pound man to weigh almost one and one-half tons. At a diameter half the size of a golf ball, the earth would become a black hole.

When a star becomes a devouring darkness, a ravenous force, nothing can ever again escape, not even light. Since nothing can escape, there is no way an observer investigating the immediate vicinity of a black hole could report back to us. Ultimately black holes could eat up all the matter in our galaxy.

Do black holes really exist? Many scientists believe that black holes are the completion of the evolution of stars that were once many times the size of the sun.

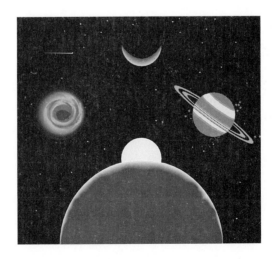

APPENDIX C-4

Prepositional Phrases

This appendix contains a list of prepositional phrases that may be used in teaching some of the most common words in the English language as well as the most common prepositions and noun words. Some teachers object, perhaps rightly so, to the teaching of basic sight words or any high-utility word in isolation. For students who are having difficulty with any of the most commonly used prepositions, you may wish to use these phrases as you would the sight word phrases in Appendix B-4. You may also make an audio tape of the phrases to be sent home with students who are having difficulties with these words. The tape may be made as follows:

1. Copy the first page, so that you will have it for further reference.

2. Number the first 10 to 15 phrases of the copy you have made. (Once you have worked with a student for a short while, you will know how many she is capable of learning. If you find that you send 15 phrases on an audio tape home and the student has easily mastered all of them, send home 20 more the next time. Increase these to the maximum that the student can successfully master in the time between meetings.) Place a 1 by the first phrase, a 2 by the second phrase, and so on. Then make an audio tape with a script much the same as the one that follows:

"You will hear some phrases on this tape recording. First you will hear a number and then you will hear the phrase. Look at each word as it is pronounced on this tape recording. There will then be a short pause for you to say the phrase. Be sure to point to each of the words as you say them. Number one, *about his dog* (pause); be sure to point to each word as you say it. Number two, *about my cat* (pause); Number three, *about dinner. . . ."*

It is important that the student point to each word as it is pronounced. This way the student makes the connection between the spoken word and the written word. The following are commonly used phrases. Most of the words are also in the Fry list of the 600 most frequently used words in reading and writing the English language.[1]

ENDNOTE

1. Fry, E. (1972). *Reading instruction for classroom and clinic.* New York: McGraw-Hill (pp. 55–63).

about

about his dog
about my cat
about dinner
about my sister
about the room

along

along the ground
along the water
along the wall
along the road
along the way

as

as a house
as a girl
as a boy
as a man
as a woman

before

before winter
before bed
before the fire
before eight
before we go

by

by the hair
by the horse
by the week
by the government
by her eyes

after

after we've gone
after three years
after work
after his mother
after the bell

around

around the garden
around the school
around here
around eight o'clock
around the trees

at

at the house
at the door
at the party
at the water
at the half

but

but the outside
but the poor
but the yard
but his head
but her eyes

down

down the hill
down the side
down the front
down the street
down the stairs

for

for the law
for the doctor
for the money
for a guess
for tomorrow

from

from the cows
from her need
from my cousin
from the cold
from the story

in

in the hour
in the music
in the spring
in the picture
in his voice

into

into the box
into the floor
into the train
into the bank
into the office

like

like the wind
like snow
like you
like her hat
like a bird

near

near the fish
near the war
near the bridge
near the farm
near the airplane

next

next turn
next president
next to me
next to him
next in line

of

of the sun
of my life
of the farm
of the paper
of the church

off

off the wall
off the water
off the horse
off the table
off of it

on

on one afternoon
on Friday morning
on her smile
on the house
on her face

out

out of paper
out to study
out of school
out of line
out in public

outside

outside the country
outside the woods
outside the town
outside the third grade
outside the grocery store

over

over his clothes

over the ice

over the city

over the thing

over his name

through

through them

through his heart

through twenty

through the day

through the water

until

until the night

until they come

until tomorrow

until this minute

until he knew

to

to the summer

to the fair

to the state

to the world

to the house

up

up the window

up the river

up the table

up in the air

up to speak

with

with his suit

with my uncle

with her aunt

with a present

with the baby

Prefixes and Suffixes

PREFIXES

Prefix	Meaning	Examples
a	on, in, at	alive asleep abed
a (an)	not, without	anhydrous anhydride anarchy
*ab, abs	*from*	abduct abrogate abstain
*ad (ac, af, ag, al, an, ap, ar, as, at)	*to,* at, toward	adapt accuse aggrade acclaim affirm
ambi (amb)	both	ambicoloration ambivalent ambidextrous
amphi (amph)	both, around	amphibian amphitheatre amphibolite

---

*Prefixes that appeared most frequently and accounted for 82 percent of the 61 different basic forms of prefixes studied by Stauffer. The italicized word represents the meaning of the prefix in the study referred to here. From Stauffer, R. G. (1969). *Teaching reading as a thinking process.* New York: Harper & Row (p. 348).

Prefix	Meaning	Examples
ana	back, again, up, similar to	analysis analogy anabaptist
ante	before, earlier date	antechamber antedate antetype
anti (ant, anth)	against, counteracts, prevents	antilabor antiaircraft antitoxin
apo (ap)	off, away from, used before	apology aphelion apocrine
archi (arch)	chief, extreme	architect archenemy archfiend
auto	self-propelling, self	automobile autotruck autobiography
*be	to make, about, *by*	belittle beguile befriend
bene	well	benefit benefactor benevolent
bi	having two, double	bicycle bilingual biweekly
by	near, extra	bystander by-pass byproduct
cata (cat, cath)	down, against	catastrophic catacomb catheter
centi	one hundred	centigrade centimeter centipede

Prefix	Meaning	Examples
circum	around, about	circumnavigate circumpolar circumspect
*com (co, col, con, cor)	*with,* together, intensification	combine copilot collect confided corrupt
contra	against	contradict contraband contrarious
counter	opposite, in retaliation, opposed to but like	counterclockwise counterattack counterpart
*de	*from,* away	deport detract devitalize
deca (dec, deka, dek)	ten	decimal decade decagon
di (dis)	twice, double	dissect dichroism dichloride
dia	through, across	diagonal diagram diagnose
*dis	opposite, refuse to, *apart*	disagree disintegrate disable disengage
ec (ex)	out of, from	eccentric exodus exaggerate
*en	*in,* into make	encircle enact encourage

Prefix	Meaning	Examples
enter	to go into, among	enterprise entered entertain
epi (ep)	upon, after, over	epitaph epilogue epicene
equi	equal	equilibrium equilateral equiangular
*ex	*out*	exile exhale exhaust
eu	well	euphony euphonism eugenic
extra	beyond	extraordinary extrajudicial extracurricular
for	very, neglect, away	forlorn forbid forget
fore	before, in front	forepaws forehand foreleg
geo	earth, ground, soil	geography geographic geology
hemi	half	hemisphere hemicycle hemistich
hexa (hex)	six	hexagon hexapod hexachord
hyper	over, above	hypersensitive hyperactive hyperacid

Prefix	Meaning	Examples
hypo	under, beneath	hypocrite hypocycloid hypodermic
*in (il, im, ir)	in, within, *into*	inbreed instigate infect
*in (il, im, ir)	no, *not,* without	illiterate immaterial insignificant irresponsible
inter	between, with	interurban interlock interact
intra	within, inside of	intrastate intravenous intramural
intro	into, within	introvert introspective introduce
kilo	one thousand	kilowatt kilogram kilocycle
mal (male)	bad, wrong, ill	maladjust malediction maladroit
meta (met)	after, change in place or form	metacarpal metabolism metaprotein
milli	one thousand	milligram millimeter milliard
mis (miso)	wrong	misplace misadventure misanthrope
mono (mon)	one	monosyllable monologue monolayer

Prefix	Meaning	Examples
multi	many	multitude multiply multiphase
non	not	nonunion nondemocratic nonzero
ob (oc, of, op)	to, upon, totally	object occur offer oppose
oct (octa, octo)	eight	octopus octagon octopod
off	from	offspring offset offstage
out	beyond, excels	outtalk outweigh outmaneuver
over	too much	overactive overheated overage
par (para)	by, past, accessory	parallel paragraph parasympathetic
penta (pent)	five	pentagon Pentateuch pentane
per	through, completely	perceive persuade perchloride
peri	around, about	perimeter periphery periscope
phono (phon, phone)	voice, sound	phonograph phonate phoneme

Prefix	Meaning	Examples
poly	many	polygon polygamy polysulfide
post	later, behind	postgraduate postaxial postlude
*pre	*before,* in front (of), superior	prewar preaxial pre-eminent
*pro	moving forward, acting for, defending, favoring, *in front of*	progress pronoun prosecutor prolabor prologue
quadr	four	quadrant quadrangle quadrennial
quint	five	quintuplets quintet quintillion
*re (red)	*back,* again	review regain recall
retro	backwards	retroactive retrospect retroflex
semi	half, partly, twice in (period)	semicircle semicivilized semiannually
sex (sexi)	six	sextant sexpartite sexivalent
*sub (suc, suf, sug, sup, sur, sus)	*under*	submarine succeed suffix
super	above, exceeding	superior superstructure superscribe

Prefix	Meaning	Examples
sur	over, above, beyond	surcoat surface surbase
syn (sym)	with, together	sympathy synthesis symptom
tele (tel)	afar, of, in, or by	television telescope telephoto
trans	across	transcontinental transport transatlantic
tri	three	triangle tricycle triweekly
ultra	beyond, excessively	ultraviolet ultramodern ultramarine
*un	*not*, opposite	unannounced unburden uncrowned
uni	consisting of only one	unicellular uniform unicorn
under	below	underpaid underworked underpass
vice	in place of	viceroy vice-president vice-consul
with	against, away	withstand withdraw withhold

SUFFIXES

Suffix	Meaning	Examples	Used to Form
able (ible, ble)	able to, worthy of	obtainable divisible breakable	adjectives
ac (ic, al, an)	characteristic of, having to do with, caused by	cardiac alcoholic comical American	adjectives
aceous (acious)	characterized by, like	carbonaceous crustaceous tenacious	adjectives
ade	action, product	blockade limeade lemonade	nouns
age	act of, cost of	tillage passage postage	nouns
al	relating to, of, pertaining to	directional fictional dismissal	adjectives
al	action process	rehearsal arrival acquittal	nouns
an (ian, ean)	pertaining to, of, born in	diocesan Christian European	adjectives
an	one who, belonging to	artisan African American	nouns
ance (ence)	act of, state of being	continuance reference performance	nouns
ancy (ency)	state of being, act	efficiency piquancy emergency	nouns

Suffix	Meaning	Examples	Used to Form
ant (ent)	one who	accountant suppliant superintendent	nouns
ant	performing, promoting	litigant expectorant expectant	adjectives
ar	relating to, like, of the nature of	regular polar singular	adjectives
ard (art)	one who (excessively)	braggart dullard pollard	nouns
arium	place relating to	planetarium sanitarium aquarium	nouns
ary (ar)	relating to	military dictionary scholar	nouns
ate	office, function	directorate vicarate magistrate	nouns
ate	acted on	temperate determinate animate	adjectives
ate	to become, com- bine, arrange for	evaporate chlorinate orchestrate	verbs
ation (ition)	state of	translation realization nutrition	nouns
cle	little, small	article particle corpuscle	nouns
dom	state of being	wisdom martyrdom freedom	nouns

Suffix	Meaning	Examples	Used to Form
ed	tending to, having	cultured versed bigoted	adjectives
en	cause to have, made of	strengthen woolen wooden	nouns
en	to make, made of	deepen strengthen fasten	verbs
ent (ence)	quality, act, degree	solvent emergence despondence	nouns
er (ar ior, yer)	a thing or action, connected with, or associated	batter beggar interior lawyer	nouns
ery (erie)	place to or for collection of	nunnery jewelry tanneries	nouns
esce	to begin	effervesce fluoresce coalesce	verbs
escent	starting to be	obsolescent fluorescent alkalescent	adjectives
esque	like, having quality or style of	picturesque Romanesque statuesque	adjectives
ess	female	patroness giantess princess	nouns
et (ette)	little, female	dinette suffragette pullet	nouns
ful	full of	hopeful playful joyful	adjectives

Suffix	Meaning	Examples	Used to Form
fy	to make, become	liquefy purify glorify	verbs
hood	state of, condition	womanhood childhood priesthood	nouns
eer	one who, calling or profession	auctioneer buccaneer profiteer	nouns
ic (ics)	relating to, affected with	alcoholic allergic volcanic	adjectives
ic (ical)	one that produces	magic cosmetic radical	nouns
ice	condition or quality of	malice justice practice	nouns
ie	small, little	doggie lassie	nouns
ile (il)	appropriate to, suited for, capable of	docile missile civil	adjectives
ing	related to, made of	farthing banking cooking	nouns
ion (sion)	result of act, state	regulation hydration correction	nouns
ise (ize)	to make, treat with	sterilize summarize finalize	verbs
ish	having	boyish purplish fortyish	adjectives

Suffix	Meaning	Examples	Used to Form
ism	act of, state of	baptism invalidism animalism	nouns
ist	practicer or believer in one who, the doer	evangelist pianist violinist	nouns
ive	related to, tending to	creative massive amusive	adjectives
ize	to become, become like	Americanize crystallize socialize	verbs
kin	little	catkin manikin napkin	nouns
le (el)	small, a thing used for for doing	icicle handle mantle	nouns
less	without, lacking	careless hopeless painless	adjectives
ling	young, small	duckling hireling suckling	nouns
ly	in a way, manner	softly quietly hoarsely	adverbs
ment	concrete result, state, process	embankment development amazement	nouns
ness	state of being	happiness cheerfulness hopefulness	nouns
ock	small one	hillock bullock paddock	nouns

Suffix	Meaning	Examples	Used to Form
or	state of, does certain thing	pallor grantor elevator	nouns
orium	place for, giving	sanatorium auditorium haustorium	nouns
ory	tending to, producing	auditory gustatory justificatory	adjectives
ose	full of, containing, like	verbose cymose morose	adjectives
ous	having, full of	religious generous poisonous	adjectives
ship	state of, office, art	friendship clerkship horsemanship	nouns
ster	one that does or is	spinster teamster youngster	nouns
th	act of, state of	growth length spilth	nouns
tude	condition	certitude gratitude finitude	nouns
ty (ity)	state of, degree, quality	masculinity priority timidity	nouns
ulent	tending to, abounds in	fraudulent flocculent opulent	adjectives
ure	act, office	exposure legislature procedure	nouns

Suffix	Meaning	Examples	Used to Form
ward	in specified direction	southward seaward backward	adverbs
wise	manner, way	likewise clockwise lengthwise	adverbs
y	like a, full of	rosy fishy glassy	adjectives
y (acy)	state of, action, condition, position	jealousy inquiry celibacy	nouns

APPENDIX C-6

Repeated Readings Chart

The method of repeated readings is described in the introductory chapter. On page 501 is an example of a repeated readings chart in which the student began reading at 35 words per minute and, after 8 trials, was reading at 120 words per minute. The student also began this passage with 26 errors and, after 8 trials, made no errors. To compute words per minute, count the number of words the student is to read and then determine the time it takes the student to read that passage in seconds.

The words per minute equals the number of words read divided by the number of seconds it took to read the passage, multiplied by 60. A student who reads 220 words in 110 seconds would then be reading at 220/110 = 2.0 × 60 = 120 words per minute. In doing repeated readings, it is recommended that you use 100 words per grade level times .75. Thus a student in the fourth grade should read 400 × .75 or 300 words; a student in the fifth grade should read 500 × .75 or a 375-word passage; and so on.

On page 503 is a blank repeated readings chart that you may wish to detach and duplicate for students' use.

Repeated Readings Chart

Words per Minute		Number of Errors	
Trials		Trials	
1 2 3 4 5 6 7 8 9 10		10 9 8 7 6 5 4 3 2 1	
140			0
130			2
120			4
110			6
100			8
90			10
80			12
70			14
60			16
55			18
50			20
45			22
40			24
35			26
30			28
25			30
20			32
15			34
10			36

Repeated Readings Chart

Words per Minute		Number of Errors	
Trials		Trials	
1 2 3 4 5 6 7 8 9 10		10 9 8 7 6 5 4 3 2 1	
140			0
130			2
120			4
110			6
100			8
90			10
80			12
70			14
60			16
55			18
50			20
45			22
40			24
35			26
30			28
25			30
20			32
15			34
10			36

Name of Student: _____

Number of Words in Passage: _____

APPENDIX C-7

Precision Reading Form and Charts

The precision reading technique is described in the introductory chapter. On page 507 is a blank form that may be used to record the student's performance during two separate precision reading trials.

At the top of the form are blank spaces to record the following information: student's name, teacher's name, date(s) of trials, the page on which the passage begins (if it was taken from a book), and the page on which the passage ends.

The form is easy to use. The numbers above the lines correspond to the sentences that the student reads. The teacher merely writes a plus (+) or a zero (0) above each line, as the student finishes the sentence, to indicate whether the student read the sentence correctly (+) or with one or more errors (0). At the completion of the reading (up to 50 sentences per trial on this form), the teacher and student count the number of pluses, then tabulate the efficiency rate.

The efficiency rate is a percentage, obtained by dividing the number of sentences read without error by the total number of sentences, and multiplying this figure by 100.

Efficiency rate = the total number of correct sentences ÷ the total number of sentences × 100.
Example: 42 correct sentences ÷ 50 total sentences × 100 = efficiency rate of 84% (or, if total of 50 sentences is always used, multiply the number of correct sentences by 2)

After the student's reading performance is tabulated, the teacher or student then completes an accuracy chart, such as the example on p. 509. If the technique is used daily, the student will see improvement in his reading of the same passage over time by looking at the chart. When the student achieves 100% on two successive readings, a new, more difficult passage may be selected.

Teacher judgment should be used in deciding what constitutes an error. In some cases, for example, the teacher may choose not to count self-corrections as errors, especially if the teacher has been encouraging the student to read carefully and go back and self-correct oral reading when necessary.

This method is designed to stress accuracy over speed. Only after the student is able to read material at grade level with consistent accuracy should the technique be modified to encourage reading speed. To do this, the same recording chart is used; however, the student is asked to read for a specified time (which may be indicated in the *Time* space on the recording form shown on p. 511). At the end of the specified time, the teacher or student then graphs the number of sentences read correctly on the second chart that appears on p. 511. Before using this technique, it is suggested that you read the more complete description in the introductory chapter.

PRECISION READING FORM
AND CHARTS

Student _____   Teacher _____

Date(s) _____   Begin on _____   End on _____

_____

TRIAL # _____

Scoring by Sentences

—	—	—	—	—	—	—	—	—	—	—	—	—	—	—	—	—
1	2	3	4	5	6	7	8	9	10	11	12	13	14	15	16	17
18	19	20	21	22	23	24	25	26	27	28	29	30	31	32	33	34
35	36	37	38	39	40	41	42	43	44	45	46	47	48	49	50	

Tabulating Efficiency   [TIME: _____]

_____ ÷ _____ × 100 = _____

correct sentences   total sentences   efficiency rate

_____

TRIAL # ____

Scoring by Sentences

—	—	—	—	—	—	—	—	—	—	—	—	—	—	—	—	—
1	2	3	4	5	6	7	8	9	10	11	12	13	14	15	16	17
18	19	20	21	22	23	24	25	26	27	28	29	30	31	32	33	34
35	36	37	38	39	40	41	42	43	44	45	46	47	48	49	50	

Tabulating Efficiency   [TIME: _____]

_____ ÷ _____ × 100 = _____

correct sentences   total sentences   efficiency rate

Graph Samples

GRAPHING ACCURACY

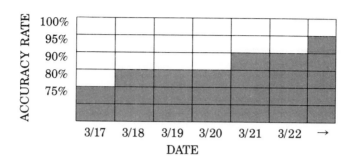

This graph begins at 75% accuracy because the student should not be reading any material at a lower rate.

GRAPHING THE NUMBER OF CORRECT SENTENCES

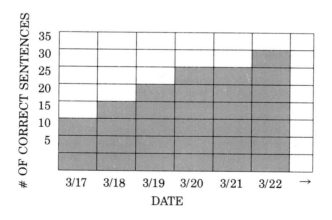

Graph Forms

ACCURACY

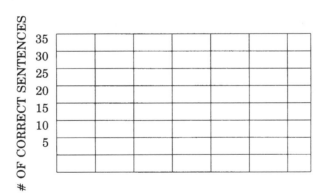

ACCURACY RATE

100%
95%
90%
80%
75%

DATE

NUMBER OF CORRECT SENTENCES

\# OF CORRECT SENTENCES

35
30
25
20
15
10
5

DATE

APPENDIX C-8

Charts for Graphing Words per Minute and Comprehension

This appendix is for students to use in graphing their reading rate in words per minute, as well as graphing their percentage of comprehension. As noted in the description of the precision reading technique in the introductory chapter and Appendix C-8, emphasis should be placed on *speed* of reading only after the student demonstrates an ability to read materials at grade level with consistent *accuracy*.

A number of available study-skills and reading-rate books present passages to be read by the student. These are usually followed by comprehension questions, most often 10, for the student to answer. You may wish to use the system of graphing each factor separately, which appears on page 516, or the single-chart system on page 515, which takes both percentage of comprehension and reading rate in words per minute into account. It will, of course, do the student little good to improve reading rate if comprehension suffers considerably in the process. In using the combination chart on page 516, multiply the number of words per minute by the percentage of comprehension and then graph the combination of these two factors. On page 514 you will find a sample of Fred's reading scores graphed for 6 trials. Note that there are blank lines on the left side of the graph to be filled in by the student. The lines have been left blank because every student will tend to read at a different rate. As the student gains in competence, he will probably improve in overall comprehension. Although percentage of comprehension may decrease as the student increases reading speed, it will usually increase after practice. Start the numbers representing the combination of the words per minute and percentage of comprehension on the third line from the bottom (as shown in Fred's example), since it is quite possible that the student may decrease in overall score slightly before beginning to increase that score. The method of computing Fred's scores is shown below the graph of Fred's reading performance. This is the system that you should, of course, use if you wish to graph the students' scores yourself.

On Fred's first trial, he read at 150 words per minute and had a comprehension score of 60%. His score was 150 × 60 = 9,000. This score was then put as the first trial using the third line from the bottom, in case his score might decrease in any future trials instead of increase.

Name __Fred__

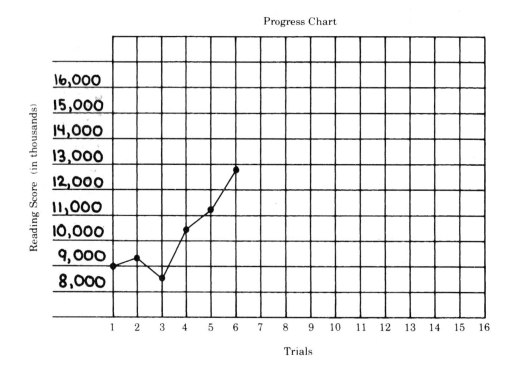

Progress Chart

On the following five trials, Fred's scores are shown below and graphed above.

Trial 2: 155 words per minute with a comprehension score of 60% = 9,300

Trial 3: 170 words per minute with a comprehension score of 50% = 8,500

Trial 4: 175 words per minute with a comprehension score of 60% = 10,500

Trial 5: 185 words per minute with a comprehension score of 60% = 11,100

Trial 6: 185 words per minute with a comprehension score of 70% = 12,950

Name _____

Progress Chart

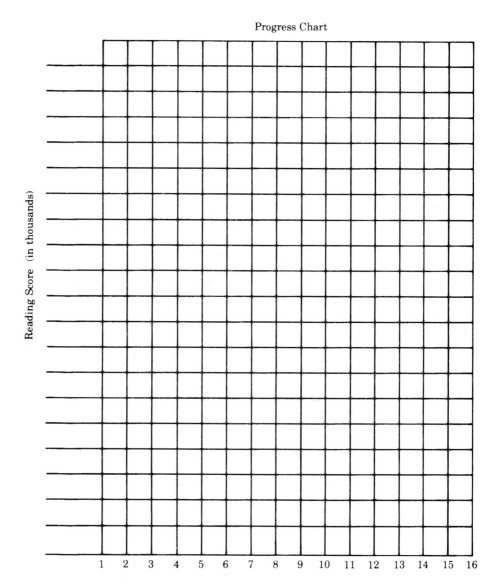

ILLUSTRATING WORDS PER MINUTE AND
PERCENT OF COMPREHENSION

Name _____

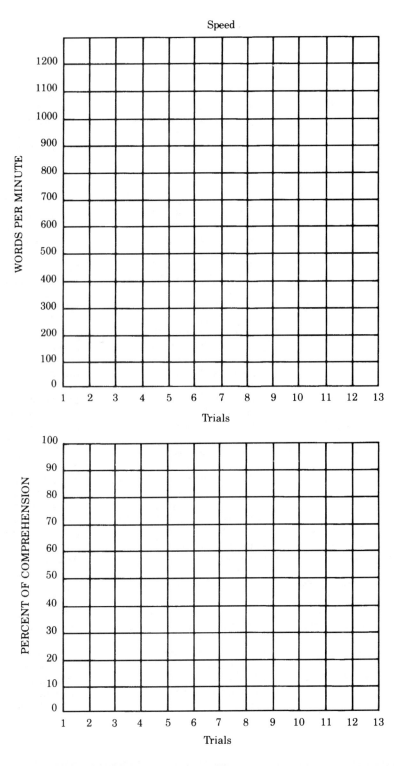

Index